DATEABLE

DATE AB LE

SWIPING RIGHT, HOOKING UP, AND SETTLING DOWN WHILE CHRONICALLY ILL AND DISABLED

JESSICA SLICE AND **CAROLINE CUPP**

hachette
BOOKS

New York

Hachette Go, an imprint of Hachette Books
Hachette Book Group
1290 Avenue of the Americas
New York, NY 10104
HachetteGo.com
Facebook.com/HachetteGo
Instagram.com/HachetteGo

First Edition: July 2024

Published by Hachette Go, an imprint of Hachette Book Group, Inc. The Hachette Go name and logo is a trademark of the Hachette Book Group.

The Hachette Speakers Bureau provides a wide range of authors for speaking events. To find out more, go to hachettespeakersbureau.com or email HachetteSpeakers@hbgusa.com.

Hachette Go books may be purchased in bulk for business, educational, or promotional use. For information, please contact your local bookseller or Hachette Book Group Special Markets Department at: special.markets@hbgusa.com.

The publisher is not responsible for websites (or their content) that are not owned by the publisher.

Print book interior design by Amy Quinn.

Library of Congress Cataloging-in-Publication Data

Names: Slice, Jessica, author. | Cupp, Caroline, author.
Title: Dateable : swiping right, hooking up, and settling down while chronically ill and disabled / Jessica Slice and Caroline Cupp.
Description: First edition. | New York, NY : Hachette Go, [2024] | Includes bibliographical references and index.
Identifiers: LCCN 2024001689 | ISBN 9780306832734 (trade paperback) | ISBN 9780306832741 (ebook)
Subjects: LCSH: People with disabilities—Social life and customs. | Chronically ill—Social life and customs. | Dating (Social customs) | Sex.
Classification: LCC HV1568 .S556 2024
LC record available at https://lccn.loc.gov/2024001689

ISBNs: 9780306832734 (trade paperback original) 9780306832741 (ebook)

Printed in the United States of America

LSC-C

Printing 1, 2024

For David, who is there, every single time. I love you.
—Jessica

And for Kevin: from the first moment, and every one after.
—Caroline

CONTENTS

INTRODUCTION

JESSICA

I joined Hinge for the first time in 2015 and kept my profile spare. While I didn't claim to be athletic and active, I didn't mention my disability either. None of my photos showed the wheelchair that I kept in my trunk. Under *occupation*, instead of saying that I was unable to work and lived on Social Security Disability Insurance (SSDI), I quipped, "Mostly book clubs."

August was tall and handsome, and I suggested that we meet at a park near my Berkeley rental for our first date. There was a wide bench there—only a few feet from where I usually parked—and I knew that I could walk there from my car and the slats were large enough to allow me to elevate my legs.

We talked for over two hours. He was even better in person—funny and smart. A business owner. I could tell that we were attracted to each other, and the conversation bubbled, easy and exciting.

He asked how I liked Berkeley, and I mentioned that my rental was pretty nice—it had windows on opposite walls, and the breeze was lovely in the afternoons. Only after he walked me to my Camry and I watched him open the door of his Tesla did I consider that not everyone would deem the converted shed that I lived in to be the height of luxury. I thought, *You're not in North Carolina anymore.*

That night he texted, and my heart skipped. Already! He asked if he could take me out that weekend; he wanted to surprise me. For me, as a disabled person, giving up control of my plans is terrifying, but I decided to push myself. I did mention that I wasn't up for anything active, and he assured me that what he had scheduled was very relaxing.

Two days later, he knocked on my shed door, and we walked hand in hand to his car. He was adorable and excited, but he drove too quickly, and I could feel my hips and back being injured with every turn. I gripped the door handle and the seat and tried to hide my discomfort.

He pulled up to a restaurant that specialized in macaroni and cheese(!) and ran inside for our to-go order. When he put it in the back seat, I noticed that he had packed white wine, two glasses, and a blanket. I loved that he was a planner. We crossed the Richmond Bridge and drove about twenty minutes to Belvedere Island.

Winding through a neighborhood of mansions, as we watched the sunset, August talked about his work and the plane that he had just purchased (uh, what?) and said that he was looking forward to Burning Man. Out of his sightline, I used my right pointer finger to check the pulse on my left wrist. Still OK. I sneaked a bite of my granola bar to keep my glucose stable.

He parked next to a wall and grinned. "We're here! Just wait in the car for a second." I sent my sister a pin with my location and his last name. He scaled the wall and disappeared, and I wondered if this was the beginning of the story that would play on the news about my disappearance. Appearing next to me, he opened my door and helped me out. "It's a little precarious but not too bad. I'll help you."

Had I been naive to try to wait until the third date to mention my disability?

Around the bend, some ramshackle steps made the climb over the wall easy, and on the other side, a short dirt path took us down a thirty-foot hill. I shuffled down, gripping August's hand. My heart was pounding from the exertion, and my vision was fading in and out. At the bottom of the hill, I looked around. The bay stretched in front of us. The Golden Gate Bridge, the Bay Bridge, and the Richmond Bridge sparkled.

We were standing on a concrete platform. A few homes dotted the hill beneath us.

He explained that a friend had started to build a house here, and due to "a long story not worth telling," construction had stopped. August set out our picnic. At this point, I was no longer afraid of him. You don't make it to your midthirties without a decent danger instinct, and I knew the nearby residents could hear if I screamed.

We shared a large pillow and leaned back against the hill, drinking wine and trading bites of our mac and cheese. Again, conversation sparkled and shifted from light to serious and back again. He looked into my eyes. "I can't believe how much I like you." And we kissed.

With one hand in my hair and the other on my lower back, he kissed me again and again, smiling and murmuring between each one. "Wow," he said.

I couldn't believe that just weeks after moving to California, I had met someone so thoughtful and funny. Someone who had planned a date like this *for me*. Someone who kissed like this. We adjusted so that I was now leaning against his chest, legs and fingers intertwined, watching the ferries and barges on the bay.

"I feel like I already know you," he murmured. "You are unlike anyone I've ever met." He trailed his thumb up and down my arm.

Maybe I should tell him now, I thought. Things are moving quickly, and I owe it to us both. "There's something I haven't told you," I started, taking a deep breath. "I have an illness that makes it hard for me to stand up for very long. I have to rest a lot." I stopped there, afraid to unload the whole truth: the dislocations and constant injuries, the nausea, the wheelchair, the awful episodes of heart pounding that wake me at night.

He paused his thumb for only a moment, but I felt it. I felt his chest tense under me. "Thank you for telling me," he said and came around in front of me, holding my face and kissing me again. "I guess I should take you home to rest," he said.

The shift was obvious on the return trip. He didn't reach for my hand as he had on the drive there. He turned the music up. After pulling up in front of my rental, he took a deep breath, not looking at me. "I think we're better as friends."

I made my way back to the shed and flopped onto my bed with my big-headed dog, Ben Nevis. I was exhausted and dizzy from my night out. My stomach roiled. But it was my shame that ached the most.

IT CAN FEEL IMPOSSIBLE TO NAVIGATE DATING WHILE DISABLED IN A SOCIETY that stigmatizes disabled bodies and minds. At the beginning we wonder, what do we owe our dates? How much of our stories do we share? For those of us who don't have evident disabilities, do we disclose at all? My body is my business, but was it shame that kept me silent? When I was dating in my thirties, I had spent years accepting my body for what it is, but that hard-fought internal acceptance was easily compromised when I had to find a way to advertise my inherent worth to potential partners.

I acquired my disability at twenty-eight, suddenly. While on a hike in Greece, I became overheated, and that one stressor instigated a cascade of symptoms and syndromes tied to what had been a latent genetic condition, Ehlers Danlos syndrome (EDS). Now, twelve years after the hike, due to dysautonomia and EDS, I use a power wheelchair when out of the house, can stand for about thirty seconds, and can sit upright, not reclining, for less than five minutes. Every moment of the day, I am in significant pain and must spend most of my time resting. When I became disabled, my twelve-year relationship ended, and I, at thirty, started to date in a world and body that had changed significantly.

CAROLINE

"Well, she'll never be president," the doctor told my parents two weeks after standard newborn blood tests revealed dangerously low thyroid hormones. The doctor muttered something about a sheltered workshop and scrawled "R—" in my medical file. In the years that followed, my parents struggled to understand why I wasn't meeting physical milestones (A spinal tumor? A stroke?) but was excelling at every intellectual one. At nine months, I could speak but not sit; by age three, my IQ was off the charts, but I still couldn't walk. Finally, the diagnoses came: cerebral palsy (CP; bilateral spastic diplegia, to be exact). My arms were not affected, but my legs were tight, weak, and misshapen (the doctor reluctantly crossed out the "R—" in my chart at my mother's insistence). In the years that followed, I learned to walk with assistance, and then more confidently with crutches. I used a wheelchair or scooter for longer distances. I stayed in my comfort zones: academics, family, and a circle of close friends, most of them established before difference came with a judgment attached.

Dating was where it became difficult. I was the only obviously disabled kid in my whole school, at summer camp, and in nearly every extracurricular activity. I had never seen anyone who was disabled portrayed as an object of desire, so I assumed I couldn't possibly be one either. There were crushes and hookups, brief relationships that fizzled, some pretty scary sexual harassment, and a whole lot of self-loathing. Every time something didn't work out, I thought it was my fault: if I could just erase my disability, everything would be OK.

Once I became more comfortable as a disabled person, dating got a whole lot better. In grad school, I found my dating groove and realized that being more confident changed the game: when I owned who I was, dates could too (including one guy who tried to impress me with his new "phone computer thing" that I said was ridiculous and would never take off). When my friends started posting profiles on eHarmony, I joined in.

JESSICA

Caroline and I have both been dumped because of our disabilities, and the sting never totally goes away. Even now, partnered and parenting, we flinched when Iliza Shlesinger joked about a person with a limb difference: "Stump doesn't get you a second date." Every few years, Ken Jennings's tweet about how sad it is to see a hot person in a wheelchair reemerges, and people rush to his defense.

The ignorance doesn't come just from a few misinformed public figures; society reminds us constantly that we are considered undateable. It's tough too because so many well-intentioned people have adopted the language of intimate connection and twisted it around when it comes to disabled people.

For example, we have so-called Best Buddies programs in schools, where nondisabled students are assigned as companions to disabled kids (because obviously all genuine friendships start with one kid being assigned to another); "special" proms for disabled students that get a zillion likes on social media; and feel-good stories about a sorority deigning to open its doors for a day to disabled college students. There are numerous negative effects of this self-serving faux camaraderie, but one of the most pernicious is that as disabled people, we don't get healthy models for authentic friendship and intimacy. Personal assistants (PAs) or publicity stunts are rebranded as freely chosen, consensual partnerships, typically highlighting the compassion and benevolence of the nondisabled organizers.

Once we throw off assigned "best" friends and like-generating pseudodates, we are forced to figure out what we actually want rather than just accepting whoever and whatever is offered to us. And it's critical that we do: when we don't value ourselves, relationships become a minefield. As disability activist Marina Carlos said, "People just think we're going to accept everything. Even not just in dating life, but anywhere."[1] Far too often, disabled people slip into the mistaken notion that anyone who has said that they want to be with us as friends or romantic partners has a right to our time and affection. That's just not true.

If you're disabled and single, you're not alone: around twenty-nine million people under sixty-four are disabled and unpartnered in the

United States, and many are actively dating. *Dateable* is for people with physical disabilities, people with intellectual disabilities, people who identify as neurodivergent, and those who are chronically ill. It's for disabled people who love casual sex, those who are asexual, and everyone in between. We look at what it means to be a disabled person seeking romantic connection, how it is to navigate dating apps, and the accessibility obstacles of dating, breakups, and long-term partnerships. In the following chapters, we share interviews with people who identify as queer and straight and as Black, Brown, and white.

We interviewed a few dozen disabled and chronically ill people in the process of writing this book, and those interviews were transformative for both of us. We discovered beautiful and creative corners of the disability community that changed how we think about ourselves and that we can't wait to share with you. We are endlessly grateful to the people who spent their time and their spoons talking to us.[2] Some people preferred pseudonyms, and some did not, and when requested, we also altered identifying details.

A note on identity: We are both white, cis women. Caroline is straight, and Jessica is queer and in a relationship with a cis man. We both grew up with financial security. Our perspectives and experiences are influenced by our identities. Like many people who went to graduate school in the 2000s, we are fortunate to be influenced by Kimberlé Crenshaw's writings on intersectionality and do our best to let that education inform our writing.[3]

Another note on content. The very nature of dating while disabled means this book discusses ableism, racism, and homophobia throughout. Please take care of yourself while reading. Some chapters also touch on sexual assault and violence. In those cases, we have included content notes at the beginning.

While we both contributed to the structure and content of every chapter, we alternated writing the chapters and focused on just one of our perspectives per chapter. On each chapter's first page, you'll see its primary author's name in italics. *Dateable* combines our stories, the stories of the people we interviewed, our research, and some humble advice based on all the above. Throughout the book, we consider how to date safely and humanely in a world that systematically devalues lives like ours. And we talk a lot about sex.

No matter what else you take from this book, we hope you leave with this message: *You are dateable.* You belong in the energizing, frustrating, beautiful, hysterical, sad, hopeful world of dating (that is, if you want to date, and if you're reading this, we'll just assume you do). Maybe you're rolling your eyes and thinking, *I'm disabled, and I've dated a gazillion people. No one needs to tell me I'm sexy and desirable.* If that's you, hooray. But if you're a person who has never heard that you are worthy as a partner, or if you've never thought of yourself as someone who could be dateable, then welcome.

Thank you for being here.

CHAPTER 1
REPRESENTATION AND RESPECT

CAROLINE

Content note: Sexual harassment.

JAY WAS A SENIOR AND, MORE IMPORTANTLY, THE OBJECT OF MY DAY'S every energy. I plotted routes to maximize the chance of a casual meetup and convinced friends in my freshman dorm to go with me to any frat party where he might be hanging out. It was a crush and, in retrospect, not a terribly interesting one (did I mention that he was a tall, blond soccer player?). But he seemed . . . something. He sought me out at parties and held me tight during slow songs. And even though I rolled through my college campus on a golf cart because it was too hard to navigate long distances with CP and while we were slow dancing, my pink crutches sat propped up in a beer-stained corner, I thought maybe he could be into me too. When he asked me to go to dinner I (screamed, told everyone, planned our wedding) thought maybe this

1

was my ticket out of undateability. That perhaps I had a future not only as chief cheerleader for everyone else's partnering but as a member of the club itself.

In the hours leading up to the date, I did all the things: agonized over my outfit, put on the eightieth layer of mascara, and bounded (or my version of bounding) out the door when I saw him pull up in his achingly cool blue convertible. I was tongue-tied on the drive to the restaurant, my stomach in knots as I tried not to say something that would disrupt whatever cosmic forces had led to this point. As we took our seats, I noticed the server looking him up and down. This was a guy people desired, and it seemed like he wanted me.

And then, while we were still waiting on our appetizers, he said, "My girlfriend thinks it's so cute that I'm taking you out."

And that was it. The future I had painted in my mind evaporated. I grinned weakly, wondering if my eyes betrayed my embarrassment. Here I was, out on what I had thought up to that moment was a date until it became clear that the whole thing was a charade. As the server refilled our water glasses and shame broiled under a surface I was fighting to keep breezy, I wondered if my relationships would always be limited to the roles of best friend or side note in someone else's story.

The thing about dating is that, by its nature, it's hard. Dating is about connection, and like all connections, it comes with a risk—essentially a certainty—of potential partners saying, "Yeah, not for me." Even when we acknowledge that each of us is doing the same calculation with the folks we meet, it doesn't erase the sting of being told we aren't a good match. Disability adds another layer of complication to the intrinsic vulnerability of dating. There are concrete accessibility issues, of course, but also the mantle of "otherness" that many of us who were born or came of age with disabilities have assumed since childhood. When there are no rom-coms featuring disabled characters, no shows or books that have a couple casually wheeling down the street, when sex ed doesn't talk about disability (or isn't even taught to disabled people), and when most of the time you're pictured as the recipient of others' charity, the message is clear: *You don't belong here.*

DATING 101

Before we get into specifics of disability and dating, imagine for a minute that every book, movie, and TV show featuring a teen romance was wiped off the planet. *Sixteen Candles, Dawson's Creek, Spider-Man, Girls*—all vaporized. Moreover, none of those books or films ever existed because no one ever thought to write them. What would the impact of that be? Yes, the species would probably continue to exist even if *Twilight* had never hit the bestseller list, but no matter how unrealistic it might be, media is important because it teaches us how to engage one another as members of a shared culture. When we were younger, watching fictional teens figure out relationships was one of the ways we learned how to be teenagers.

Consuming content that showed kids our age dating, even in the most fantastical or unrealistic circumstances, gave us frames for basic life lessons like expressing interest in a partner, figuring out the mechanics of sex, navigating parental expectations, and establishing boundaries. It's why representation matters so much: the seemingly innocuous act of watching a silly TV show actually helps us figure out how to navigate our culture (for good or for ill!). When we see people screw up, we learn from their mistakes. When we see them succeed, we take guidance from them. This is particularly critical when it comes to dating, which we tend to learn from our friend groups and TV shows rather than parents or professionals. For example, few parents sit their kids down for a lesson on how to flirt. We see other people flirt, and we imitate them until we find our own style and figure out what works for us.

All of this means that when disabled people aren't represented in romantic roles in movies, TV shows, or books, we miss out on a lot of learning when it comes to relationships. We don't get to see people in wheelchairs kissing or one partner lifting the other onto a bed. We don't get to listen in to how people who employ PAs communicate with them about what they need before or during a sexual encounter. We don't get to see what a healthy breakup looks like between an interabled couple or how people demonstrate consent using assistive technologies. We don't get to see a bride figure out how to make her crutches match her wedding dress (I'm still mad about that one). That's not to say that there aren't other ways to learn these things, but the media has a way of both authorizing relationships and normalizing them.

Before *Will and Grace*, few people had ever seen an out, upper-middle-class gay man navigate relationships, though millions of people are doing that every day. *Sex and the City* pulled back the veil on women as the initiators of sexual relationships (um, yeah—from the dawn of time). *Orange Is the New Black* showed the pain and resilience of living as a trans woman in unjust systems (hopefully that brand of injustice will be history, rather than reality, in the near future). There are huge numbers of disabled people dating, hooking up, and marrying. But if we don't see that playing out on-screen, especially if we operate in actual communities made up of predominantly nondisabled people, it can feel like we're the only ones on earth trying to figure this out. The old saying "I think, therefore I am" could be translated to "I am authentically represented, therefore I am." When we're erased, the message is that we don't belong; there's no place for us here.

And that's bad, but what can feel even worse is when we are represented, but as punchlines or objects of charity. We could fill a whole book with all the terrible portrayals of disability when it comes to romance. How when we are represented at all, it's often as objects of voyeurism, pity, or disgust (I'll never forget one of my favorite comics casually remarking that a person who can't walk shouldn't reproduce). Major media outlets regularly share inspiration porn to lure in their audiences, seemingly without concern for the damage these stories perpetuate. Disabled people suffer real harm from these displays of artificial inclusion, and stories about contrived "friendship" teach disabled people that we should be grateful recipients of whatever attention is thrown our way, no matter how pathetic it makes us feel.

An example of the messes that happen when people internalize these images: My first job out of grad school was a caregiving role in a hospital, so I was ultrafriendly and worked hard to spend time with people who seemed to need extra attention. One of those folks was a man in his fifties who was a volunteer in our department. Robert was a favorite of my boss and seemed to be a little lonely, so I intentionally engaged him at work. Without my knowledge, he found my personal number in the staff directory, and his calls quickly became relentless. Robert showed up at work when he knew I would be the only one in the office. When I declined his advances and stopped answering his calls, he presented himself for care in the hospital's emergency room and requested my unit's services, seeing from the on-call schedule that I'd be the one assigned to visit him.

I went to my boss to report what was happening, and his response was to gently remind me that it's "completely normal" for relationships to start at work, and this man was just expressing appropriate interest in a single woman. Behind his enraging and paternalistic response, I heard the voice of a person who thought maybe this was pretty much the best I was going to do romantically. I should accept relentless harassment from a dude twice my age because it was my best chance to be in a partnership. Fortunately, there were a number of people who called my boss on his BS and forced him to change course, but his tacit assumption stuck with me. Was I so worthless that any attention was good attention? Too many disabled people answer that question with a tragic "yes." We end up in relationships that are destructive because we internalize the message that we're lucky to have someone willing to put up with us. Again, if you get nothing else out of this book, please take this to heart: *you deserve to be in relationships that make you feel valued, whole, and safe.* Don't ever settle for situations that make you feel awful about yourself.

A WORD ABOUT PARENTS

Sometimes the relationships that make us feel safest come with their own set of emotional baggage. To that end, a word about parents and guardians: growing up with a disability often impacts your relationships with the adults in your family. At a time when many nondisabled teens are out there taking driving tests and scoring bad booze with fake IDs, we're still dependent on our moms and dads for things like toileting, dressing, and getting where we need to go.

Parents who have spent the past decade-plus fighting tooth and nail to get us necessary services may have a tough time loosening the reins at a time when our emotional well-being depends on increasing independence. Parental overprotection has real and lasting consequences, among them social isolation, depression, and low self-esteem. Feelings of being different and less-than that start in adolescence don't soon go away. Kids who are overprotected can turn into adults who have difficulty making decisions about their own lives, especially without an authority figure's input.[1] Low self-worth plus not trusting our own gut can impact how we approach dating too.

A small example of this happened when I was a teenager. My friend wanted to go on a date with a guy at another school, and because he was bringing another boy along, she asked me to come too. My parents had a very strict "No dating until you're sixteen" rule (it was the 1990s), but I was within a month or two of turning sixteen, and this wasn't even technically a date. I asked them if I could go, and they said no, but I kept pressing because it didn't make sense—after all, this was just a random person, it was my friend who was on the date, *yada yada*. They kept hemming and hawing in that way that people do when they don't want to tell you the thing they're really worried about (which enraged me and goaded me even more) until my mom finally blurted out, "He doesn't know you have a disability—what will happen when he sees you?" I knew their fear came from a place of love, but it also terrified me. The message I received was that this thing—this disability—was so scary, so undiscussable, that it would be better to hide at home than to risk a hurtful encounter.

Now that I'm a mom, I have more compassion for what my parents were facing as they sent their disabled daughter out into the world, but that encounter stayed with me for a long time (probably because it confirmed everything I already feared about myself). Disability was scary. It put me outside the bounds of normal social situations. I couldn't handle the inevitable hurt and disappointments that are part and parcel of dating.

LEFT OUT

One thing I didn't struggle with (thanks to my super-liberal hippie high school) was access to information about sex: by senior year, we were practically begging our teachers to stop talking about it. Way too often, people with physical disabilities receive far less sexual education than our peers. Typically, teens get information about sexual development and behaviors from friends, parents, teachers, physicians, and digital media. However, studies have shown that evidence-based sex ed is greatly restricted for all young people (only 60 percent of states require that it be taught at all), and it's especially limited for those with disabilities. At the time of this writing, only five states mandate that disabled students be included in their sex education curriculum, and thirty-six states don't include disabled youth at all.[2] Reproductive education is poorly funded and resourced across the nation, and when asked, teachers report feeling utterly unequipped to teach disabled students about these issues in meaningful and supportive ways.[3]

The lack of information seems to especially affect women with disabilities; in a study on service barriers for women receiving gynecological care, researchers found that women with physical impairments were twice as likely as men to receive no sexual education whatsoever.[4] One researcher commented, "Without the benefit of sex education from peers or parents that many nondisabled teenagers have, those youths with spina bifida or [CP] who are not reached through schools are less likely than peers to receive *any* sex information."[5] Clearly, the vast majority of adolescents with disabilities are receiving at best minimal information on sexual development and virtually no condition-specific knowledge related to sexuality.

We also need to acknowledge that for many of us, sex, intimacy, and the weirdly specific ways our bodies work are tough things to talk about, particularly in the public sphere. My college roommate had a colostomy bag for a while, and she was like, "Yeah, everyone's fine talking about the time I got pneumonia, but who am I going to chat about my bag of shit with?" It's easy to wave a sign to say that Alex should be able to go to school. It's harder to wave one that says that Alex should be able to get laid. Parents and teachers aren't, by and large, going to stand up for the sexual rights of their kids.

Sure, doctors should provide education and appropriate reproductive health care, but few people are out there going, "What I really want and need is to be able to talk with my family doctor about how to seduce the dude I met on Hinge." Aside from the basics, most of the sex knowledge that makes a meaningful difference in our lives isn't the kind you get in a pamphlet or during a routine exam. A lot of it is super-tough to talk about (especially if you are, like me, a total prude at heart). There's not a total fix for this dilemma. Some things are, by nature and nurture, difficult to discuss. But we also know that bringing intimate and uncomfortable topics into the light tends to make them a lot less scary.

GOING SOLO

Disabled teens also face social barriers. While huge strides have been made in desegregating our education system—meaning that people with physical impairments are now allowed to attend public school (seriously, not until 1975) and not automatically put into special education classes (whether we'd benefit or not)—a side effect of mainstreaming is that we're often the only evidently disabled people in our classrooms. No one would ever say that the goal of desegregating schools would be to have one Black or Indigenous student in a room of otherwise all white kids or that coeducation means a single girl in a classroom full of boys. This is especially true if racial justice or women's history were never addressed in the classroom.

The massive gaps and losses in that hypothetical situation are obvious. But outside the academic world, we rarely stop to think about the harmful side effects of mainstreaming on disabled kids. Being the only one in a class who uses assistive technology, particularly during stages when conformity is a big deal, means that we can be socially isolated. There's no sense of shared culture, no watching how our peers navigate or adapt. I was the only disabled kid in my class from pre-K through twelfth grade; at the time it didn't strike me as weird, but now I think about the ways I'd sneak glances at the other kids at the CP clinic and just long to connect with them. The first time I watched *Crip Camp* and saw all these disabled teens hanging out together and being silly and hooking up, it made me realize the extent of our collective loss. Yes, disabled kids should never be forcibly segregated from nondisabled ones. At the same time, we need access to disabled peers, mentors, and teachers so that we can learn who we are as members of a disability culture.

LEARNING OUR HISTORY

This is especially true because people with disabilities are often (though not always) the only disabled member of their families. Because of that, we don't get disability history passed down to us, as members of many ethnic and religious groups do. We learn about our culture and accomplishments from people outside our immediate circles, and some of us find that info really late in life. I was in college before I knew that the disability rights movement existed, and it totally blew my mind. As a person of Jewish ethnicity, I grew up on a steady diet of my culture's foods, stories, books, and heroes (I still kick butt in the "Famous Jewish Athletes" category in *Jeopardy*). But by the time I had learned about my other cultural group's history, accomplishments, and ongoing work for justice, I had already traveled abroad and developed an affinity for menthol cigarettes.

It wasn't because people were keeping this information from me; it was because those closest to me simply didn't know it. Disability history isn't taught in schools, and for most of my life, it wasn't celebrated publicly. Having a disabled kid doesn't automatically give parents entrée into this world; on the contrary, they quickly become steeped in a medical model that encourages them to keep their child as "normal" as possible—meaning focusing less on disability and more on trying to fit in. Thus, growing up, I had no idea who Judy Heumann was, or Ed Roberts or Justin Dart Jr. or Nancy Eiesland (if you don't know them, look them up!), or that Frida Kahlo was a disabled artist and Sarah Bernhardt a disabled actor, or that the Fannie Farmer cookbook in my kitchen had been written by a disabled entrepreneur. I knew about Franklin Roosevelt but had mostly heard about how skillful he had been in hiding his polio from the American people. I knew about Stephen Hawking, but not that he was married (twice) and had a few kids.

All this is to say, if you haven't had a chance to learn about disability history yet, or to engage with other people with disabilities online or IRL, put down this book and do that first (we've provided some suggestions for starting places in the Resources section at the end). While you're at it, jump onto Instagram and Twitter and start following some brilliant, badass disabled people (also in the Resources section). At the end of the day, dating is all about putting yourself out there as you are, and if you don't have a full picture of what's shaped you, you're going into the game with only a few of the resources that are yours to enjoy.

The good news is that all this representation stuff is getting better—one could even say that despite the statistics, disabled people are really having a cultural moment (a moment that will hopefully extend to actual inclusion in the years ahead). While disabled characters are only about 3.5 percent of people in TV series (and most of those characters aren't played by disabled actors), that number is increasing fractionally year to year.[6] The portrayals of disability are becoming more nuanced and authentic—a simple search will yield everything from Ryan O'Connell's hysterical antics on *Special* to Judy Heumann's powerful autobiography or Shane Burcaw and Hannah Aylward's YouTube channel. If you're an academic type, there are some great books out there on sex and disability written from a scholarly perspective. There are also awesome memoirs, YouTube channels, and essays (again, check the Resources list at the end of the book). Disabled writers are addressing specific subjects such as relationships, parenting, faith, and spirituality in ways that don't center on the clichés of healing or sainthood. People with disabilities are hooking up, dating, getting married, and writing about it. We're getting busy with one another, with nondisabled people, across genders, and in groups of two, three, and more. We're also happily asexual, aromantic, child-free, or single. The point is, there are as many ways to be a person with a body as there are people with bodies.

CHAPTER 2
WE'RE HOT*

CAROLINE

*Most days. When we've had enough coffee, and our allergies aren't acting up.

"HOW'S BIG KNEE DOING? TIME TO GET IT DRAINED?" MY HUS-band asks as we sink onto the couch. Although Kevin's generally capable of coming up with nicknames that straddle the witty/affectionate/mildly annoying line, Big Knee's clunky non-name entered our lives with a thud and stuck because, much like Big Knee itself, there's nothing charming or delicate about it. Big Knee is a hot (sometimes literally) mess.

My left knee (as it's otherwise known) has been the subject of count-less injuries and surgeries over the years, some that I remember well and others that occurred invisibly in its murky depths and failed to earn a diagnosis. Since middle school, Big Knee has been a wearable anatomy lesson on the lesser-known ligaments, a surprisingly accurate barom-eter (*rain again?*), a subject of inquiry for solemn-faced med students, and a tyrannical overlord that sends pangs of pain up my leg when I DoTooMuch with my body. After I got pregnant, this knee became so painful, so filled with dread-inducing clicks and snaps, that I could barely drag myself across the room. Then, with a twisted sense of mercy, it decided that instead of keeping up its masochistic tendencies, it would sail off into bloated retirement as some kind of balloonish, arthritic sea creature taking up residency above my calf.

Touching Big Knee feels like being fondled through a waterbed, an odd and unsettling sensation to be avoided if possible. Sometimes I forget what my knee looks like, catch a glimpse of it in the mirror and think, *Oh—that's pretty awful-looking*, and then start folding the laundry and forget about it. The thing is, ever since it blew up like an engorged puffin, the pain's been a lot better (and those draining needles are enormous), so my motivation for changing anything is on the low end.

I say all this not because Big Knee needs to take up more space in the world (or this page) than it already does (less space would be good), but because even with widening views of beauty, many of us disabled people still don't feel like our bodies fit. Western culture may have (incrementally) graduated from single-hued "nude" undies and started to expand its range of acceptable body types to include both Melissa McCarthy and Zendaya, but we still don't see *Vogue* splashing our arthritic joints, colostomy bags, stumps, and drooling faces across its covers.

Beauty standards are expanding by size and hue, but disabled people continue to be erased as objects of desire. And while we know that everyone is filtering and photoshopping the heck out of the images we see and that half of the features that are held up as ideal can't be achieved without unsettling amounts of silicone being injected into lips and booties, we still look at those images and wonder where our disabled bodies fit. Is the big tent of beauty big and wide enough to include us?

Before we dive in, a few important points are probably super-obvious, but we should highlight them anyway:

1. *Mass-market beauty is about selling us stuff.* It's rooted not in who or what is beautiful but in insecurity. The more we dislike how we look, the more stuff we buy to make us feel beautiful. While the images offered to us continue to expand in color, size, and gender presentation, we know that it's not because cosmetic company executives have suddenly seen the light but rather that they want to capture a wider share of the makeup/filler/designer-clothing market. As we'll discuss elsewhere in this book, due to systemically unfair finances, disabled people often have less disposable income than our nondisabled peers.

   That means we have less money to spend on everything, including fancy mascara. Thus, there is no incentive for the powers that be in the beauty industry to feature people who look like us. If a group of people sitting in a boardroom somewhere doesn't think we'll spend our money on their products, then they don't have any motivation to include our images in their ads. The fact that we're not rolling down runways has everything to do with how much money is in our bank accounts and nothing to do with how we look. If people with CP were suddenly handed a million dollars each (yes, please!), you'd better believe we'd be limping down those runways, and The Row would come out with a line of designer crutches.

2. *Everyone has complicated relationships with their bodies.* That's true for us as disabled people and for nondisabled folks as well (or so I've heard). Maybe there's a magical person out there who loves every pimple, toe, and hair follicle and always has and always will, but for most of us, there are parts of our bodies we find beautiful and other parts (ahem, knee), that we appreciate a lot less. We talk a lot in this book about how sexy we are as disabled people, but obviously, no one feels

attractive all the time. Claiming our hotness doesn't erase the fact that there are days, weeks, or even years when we feel anything but. Naming our beauty is about claiming our place within a broad spectrum of common feelings about our bodies.

3. *"Beauty" (in the mass-market sense) and engaging in fulfilling, healthy relationships are two totally different things.* If being born with a body that closely matches the current cultural/market ideal were a predictor of happy marriages, no celebrities or reality TV stars would ever get divorced. As every gossip site and Instagram breakup post reminds us, conventionally attractive people break up, get cheated on, and are unhappily or happily single. People who don't meet arbitrary beauty standards, including those who have facial differences, are in joyful partnerships full of mutual attraction.

OK, now that we're on the same page, let's dive in.

BEAUTY MEETS RIGHTS

Beauty Always Recognizes Itself.[1]

—*Patricia Berne*

Let's talk about beauty and desire. It's more difficult than it might first appear. As hard as disabled people and our allies have fought for basic human rights, there's something that's clear and well-defined when we're operating in the realms of physical access, education, and work. We might disagree on the specifics of what we need and how we'll get there, but we're talking about things that can be measured, legislated, and enforced.

It's a lot harder when we start talking about the parts of our lives that don't fit that mold, like perceptions of beauty, authentic relationships, and feelings of desire. This isn't restricted to issues around disability: we know that the civil rights movement created laws around voting and desegregation but didn't stop bigotry and violence toward people of color. Even though all people now have the right to marry, there are still folks who are carrying prejudice toward members of the LGBTQ+ community (and it's a lot harder for many disabled people to marry, but more on that later in this book). In the same way, we can demand legislation mandating that a building must have an elevator, but we can't make laws about attraction, love, or self-confidence. Regulations are critically important, but as much as we need curb cuts, medical funding, and accessible restrooms, it is just as critical to experience affection, authentic connections, and intimacy.

We also know that none of this can be forced. If I commanded you to see every part of your body as fabulously gorgeous exactly how it is, you couldn't just magically do that because you decided to. The same would be true if I said that you must find the body of the person across the room attractive or desire a romantic encounter with them. This free-will element is what makes dating so stinking hard—it's one of the most important parts of seeing ourselves as whole human beings, and much of the work lies within our own hearts and minds rather than in the courtroom or on the picket line.

CRIP-ZONED

When you grow up with small children looking at you and then asking their parents, "WHAT'S WRONG WITH THAT MAN?" you become a little jaded.

—*Ryan O'Connell*[2]

Many of us who grew up disabled have to contend with the dual messages we receive from peers and strangers: we're both captivatingly interesting and utterly invisible. On one hand, our bodies are objects of curiosity, invitations for comments that suggest we're alien beings on some kind of intergalactic exchange program (my five-year-old neighbor popped into the room the other day and instructed me to get two good nights of sleep so that my back wouldn't be twisted anymore, and honestly, that's some of the better advice I've gotten from random people over the years).

Many of us are prepared for strangers to offer to pray over us, ask us intrusive questions about our health, or grab our arms if they feel that we could use their assistance. The flip side is that we can go from way too visible to utterly invisible in a hot minute. Disability rights activist Judy Heumann spoke about a time in college when a guy asked her if she knew any girls who were free that evening and interested in going on a date. He was looking right at her, this person who was clearly both a woman and sitting in a dorm room with no discernible plans, and because she was using a wheelchair didn't clue in to the fact that she was exactly the available, single female student he was looking for. Judy was so blindsided by the blatancy of her erasure that she said nothing in response, but the gut-punching impact of that moment was still fresh years later. She described herself, in the eyes of her fellow students, as a "kind of non-sex," someone who was presumed to have no interest in dating or having a partner, though that was not at all the case.[3]

My husband (who also has CP) put this slightly differently: "It's like there's the dating, and friend-zoned, and then way over here there's this other category of disabled people who are off on our own." In other words, we're crip-zoned. There are no romantic comedies where we cast off our crutches (or don't), get a makeover, and suddenly become portrayed as desirable. There were plenty of times over the years when I wondered whether some guy I was friends with would have asked me out had I not used a motorized scooter to cruise the high school hallways, and based on our conversations with other disabled people, this wondering seems pretty widespread.

One woman with CP said that in high school, her sister always had boyfriends, while she had platonic guy friends, and she wondered how much of that was about her disability. She also had the sense that things would get easier as she and her potential partners grew up: "I knew that as I got older and people matured, things might be different. I'd meet someone who would see me. See my beauty. If someone doesn't love you for who you are, they're not the right person."[4]

Plus when we're objectified or erased, it can be difficult to figure out a healthy way of relating to our beauty and vulnerability. As we talked with lots of disabled people about their bodies and reflected on our own, we noticed that there are some parallels between how we're objectified by others and how we choose to engage those around us. Especially the ways we magnify parts of ourselves and hide other parts of our experience. One theme that comes up over and over is the idea of overcompensating.

YOU'RE AMAZING

Jack, who is a spinal-cord injury survivor and uses mobility equipment, spoke about his sense of constantly having to prove he's "not stupid" by being the funniest, smartest, most professional guy in the room.[5] Ryan O'Connell pointed to CP as a motivating factor in his preference for eye-catching clothes that would distract from his gait,[6] while a woman we interviewed talked about the pressure to always look pretty, dress well, and have impeccable makeup.[7]

I constantly had to be the bright shining star, the darling of teachers, and the funniest, kindest person in the room. Not being liked was (and to some degree still is) terrifying for me, an existential threat to every overcompensating atom in my very soul. It doesn't help that as cute disabled kids, we are told just how AMAZING we are for every freaking thing we do, which makes staying AMAZING in the eyes of others a habit that's difficult to break (and dating particularly challenging because, generally, the people we go out with find us JUST OK, which, if you're addicted to being adored, feels slightly devastating).

While some of us overcompensate to distract from what made us look different from our able-bodied peers, others lean into their disability and invite the public's engagement with it. Andrew Gurza is the founder of the sex podcast *DisabilityAfterDark* and originator of the #disabledpeoplearehot hashtag. Gurza has said that they feel compelled to be "more queer, more outlandish . . . Fuck you, this is who I am. If you can't deal with it then get out."[8] In other words, whether we point away from it or toward it, many of us are taking the "go big or go home" approach to engagement with others.

At one point in my twenties, I would have gladly traded every award, accolade, and fancy degree for a totally boring, unremarkable, nondisabled existence. I don't feel like that today, but it seems important to acknowledge that normal, however it's defined, felt foreign and unattainable for me as a disabled person, and that led to an almost frantic quest to earn membership in a culture where I assumed I was a burden.

Again, I don't feel like that now. Instead of thinking of my disability as a liability, a reason why I have to earn my place, I see it (on most days) as a sometimes painful, always inconvenient gift that enabled the most fulfilling and authentic parts of my life to come about. But that involved a huge shift and a lot of maturing, and it didn't happen overnight.

My totally unscientific observation is that those of us who grew up disabled carry a bit more of this pressure to overcompensate and try to earn our places than those who acquired a disability later in life, but that's up for debate—there are likely plenty of instances where people are plunged into a new role and feel that they have to prove how amazing and brave and special they are for doing stuff that no one thought was miraculous before.

The other side of this is that just as we can be erased by those we encounter—especially as people who want a typical set of things like friends and relationships and intimacy—we often end up hiding important pieces of our physical and emotional experiences from others. We learn to segment parts of our lives that we don't think people will understand or that we feel would make us less attractive.

The super-obvious example is anything having to do with toileting. As you are probably well aware, many of us have all kinds of delectable little bathroom rituals ranging from the frequency with which we need to relieve ourselves to the special equipment or personal assistance that may be required. The intricate dance we must go through to relieve our body of waste would make us prima ballerinas if applied in a different setting. And yet these things that consume quite a bit of energy in our lives are rarely, if ever, spoken of openly.

When I met and had just started dating Kevin, he was showering in his one-bathroom apartment, and I had to pee. Without a ton of pelvic floor control, peeing is not something that can be put off indefinitely, so I realized quickly that it was either urinate on his floor or burst into the bathroom of a guy I barely knew and pee in front of him. Weighing my options, I chose the second, but even then I tried to brush it off as some kind of personality quirk—"Oh, look at me, so uninhibited, so delightfully free with my body"—rather than the disability-related choice it was.

Far from uninhibited, I am in fact a huge prude, would never choose to pee in front of a person I had just met, and was totally mortified. But I didn't feel that I could talk to this dude about my pee issues without making myself sound weird, so I just laughed it off as a charming little idiosyncrasy (I now pee in front of him on the daily, so we're OK there).

In this same vein, one person we chatted with has a preferred way of holding his suit jacket so that when his catheter inevitably leaks, the wet spot remains covered and he can continue whatever it is he's doing without running off for a change of clothes. Others have figured out ways to change diapers in public spaces without drawing attention to themselves or adjusted their food or drink intake with new people so they don't have to navigate cath changes or find an accessible restroom in a new space.

MASTERS OF DISGUISE

Sheltering people we meet from our experiences is broader than which biological substances emerge from us and how. It can be difficult to talk about surgeries or therapies with people who haven't gone through them. When I was young, many of my little friends took riding lessons, while I went to a therapeutic riding class for disabled kids. I never told these friends that I was in a "special" class, just that I went to a different barn.

As I got older, I continued to edit what I revealed to people about my life and how I navigated the world, trying to take out anything that would make them remember that I was disabled. There was one sleepover where all the girls were sharing who their crush was, and I refused to answer, passing it off like I didn't have one (I did!). I had it in my head that it was so ridiculous that a guy would like me, it would be easier for me just to pretend I wasn't interested in such plebeian topics.

As adults, we might say that we're just too busy to date, too independent, or waiting for the right time, when, if we were honest, we'd admit that it's just so freaking vulnerable and frightening to put ourselves out into the dating world with a disability. That kind of editing is a really tiring way to live, and it's a shame because life becomes so much easier when we're not working hard to keep parts of it hidden away. And that openness, paradoxically, can free up some of our energy to actually connect with other people.

It becomes even more exhausting when we try to hide our mobility needs from others. If you're not disabled and you're reading this book (welcome, friend), you may not know that there's traditionally a bit of a hierarchy when it comes to disability and how we move around the world. At the top of this hierarchy are people who meet traditional Western beauty standards and do not have any apparent disabilities, like Deaf model Nyle DiMarco.

If you didn't know Nyle and just saw his picture, you would have no idea that he is a member of the Deaf community. The next step on the hierarchy is people who look like nondisabled folks who are sitting down—your Paralympic athletes with lower-spinal-cord injuries, for example. Fit, healthy, breezy, sitting in the wheelchair equivalent of a McLaren.

And then you start moving down the rungs—people whose disabilities are more apparent; those who need canes, crutches, walkers, scooters, service dogs, helmets, motorized wheelchairs, sip-and-puff chairs, or communication devices; people with facial differences; etc. We're not cave dwellers here—we all know that there is no true hierarchy of attractiveness or human worth. But that being said, many of us with disabilities feel pressure to get as close to the next rung up the ladder as we can, even if it means we don't use a device that would be a huge help to us physically, or conversely, that we subject ourselves to painful procedures in the hopes of looking more conventionally attractive or nondisabled.

For a long time, I used nothing to get around—I just kind of cruised on furniture and fell a lot. And then my doctor said that I really should use crutches and I balked, because forearm crutches are for *really* disabled people and I'm just a normal person who can't walk. And then I got crutches and realized I'm a person who can walk—with crutches.

But then I found that while I can move with crutches, I can't move as fast or for as long as I'd like to, so a motorized scooter would be a huge help. But I'm either super-vain or have internalized a lot of ableism (or maybe both), so actually renting one felt like walking around the city with my undies over my jeans—just this really vulnerable, out-of-place feeling. It helped me physically but also felt like a giant billboard announcing I'd given up all pretense of minimizing how much space I was taking up in the world.

All of this is to say that if you're disabled (or maybe just if you're me), you may be so used to hiding big chunks of your life and discounting your needs that you don't even realize that that's a kind of weird way to live. All of us might not get to the Andrew Gurza "Fuck you, this is who I am" level of comfort with themselves, but there's a happy medium between that and "Please don't mind me; I'll just be in this corner."

WE'RE COMPLICATED

It's an act of rebellion to like my body.[9]

—*Sarah Todd Hammer*

If relationships are complicated, beauty is too. As disability educator Emily Ladau reminds us, disability is but one of the many intersecting parts of our identities.[10] Other parts include race, ethnicity, culture, religion, body size, age, and gender. The closer we are to the ever-shifting Western (white) cultural ideal, the less work we have to do to find ourselves perceived as an object of desire. Tellingly, the majority of the disabled people we spoke with who referred to themselves as beautiful were white, slender, and cisgender with symmetrical facial features.

That's a pretty revealing statement about the power that being white, thin, and gender-conforming continues to hold in our culture. Another common theme we found was that people's perceptions of their own attractiveness deepened over time. Folks who had never thought they were desirable as teens or young adults developed more appreciation for their appearance as they matured.[11] Becoming older also gave people a wider view of the insecurities that are shared by every human; when you realize that pretty much everyone is dissatisfied with aspects of their bodies and yet still hits up their local happy hour, there is less sense of isolation.

Humans are complicated—we have lots of overlapping feelings about who we are, some of which may conflict with each other. This is especially obvious when we think about how our bodies are perceived by others. Recently I was struggling down a set of steps, and an older man paused to look at me and said something about my being disabled and then added, "But you're still pretty." Part of me wanted to rise up with Gurza-esque indignation: "I'm disabled, *and* I'm pretty, asshole." And the other part was like, "Oh, wow, even though my body is shaped like fusilli, a random senior citizen thinks I'm pretty!"

One disabled scholar reflected on an interaction in which a person remarked that "Nobody who looks as good as [she does] can be disabled." She noted that part of her reveled in the accusation—even saw it as affirmation that she had successfully passed as nondisabled, even though another part of her felt horribly complicit in this ableist claim.[12] Some people may feel conflicted about the positive attention their body receives because the source of what's being praised is painful. A person who uses a feeding tube might be complimented on their thin physique, or someone might develop highly toned, muscular arms from using crutches or a racing-style wheelchair. Compliments on such features may be experienced as both welcome and uncomfortable at the same time. (Granted, some of you might be reading this and saying this is all just way too emo and you love any and all compliments, so just lighten up—that's fine too!)

For many of us, being at least vaguely in line with current fashion trends impacts how we feel about our appearance. Post anything online about disability and fashion, and you'll get a million (mostly negative) responses, especially when it comes to shoes (if anyone figures out the holy grail of a brace-accommodating shoe that's also cool and attractive, please let us know!).

While designers are making their lines more accessible with different types of closures, back-entry sneakers, and pull-on styles, we know that it can be challenging (and expensive) to find clothing that works for us, especially when standard sizes and silhouettes don't conform to our bodies. And finding clothing that we love, if and where possible, is super-important. No matter whether we're more cottagecore or Y2K, we all deserve clothes that not only fit our bodies but also make us feel attractive.

This might mean asking a little more time of PAs, for whom loose, slip-over styles are easier and less time consuming to navigate. Makeup-inclined people with disabilities or chronic health issues may find that some products irritate our skin or are challenging to apply (ahem, eyeliner). One woman we spoke with said after she developed a chronic illness, it took a long time to find a few cosmetics that she could use without irritation. Living without makeup for someone who had always loved using it was tough, and when she finally found a few items she could use, she felt really excited (though the experience helped her better appreciate how she looked with nothing on at all).[13] For those for whom fine-motor coordination is a challenge, there are some good adaptive cosmetics brushes out there that make application a little easier that we put in the Resources section. You may also want to follow disabled folks on the socials who have a lot of great things to say about fashion and makeup (check out @karin_recovers and @nina_tame).

All this is to say, it can be tempting as a disabled person to say that we somehow don't deserve to take pride or joy in our appearance, that we haven't earned the God-given right to treat ourselves with delicious-smelling lotions and vibrant lipsticks and think that we're delightful to look at. If you've been waiting for a sign from the universe that it's totally OK to play up those features you love, consider this that sign.

SUMMING UP . . .

Many of us reading this will always have uneasy relationships with our bodies. At times they'll be more friends than foes, and on other days we'll look in the mirror and say, "Wow, that's a big knee." Perfect symmetry and effortless grace may always be out of reach. The thing is, that's OK. It's more than OK. Because beauty is not about matching some marketing manager's idea of a mold but rather is found in occupying the bodies we actually have with integrity and appreciation. It's about seeing our bumps and scars, twists and turns, shrunken places and bulging joints not as liabilities to be hidden or apologized for but as part of the way we tell the stories of our lives.[14]

And it is those stories that make us desirable to ourselves and to others. As disability advocate Sarah Todd told us, "I am more confident now than I was before. . . . I know I look different because of scars on my neck and back and muscle atrophy and scoliosis. . . . There isn't anything I can do. I love how my body looks."[15] Our stories are cool and funny and fun and awful and beautiful and deserve to be shared, not hidden. So get out there, claim your space, don't apologize, and be your hot self.

If all of this is inspiring you to join the conversation about disability, beauty, and fashion, here are a few folks to have on your radar:

Imani Barbarin: @crutches_and_spice
Melissa Blake: @melissablake81
Marina Carlos: @marinacpom
Nyle DiMarco: @nyledimarco
Andrew Gurza: @andrewgurza6
Ariel Henley: @arielhenley
Karin Hitselberger: @karin_recovers
Emily Ladau: @emilyladau
Ryan O'Connell: @ryanoconn
Nina Tame: @nina_tame

CHAPTER 3
AM I (UN) DATEABLE?

CAROLINE

FROM 2012 TO 2020, A BRITISH TV STATION AIRED A REALITY SHOW called *The Undateables*, which followed disabled and neurodivergent people as they navigated romantic encounters. While many of the participants came off as thoughtful and wise during the on-camera interviews, the production and marketing were predictably cringey (picture giant billboards showing people with facial differences with the word "undateable" splashed across them). The show's title was a loudspeaker blasting the question that so many of us have quietly asked ourselves: *Does my disability make me undateable?*

Clearly there are millions of folks out there with all kinds of disabilities who are partnered, so the idea that being disabled rules out any chance for romantic love is just plain wrong. But "Do disabled people date?" is a whole lot different from "Will *I* date?" That's a question that no one can answer for sure, regardless of how their body or mind works. There are people I always assumed would be married by twenty-five who are now in their forties and still (reluctantly) single. There are others who did find a partner, but the relationship ended. Life is unpredictable, and so much of what we deeply want is outside our ability to orchestrate or control.

We also recognize that not every disability impacts dating equally. I love that disabled and interabled relationships are hitting the mainstream more and more, but it's interesting how many of the ones that end up being featured show couples who fit pretty narrow bands of white, straight, thin, hetero, and conventionally attractive. Facial differences, aphasia, cognitive abilities, how closely our bodies conform to what's "normal," and reliance on health assistants—all of these things impact how we navigate the dating world. It's entirely unfair, and it shouldn't be that way. But it can feel like a relief to acknowledge that the unfairness is out there and that it impacts our experiences of dating.

To make things even more complicated, our current "positive vibes only" culture doesn't leave much room for the emotional nuances of being an actual human person. Whatever state we happen to find ourselves in, the expectation is that we're *all about it*. Dating or single, parenting or child-free, religious or atheist, Republican or Democrat . . . you get it. We're supposed to be celebrating ourselves all the freaking time.

Parts of that invitation to self-love are really positive, but the opposite of shame culture can be . . . more shame. We don't leave a lot of space for discontent, longing, or grief, for rough edges or not feeling #blessed. For hesitancy around being just who we are, right at this moment. And so saying "Hey, I'm single and I don't want to be" can feel wildly vulnerable. Add to that the ambiguities of *I'm single and maybe I'm OK with that but sometimes not and perhaps I'd like to kiss someone but also not on Tuesdays because that's when I listen to podcasts while plucking my eyebrows* . . . and all of a sudden we're like Dorothy in *The Wizard of Oz*, only the cyclone whisks us off to a strange land where there are no reductive hashtags, and we have to sit with the ambiguity of a life that happens along a wide spectrum of contentment and yearning.

DISABILITY-ZONED

Jessica and I are both in long-term relationships. We got to that place along different paths—she always assumed she'd end up partnered, and I doubted I would. Some of that comes from our different histories: she grew up nondisabled, and I was born with CP. I have a few decades of internalized ableism coursing through my veins that makes being (achingly) single something that feels very close. But there's nothing quite so groan-worthy as having a couple of married ladies dish out platitudes about finding your soulmate (#couplegoals), so we turned to two folks we admire to speak with us about their experiences around (not) dating.

One of those people is international disability advocate Melissa Blake (@melissablake81), and the other is a man I'll call Gilead.[1] Both are in their early forties. Gilead has CP that affects his speech, movement, and mobility; Melissa has Freeman-Sheldon syndrome, a genetic bone and muscular disorder. Melissa has not dated but would be open to it; Gilead has dated a little but is currently single.

Melissa spoke candidly about growing up with a disability:

> My teen years felt like an endless parade of watching my classmates and friends going on dates and coupling up; they made it look so easy, and yet here I was watching from the sidelines, not knowing or even understanding why those things were so hard for me. I figured it must have something to do with my disability, and everything I absorbed from society confirmed that. I wrestled with so much internalized ableism, although I didn't know that term back then and wouldn't learn about it until years later!
>
> I've noticed that guys have no trouble being friends with me, but it seems that anything romantic is unfathomable to them. And I can't

help but feel like it definitely has something to do with my disability . . . hello, disability-zoned! As I like to say . . . always the girl friend, never the girlfriend.

Gilead also described wanting a romantic relationship but being slotted into the friend category by women he was interested in. He noted that whereas other people seemingly have a plethora of options when it comes to dating, he felt that very few people are willing to see him as a possible partner.

Melissa wondered to what degree her own fear of being rejected held her back:

> I've had a few serious crushes over the years, and the pattern has always been the same . . . I'm too scared to say anything. I know so much of my hesitancy has to do with my own insecurities and internalized ableism, but I do often wonder: Am I not sharing my feelings with them because I'm afraid of rejection? Am I sabotaging myself before anything even gets started?

When we get knocked down over and over, it's understandable that rather than risk rejection, we take ourselves out of the game altogether. Andrew Gurza talked about this in an article he wrote on being intentionally single. After going on date after date with dudes who were clearly uncomfortable with his disability, he wrote, "I simply don't want to go through that anymore. As a proud disabled man, as a person, I deserve and need better."[2]

For Gurza, being single does not mean being celibate. He's been public about his relationships with sex workers and advocates for access to professional sexual surrogates for disabled people. On the other hand, Gilead, who comes from a religious background, says that he only wants to make love within the context of a committed, monogamous relationship. He had a sexual encounter with a woman he was dating casually but said that they stopped short of intercourse. Every person, disabled or not, has to figure out how their relationships fit into the larger picture of their commitments and values.

NEEDING VERSUS WANTING

While a person may choose to be celibate due to personal preference, culture, or tradition, it's not a requirement of singledom. Many single people still have a satisfying sex life on their own or with other people. Depending on where you live, it may be legal to employ a sexual surrogate or sex worker.

One thing that both Gilead and Melissa stressed was the idea of embracing where they are at this moment while not closing any doors. Gilead said,

> I hope that I'm not single forever, but I also know that I have to be grounded, and I have to be OK if I am single for the rest of my life. The idea of being hopeful of not being single but also being grounded in being single.

Gilead spoke about his current life as being filled with friends who provide companionship and emotional support. He said that regardless of whether he ends up with someone, he is confident in his friendships and is sustained by them.

Melissa echoed this:

> I'd love to have a romantic partner, not to fill some empty hole in my life but to add to my life that is already full in so many ways! In other words, I don't need a boyfriend, but that doesn't mean I don't want one.
>
> I like to use the analogy of ice cream. I don't technically need ice cream—it's not an essential food group—but that doesn't mean I don't want it. Ice cream is rich and delicious—having someone special in my

life could be rich and delicious too. And there's nothing wrong with that, with wanting to experience that at least once in my life.

As much as I would welcome sharing my life with someone, I'm also just as truly content *not* being one-half of a couple; I embrace my singleness and feel empowered by it. I loved my thirties—it was a decade where I really came into my own and became comfortable in my disabled body and with my disability in general. Not to mention, I feel like I discovered who I am, so it was sort of like I was meeting myself for the very first time. Would all that have happened if I'd been in a relationship? I don't think it would have. . . . I always say that if I meet someone and we click and I could see myself being in a relationship with them, then great. And if I don't, well, then, that's totally fine too.

(That bump was the sound of Melissa's mic drop.) Seriously though, it's OK to be single and not like it. And none of us should be forced to pretend we're totally cool with being unpartnered, even if we're disabled and it feels like the messages we get from the world are that singledom is the default. Whatever it is we're hoping for, we have a right to want it—and to keep the door open.

CHAPTER 4
UGH, APPS

JESSICA

TEXTED MY HUSBAND WHILE WORKING ON THIS CHAPTER. DAVID, WHO is quiet and thoughtful and deeply principled. Who respects and supports me and never acts as if our relationship is anything but a gift to him. David, who since we've been married has learned that he is autistic and, for the past decade, has been blind in one eye. Who is, in other words, disabled.

Jessica: Do you think you would have messaged me if I had mentioned my disability? If I had been in a wheelchair in a photo?

David: It's hard to say, since I'm such a different person now, but I think statistics would suggest no. I hope I would have.

Jessica: Right. I was thinking you probably wouldn't have. Even though you are a really kind and open-minded person.

David: I don't recall ever seeing anyone on dating apps in a wheelchair.

As we texted, I felt tears forming. This whole life that we have built—our kid and our house on the water and the laughter. I could have missed it. He could have missed it. I felt betrayed, as if his love and commitment are less real because I, at least initially, tricked him into it.

We met on December 27, 2015. I ended our date after about an hour because I couldn't sit up for longer than I already had, even with my legs tucked under me on the bench. On our second date, while eating takeout at the house where I rented a room, I told him that I was disabled. On our third date—tacos on Telegraph Street—I told him more, and while I talked, I could see in his eyes that he was falling in love with me. Despite having had multiple people break up with me because of my disability, I never wondered whether David would be scared off. I recognized his loyalty immediately.

But now, eight years later, I have to consider that if I had told the truth up-front about an essential part of who I am, something I do not consider to be a problem, he never would have messaged me that first time. His first message was *You seem really great.*

I didn't lie in my profile. Because I couldn't work, I supported myself on SSDI payments, so under *occupation*, I wrote, "Mostly reading," and when asked to list my favorite ways to spend the day, I wrote, "Sitting down." I just didn't mention that I was usually sitting in bed or in a wheelchair. None of my photos showed me standing—I picked them carefully. But I also ensured that you couldn't see my wheelchair, a heart monitor, or a hospital bracelet.

In one, I sat at a picnic table in the courtyard at a downtown Oakland bar, leaning against a brick wall, reading. In another, I sat on the floor of an Oakland bookstore, again, reading. You would not know I was disabled by looking at my profile, but you would certainly know that I love books.

In part, I didn't mention being disabled because I didn't yet identify as disabled. I considered my Social Security *Disability* Insurance income to be a kind of incidental term. I knew I used a disabled parking placard because I couldn't walk, but somehow, I still considered it a technicality. Sure, "disabled" may be the best word for my body, but it wasn't essentially true, at least in the way that it was true for other people.

When I met David, at thirty-two, I had been, as I would have called it, "sick" for four years. For the first two years, doctors had told me that my physical symptoms must be psychological. For the second two, after finally having been diagnosed with postural orthostatic tachycardia syndrome (POTS) and EDS, I had worked relentlessly (and unsuccessfully) to recover. I was still settling into my new body. I still thought of myself as a runner taking a long sabbatical.

Over the first few years of our relationship, as I wrestled with accessibility obstacles in grad school and we became parents, my perspective on my own identity shifted. Rather than being a technicality that described the type of parking spot I used, "disability" became more. It is a community of brilliant, powerful, engaged, and creative people who live in bodies like mine and who have been paving a path for us all for decades.

I started to read disability theory and looked at my own encounters with ableism in the context of a larger story. I inhaled firsthand accounts of other disabled people and spent hours a day learning about models of disability and the complicated interplay between our bodies, minds, and societal structures. By the end of 2017, I was proud to be disabled. The shame I felt about my body's needs and its pain shifted—my picky and demanding body aligned me with the most extraordinary people and thinkers I had ever known.

If I had started dating, I would not have been able to leave my disability out of my profile and my photos. It had become too essential to my identity. It would have felt like a betrayal of myself. So I go back to that question—how, then, do I reconcile the fact that I would never have met David? That something that I love about myself, that is essential and interesting and creative and powerful, would have caused him to scroll right on past me.

TO DISCLOSE OR NOT

Many disabled people whose identity is not visually apparent choose not to disclose their disability or illness on their dating profiles. Reasons vary, but it's at least in part because the tools we use to date online don't ask. While writing this chapter, I signed up for a dozen dating websites and phone apps and could not find even one question about disability. This omission is indefensible. Dating applications ask about gender, race, ethnicity, food preferences, kids, sexuality, job, cannabis use, and even pet preferences! Twenty-five percent of Americans are disabled, and somehow, it doesn't make the cut. I can't recall a single person mentioning a disability or chronic illness in a profile.

I spent hours on Reddit boards associated with the more popular dating apps, reading threads about whether one should or should not include photos of mobility equipment or mention a disability in a profile. Responses circled the same advice: "Why would you present yourself by highlighting a negative characteristic?"

That's the thing, though, isn't it? I do not consider my disability to be a negative trait. Of course, every person, disabled or not, has the right to perceive their *own* body and mind the way they want, but many of us are proud to be disabled. I credit my disability with my ability to find joy in small things and my capacity for empathy. My pride in my identity is not based on some equation of whether my disability has brought "good things" into my life; rather, it's because disability is an indispensable fact about me. It's integral and true. Not being asked whether we are disabled implies that it's something to be ashamed of. It's not. It's not. It's not. IT. IS. NOT.

It's not only the app designers who imply that being disabled is shameful. After talking to dozens of disabled people who date online, we learned that those who do mention their disability receive heart-breaking and brutal responses. Many disabled people, with more apparent disabilities than mine, receive no messages at all.

People who talk openly about their disability on dating websites are often ignored. Some have even run small, unscientific experiments—changing nothing in their profile except a mention of their disability. Without exception, adding a disability causes interest to plummet. Many whose disabilities are apparent and who cannot exclude them from profiles say that they have never had someone express interest on a dating application or website—they have found romantic connections in other ways.

Dating apps not only ignore disability when asking about identity but also are often inaccessible to disabled people. A 2019 survey at Arizona State University found that dating apps are particularly unusable with screen readers and that blind or low-vision people were unable to access many of the features.[1] Again, it's self-perpetuating. If someone cannot use the app, they cannot be represented on the app.

DATING APPS FOR DISABLED PEOPLE

An autistic Canadian web developer, Christie Faye Collins, has been working to create an app that is more inclusive than those she was able to find when she was dating online. Christie hopes to create something similar to Hinge, but accessible. As of 2023, her app, called NOMI, is in the development stage. As she shared in an interview with me, "The premise is that disability and neurodivergence is centered and celebrated and the default is disability or neurodivergence, rather than able-bodiedness and neurotypicality like it is in the mainstream dating apps."[2]

I followed up with Christie over email and asked what issues she had encountered in mainstream dating apps and which accessibility and other features she was developing in response. Her answers brought tears to my eyes. Her response was evidence that the "nothing about us without us" refrain from disabled activists is paramount. A nondisabled person could not have designed something this thoughtful.

Accessibility is, obviously, a priority for Christie, and she acknowledged that the app will evolve with technology and as she becomes familiar with other needs and features. In the meantime, accessibility features include the following:

- App content will be compatible with screen readers (every icon will be labeled, and all images will have "alt text" to give users a "holistic impression of people's profiles and the story they are telling").
- Profiles will include the option to record audio for those who cannot or prefer not to read. All audio will have a transcript.
- Text will be large with high contrast.
- The color palette will be calm.
- The payment structure will be pay as you can.
- Personalized assistance will be provided for app navigation.
- All profiles will be verified.

When interviewing people for this book, I found that disabled people are much more likely to be in nontraditional relationship structures. Unprompted, Christie commented,

> So many people in the disability & especially the neurodivergent communities identify as LGBTQIA2S+ so we have a very wide range of gender and sexuality options to choose from as well as the opportunity to add your preferred relationship structure and filter for folks with a compatible relationship structure to yours.

Authentic connection is crucial, and NOMI plans to foster that through thoughtful profile prompts, connections based on interests, and deliberate opportunities to disclose disabilities. The feature I found most compelling is the complete absence of swiping. Unlike in other popular apps, you won't have to make a quick decision about someone. You can even flag a profile to return to later. She designed this feature especially for those with anxiety, but I think it helps to remove artificial urgency and imposed superficiality from the experience.

NOMI is not the only new app created by a disabled or neurodivergent person. Jacqueline Child, a woman with a nonapparent disability who lives in Colorado, found dating to be disheartening. Jacqueline, who has lupus, rheumatoid arthritis, and EDS and has had over forty surgeries in recent years, felt implicitly excluded when using mainstream swipe-based apps.

She decided, with her sister Alexa, an attorney, to create her own app: Dateability—a place where disabled or chronically ill people can gather and meet. They hired developers and emphasized the importance of making the app as accessible as possible. Before their October 2022 release, they tested it on a variety of users with different needs. They also ensured that Dateability works on computers as well as phones since small screens are not accessible to all.

While other apps don't even mention disability, Dateability profiles include a long list of diagnoses, mobility equipment, and other illness- and disability-related options. Users are not required to disclose the details of their condition, but Alexa and Jacqueline hope that the app will celebrate disability in a way that encourages disclosure.

A dating application for disabled people is not without risk, though. As we discuss in chapter 8, there is a small but often dangerous culture of disability fetishization. It's crucial that any app for disabled people also has robust safety precautions in place.

There are already some cringe-at-best and predatory-at-worst dating apps designed for "special people" (eye roll) that should be avoided at all costs. In addition, a few decent disability-focused apps have failed to gain a foothold but have managed not to be aggressively cringey.

For example, Jamil Karriem, an entrepreneur, developed Hiki for autistic people. When he was interviewed by *Forbes* in 2021, he said that he developed the app to be a place "where neurodiversity is celebrated,

and the lived experiences of Autistic adults are honored and validated."
Jamil is not autistic but had the idea for the app after his cousin, who is,
lamented that he was having trouble meeting people.[3]

Jamil said it was tough to obtain funding because venture capital-
ists can be reticent about betting on products designed for groups they
do not understand. He acknowledged that it's essential that the app be
designed with and staffed by neurodivergent people and has prioritized
that when hiring. Seventy percent of his staff are autistic.

Glimmer is another app designed to help disabled people connect pla-
tonically and romantically. Its founder, Geoffrey Anderson, was inspired
to start it because his brother has an intellectual disability. Glimmer
allows members to disclose their disability however they'd like and gives
various disclosure options. Glimmer welcomes all people, not only those
with disabilities.

When you sign up for Glimmer, you have the option to select from a
long list of diagnoses and identities. The sexual orientation options are
quite limited and dated: heterosexual, bisexual, homosexual, or asexual.
This is a glaring oversight considering the overlap between queerness
and disability, which we discuss in chapter 10. Unfortunately, Glimmer's
marketing frequently crosses into inspiration-porn territory.

Even though the quality and representativeness of disability-specific
apps have improved with NOMI and Dateability, it's important to stress
that disabled people should not be relegated to our own, separate applications. We should have that option (like Jewish singles who seek out
those who share their identity on Jdate), but having apps designed specifically for us does not excuse our explicit and implicit exclusion from
the most popular options.

THE PROBLEM WITH APPS

A more accessible and inclusive approach to dating applications would
benefit more than disabled people—we aren't the only ones who find

dating apps demoralizing and dehumanizing. All apps inherently flatten people to a collection of attributes. Swiping right or left in a split second on an entire, complicated person is, at its core, degrading. But the insult of these platforms is heightened when a whole group of people is, in effect, excluded.

Hardly anyone would argue that dating apps provide a humane system in which the beautiful nuances of people are celebrated. Every person is commodified into visual indicators of their superficial worth— conventional attractiveness, socioeconomic status, education. While scrolling, we fire off our most insecure and unexamined judgments in order to find a romantic connection. Sloppy. Dangerous.

But these apps have earned an entire chapter of this book because of their ubiquity. A 2017 Stanford study showed that 39 percent of committed heterosexual couples met on dating sites. They are the most common source of romantic connection by far. That number has only continued to grow, spurred, in part, by the pandemic. Other researchers have found that queer people are twice as likely as straight people to use a dating app.

Disabled people are, in many ways, incentivized to make our way to apps. The physical world outside our homes is often inaccessible, and meeting people in physical settings that don't accommodate our bodies and minds can feel impossible. For many of us, virtual connections (at least to start) make the most practical sense.

Unfortunately, as I've discussed, the platforms on which we could look for romantic partners are unwelcoming and fraught. Without the option to even claim, much less celebrate, our disabled identity, dating apps reinforce that we should be ashamed of who we are. If we insist on mentioning our disability, we are often ignored. When we aren't ignored, we are objectified and disrespected.

In 2016, on the website Refinery29, Kristen Parisi, a wheelchair user, wrote about her experience on Tinder. She tried a few approaches. For months, she hid her chair and just told people about it within a few minutes of exchanging messages. Later, she decided to wait a week or more until a good rapport had developed with a match. Finally, she included photos with her chair. Every approach was a disaster. People made fetishizing and inappropriate comments, ghosted her, and worse.

When she explained that she was paralyzed, men frequently, and bizarrely, asked about anal sex, wondering if a lack of sensation in the lower half of her body might make her sexually adventurous. Others questioned her right to even be on Tinder, stating that they thought she was supposed to date other people in wheelchairs. One match, a doctor with whom she had developed fun banter, blocked her after she said she was disabled. "Gross, no," he replied before disappearing.

Faith Martin, a wheelchair user with CP, joined Tinder at eighteen. She recalled that nearly every person who matched with her asked, within minutes, if she could have sex. The question itself assumes a specific and narrow view of sex and, more importantly, presumes that the details of a stranger's body are your business.

Like all solutions, this one is multifaceted. First, we must insist that app creators and funders include disability as an identity option. Disability is nothing to be ashamed of. We should list it, if we choose, alongside our race and sexual orientation. Second (and this is something we champion throughout this book), we must continue to advocate for increased media representation of disabled people with full and exciting romantic and sexual lives. We exist.

BOOTS ON THE GROUND

Despite their downsides, some disabled people do find apps to be exactly what they need.

In 2016, Josh Hepple, a gay man with CP who lives in the UK, wrote a piece for the *Guardian* about his time on Grindr. Josh uses a wheelchair full-time, requires 24/7 assistance, has a speech impairment, and defines his movements as "jerky." He also has casual sex with around three different people most weeks. His profile is very detailed about his needs and sexual preferences, and he has found that men over forty are the most receptive. Josh cannot masturbate and has found dating online incredibly rewarding, both emotionally and physically.

He chooses to present himself with pride on Grindr and to describe what he's looking for. Josh looks past the overt and covert ableism and makes Grindr work.

Caroline told me that when she first considered dating sites, it was after years of feeling rejected and believing that her expectations for relationships didn't line up with the men she wanted to date. She found herself repeatedly friend-zoned and suspected that her disability was preventing people she liked from seeing her in a romantic light. She said,

> By the time I was looking into online dating (this was the pre-app era), I had spent years trying to minimize my disability and hide as much of it as possible with romantic interests. During those years, I started to believe that there was something fundamentally wrong with me. I initially joined Match and eHarmony as kind of a joke with some friends who were all checking it out.

The lightness around these websites made the stakes feel low enough that she could change her approach to dating. Instead of hiding her disability, she led with it. She mentioned her crutches straightaway:

> I blasted every single thing I thought would turn someone off: I am disabled, use crutches, went to seminary, and work as a religious professional (say those things in a bar and you'll find yourself . . . alone in a bar). I wasn't confident, but this was a joke, right? So I just pretended I was.

To her surprise, her confidence seemed to work. She received lots of messages, started a few promising conversations, and had some good dates. This all bolstered her confidence even more until one day, she heard from Kevin, her now husband.

Most disabled people have mixed results when dating online. D'Arcee, who uses both they/he pronouns, has taken a few approaches to online dating. He has CP and uses a wheelchair but found that when he included the chair in photos, he got very few messages. They also observed that many men don't know what CP is, and D'Arcee prefers to talk about his diagnosis when he has more space to explain and answer questions.

Including absolutely zero mention of disability didn't work for D'Arcee either, and he grew tired of fielding ignorant and harmful responses once he disclosed it. Their current approach is to say, in their profile, "+50 points if you're open-minded." This strategy narrows the responses to those who identify that way. I think this is brilliant because D'Arcee has primed the men who message him for receptiveness. Claiming to be open-minded and then acting like an asshole when someone mentions their wheelchair is not a good look.

When traveling, D'Arcee has also used Craigslist to coordinate casual hookups. In that case, he always discloses his disability.

Like D'Arcee, Sarah doesn't mention chronic illness or being 75 percent deaf in her profile but does talk about disability advocacy work, which serves to prime those she communicates with to at least accept people with disabilities. In addition to being hearing-impaired, Sarah is neurodivergent and has chronic vertigo.

Sarah has the option to disclose or not disclose a disability because it isn't apparent to those who aren't looking for it. She doesn't use mobility aids, though her skin has some discoloration and her weight fluctuates because of her conditions. From her perspective, her presentation on apps is impacted by her disabilities, though people who do not know her wouldn't necessarily see that.

She does talk about her disability early on, usually while messaging—it's not worth wasting time on someone who won't accept her for who she is. Also, because of her hearing loss, she often requests a quiet location for the first date.

Some disabled people enjoy chatting on apps but find it difficult to transition to in-person meetings. Sarah Todd, a dancer and college student from Atlanta who was diagnosed with acute flaccid myelitis as a child and has partial paralysis of her hands and arms, initially joined Tinder during her freshman year of college as a joke. She didn't mention her disability but also had no intention of actually meeting up with anyone.

In sophomore year, she joined again, this time actually hoping to meet someone. If you look closely at her photos, you might be able to see her muscle atrophy, but she didn't specifically mention that she is disabled. She did say that she values disability advocacy, which she thought might be a hint. Despite long conversations with matches, her disability never came up. In one case, after talking for weeks and feeling a particular connection, her match asked her to meet in person. When it came time to meet, she canceled. She didn't feel up to managing the inevitable awkwardness of watching him realize that she is disabled.

OTHER OPTIONS

For those who cannot find what they are looking for by swiping or who find that the process causes more emotional distress than they want to bear, I suggest looking outside apps for people to date. While researching this book, I talked to several disabled people who met partners in online kink communities, which I will discuss further in chapter 6. In short, they found that kink culture often has an inherent acceptance of and openness to needs, limits, and preferences.

I think that if I were to date now, I might try to find people through my primary interest—reading. Certainly, there are online book clubs or discussion groups where I might meet a like-minded person.

There is also the reality of existing as a person online. If you have the capacity and are interested in maintaining a social media presence (and can handle the trolls), it can be a great way to meet people you might connect with. Let's use those creepy algorithms for good! If someone comes across you on Instagram or TikTok and likes your personality and witnesses the way you interact with others, they are more likely to see your complex reality.

Also, you can be the one who slides into someone's DMs! They can look at your profile, photos, videos, and witticisms and gather a more complete picture than Tinder allows. Socials, despite their many flaws, can bring compatible people together and allow us to reveal a more comprehensive version of ourselves than a swiping app allows. For those who love gaming, there are robust online communities around certain games, and I've talked to a few people who found romantic connections that way.

If you do want to stick to the apps, the first step is to do the internal work of accepting your body and mind as they are. It's critical to fortify yourself and know your worth before subjecting yourself to the rapid-fire judgments of strangers. Joining an app during an emotionally precarious time could easily lead to distress. This is true for anyone. Don't join an app to find evidence of your worth.

And when you do encounter the ableism that the very structure of apps seems to invite, know that it's not you. It's a broken and inhumane system. Consider how you can use this flawed system for your own needs, but remember, the version of you reflected through the snap judgments of others is not real. You are so much better than that.

When it comes to disclosure, say what you want. You don't owe anyone anything. You can be proud of your disability and still choose to keep it to yourself. When we operate within a structure that oppresses us, we don't owe the system anything.

Remember, the stories shared in this chapter are a tiny portion of those I heard and an even tinier fraction of those that exist. Dating while disabled, particularly online, can feel lonely and humiliating. Allow the shared experience of other incredible disabled people to bolster you. You are not alone.

MY OWN WHAT-IF

I emailed David after working on this chapter for a few weeks, "How do you feel when you think about the fact that if I had been honest, we would never have met?" I worried about his response because despite all of my work on disability advocacy and my hard-won self-confidence, internalized ableism waits just around the corner. David and I often start hard conversations over email. As an autistic person, he's found that having time to process and consider questions helps him feel less flooded. I usually email him and then wait. Inevitably, he emails or puts a meeting on our shared calendar where we can discuss.

After sending the email, I thought about all the time and energy he spends caring for me. About the household tasks that I can't do and how hard it must be to navigate my ever-evolving body. Does he feel duped? Sure, he loves me now, but does he look back and wish he could have scrolled past? Avoided my messy life?

Even typing that, I'm horrified to note how deep the well of internalized ableism runs. I reflect on how much the inherent ableism in dating apps impacted me—the long-term impacts of platforms that ignore disability and exclude us with inaccessibility. How they perpetuate the fear that we aren't worthy. The small voice that wonders if all the people who swiped left had a good reason for doing so. I can hold two opposing beliefs: *I am worthy. I am not.*

One grows from the truth and the other from fear.

A few hours after emailing, I hadn't heard back from David, but we ran into each other in the kitchen, and he asked for clarification. He was standing by the counter, and I sat on the floor. I took a deep breath and tried to sound casual, but my heart pounded and my cheeks flushed.

"Do you wish you had waited for someone else? Do you feel like I tricked you by not disclosing?"

Later that day, I got his response.

> I don't wish I had waited for someone else. I love you. There are things about your disability that make life difficult, yes, things that I wish could be easier. For example, I wish we could travel together: go to Italy, no big deal. But I would rather not-travel with you than travel with somebody else. You are beautiful and funny and wise and kind and relentless (!). I have learned a ton from you, and we laugh all the time, and we are compatible. You take care of me in ways that only you have and only you could. I talk with you more freely and more easily than I ever have with anyone else. Why would I wait for someone who can go to Italy but lacks all your wonderful qualities?
>
> Now that I love you and am married to you, it seems very weird to me that disability is so othering.
>
> Before you get to know someone, when you're in dating mode (or, worse, swiping mode), you (or at least I) tend to think someone is perfect. But what you really mean when you think that is that they will add exactly what you want to your life and hardly change you at all. Of course, that is ridiculous. Everyone is a person. Everyone needs things. Everyone is annoying sometimes, everyone is mean sometimes, everyone has health problems, everyone needs to be driven to the hospital, everyone changes you, everyone makes you grow.

Being married to a disabled person is being married to a person. Maybe you know about their "health condition" upfront. That's the main difference. The "perfect person" has "health conditions" too, or if they don't, they will soon. Disabled people have needs. Non-disabled people have needs. Disabled people can be annoying. Non-disabled people can be annoying. Living with and loving someone presents them to you under a microscope, at a zoomed-in resolution that is unlike anything you can conceive of while swiping.

Loving you is loving a person. Your disability dictates some of how our abstract life gets concretized. But it is not A Different Thing.

I believe him. Thank goodness I can. And I believe that disabled people who want long-term partners, casual sex, and everything in between deserve to find what we are looking for. And we have the right to start that search on our phones if that's what we want. We cannot let a broken system that tricks us into thinking our value is quantifiable and swipable win.

CHAPTER 5
MEETING UP

CAROLINE

"I FELL."

"Wait, you fell? Like 'laying on the ground' fell?"

"Yeah—totally wiped out. Blood everywhere."

"Oh, crap."

My sister went on to describe the rest of her date with the guy she'd had a crush on for a year: tripping over a grate, which led to torn pants, a busted knee, and an emergency trip to the corner store for Band-Aids and antibacterial lotion. Trying to help, I trotted out all the clichés: if he's the right person, a few bodily fluids and changed plans shouldn't be an issue; this whole thing is just the universe testing to see if he's a jackass; screw him if he misses his chance with you.

Sis wasn't convinced (big surprise—is anyone ever?). She wondered whether this guy—someone who until then had been exposed only to the carefully curated image she'd presented at work—could make the leap to the messiness of real life. Was all that flirtatious mystery gone for good?

Did I mention it was my nondisabled sister asking these questions?

Fortunately, her concerns were overblown; my platitudes were, for once, right on track; and the two of them are now married and parenting young kids (a bodily fluids–centered endeavor at the best of times). That dramatic first-date fall foreshadowed the depth and complexity of the real life they'd share together.

My sister's questions also captured the reality of dating: it's inherently challenging, subjective, and vulnerable. To meet up with someone, even if it's just for a casual fling, is to put ourselves in a position to be rejected for anything, from our taste in music to whether we vote in the midterms. And if we're looking for something serious, then dating is, essentially, standing in front of another human and asking, "Hey, am I a person you could see sharing flu germs and a mailbox with for the next few decades?" Statistically, there's a strong likelihood that the other person will decline. And obviously, it's true in reverse—we date plenty of lovely people whom we just can't imagine sharing a life with. I didn't call a guy back one time because he worked for a weapons developer, and I couldn't see eating dinner and being like *So, honey, how many villages did you say that missile can take out? More than the last one? Marvelous, well done.* Most of the people we go out with will not be into us, and vice versa. And being rejected sucks. There's no piece of advice or book or technique that makes dating emotionally risk-free, just as we can't swim without getting wet or skydive without falling. Vulnerability is part of the package.

While their first-date bloodbath is now a charming little anecdote in the larger story of my sister's relationship, what strikes me is how I both totally related to her falling experience and at the same time felt utterly distant from it. As the disabled half of our sister duo, I'm the one who tends to wipe out, and I have the scars to prove it (including a fairly dramatic one from a broken beer bottle I landed on in a bar, which I secretly love because it makes me feel so badass). One of my first dating memories is holding hands with my crush in high school, tripping on a backpack someone had left in the hall, and hitting the ground. I don't remember whether he distanced himself from me after that or I was so mortified that I just avoided him, but that was the end of whatever it was we had going on. That sickening feeling of being upright and then on the ground (in body and spirit) is something I know at my very core.

In my sister's mind, a big fall was something unfortunate that happened *to* her—an aberration, a quirk, a little story to talk about during a wedding toast. For me, falling is part of who I am. Or, more accurately, falling is an aspect of my disability, and disability is part of who I am. I can't imagine someone talking about all the times I've fallen in front of my husband during our wedding toasts (and if they had, the guests would probably have been like, "Dude. That's messed up."). When my sister falls, it's a story. For me, it's "Oh, that's Caroline."

For a big part of my life, when I fell in my dating relationships (or really anywhere in proximity to another human), it wasn't just embarrassing, it felt like confirmation that I wasn't supposed to be part of the dating world. That I should bow out gracefully and cede the romantic territory to anyone who could type "hiking" into their online profile under *interests* and not worry that someone would actually take them up on it.

I wish I could say that there was some big secret for shaking this whole "I'm sorry for existing; I'll just sit over here and try not to breathe too hard lest you need the oxygen" attitude. All I can say is that I felt like that at one point, and now I don't (or, more accurately, don't much of the time). And talking to lots of other disabled people while writing this book revealed that this evolution seems to be fairly common. Whether it's a few more years of living, a little more experience, or simply dating a bunch and realizing that the whole "Yeah, I'm just not super into you" is a two-way street, a lot of people we spoke with for this book said that they felt a lot less self-conscious as they grew older. And also that they didn't have any kind of ten-step plan to get there, so if you don't either, join the club.

While no one has all the answers when it comes to first encounters, we learned some things from talking with a lot of disabled people about this aspect of their dating lives that seemed useful to share. (Sidenote: talking with a lot of disabled people about their dating lives is one of the best ways to spend one's time.)

Before we jump into the collective wisdom on this topic, a quick aside: not every person who's reached adulthood has dated (that's true for disabled and nondisabled people, though anecdotally, it seems that we disabled types carry a bit more shame around it). There was sometimes a moment in these interviews when people would be like, "Um . . . yeah . . . dating, you say? Theoretically?" And to that, I say, theoretically is just fine. Maybe you haven't dated before. Maybe you've wanted to and never had the opportunity, or maybe you've never wanted to. Maybe that thing you did with that one dude five years ago might technically count as a date, but you're not sure whether the other person thought of it that way. Maybe you've done the dirty with a bunch of people but never been out to cocktails with one. You're far from alone. If you are remotely interested in dating, you should try it, even if you're making a first attempt in your golden years. Because the thing about dating is that, despite the vulnerability and subjectivity and the off chance you'll pee on yourself in front of a relative stranger, it's also great fun. And fortunately for all of us, there are disabled people who are willing to give us a window into the delightful and complicated world of pairing up.

PREPPING FOR YOUR MEETUP

So you've swiped right, exchanged Snaps, and decided to meet IRL. All that flirty texting needs to make the leap to face-to-face communication. What now? If your first encounters have been online, you may want to think through what aspects of yourself you want to share with someone prior to getting together. While there are no hard-and-fast guidelines as to what to tell people about yourself in advance, a pretty good rule of thumb is to think about what level of disclosure you would appreciate from a person you're meeting for the first time.

For example, would you want to know before a date if the person you're meeting up with isn't entirely comfortable communicating in spoken English? What if they don't like to be touched? How about allergies to common foods that might impact a restaurant choice?

Maybe you're one of those go-with-the-flow folks who can pivot in any situation and don't need a lot of preliminary info to feel at ease. In that case, not disclosing much is fine—if the other person does, great, but you're not expecting it. Or maybe you're the kind of human who needs to know your date's blood type, astrological sign, and kindergarten teacher's name before you meet in person. In that case, you might be more on the "let's get this all out in the open" end of the spectrum, and you would disclose as much as possible prior to your first meeting. Most of us are somewhere in between: we want to know enough to set expectations around communication and acceptable activities but don't need an itemized list of our date's favorite burger toppings before grabbing a coffee together.

The point is not that the other person will match our predate preferences exactly. What I consider respectful to share may be, to them, totally insignificant or way TMI. Rather, the aim of this exercise is to know ourselves better. If I feel pressure to hide important parts of who I am but would be totally put off if a date did the same, what does that say about how comfortable I am in my skin? Are there things I consider nonnegotiable that we should get straight before we meet? Am I fearful of being hurt and channeling that fear into overdisclosure to reduce the chance that someone will be taken aback by the real me and bolt?

When we asked people how they chose to talk about disability prior to meeting with someone they'd met online, there was a general consensus that giving someone a heads-up that you use a mobility aid or a service animal is helpful. First, wheelchairs and animals are blatantly obvious. It's kind of like, "Oh, you'll recognize me by the tiny blue earring in my left ear" without mentioning that you also have a big ol' tattoo of Paul Newman on your cheek. Anything that will come to light within three seconds of meeting each other is best introduced before the date, if only so you're not spending energy anticipating the other person's reaction.

If your date suggests an activity that doesn't work for you, it's also wise to be up-front about that (or, as one person suggested, to suggest something as a starting point so you are less likely to have to say no to what they offer as a first option).[1] If a date asks you to go on a cocktail cruise and you tend to get horribly seasick, for everyone's sake, let them know. Same if they want to go to a Brazilian steakhouse and you're vegetarian, or hike a rocky trail and you use a wheelchair. Gracefully suggesting an alternative activity with a brief explanation of why projects confidence and builds trust from the get-go. Every human has stuff that we can't or won't do (ahem, karaoke . . .). No big deal. No one's giving out prizes for "ability to choke down one's true self and hide your misery while dating." If there's absolutely no chance in hell that this will be safe or fun, what exactly is being accomplished? We talk about this a lot more in the chapter on safety, but one way people tend to get into sticky situations is saying yes to something that they aren't entirely sure they can do and then spending the rest of the date either worrying or in pain. That's not a recipe for an enjoyable experience, so just be honest.

If you're on the fence about meeting up with someone or location is an issue, video chats can be an enticing option. Now that the world has grown accustomed to conducting everything from business meetings to Thanksgiving dinners over Zoom, using video to make the leap between texting and meeting in person has significant appeal. The COVID-19 pandemic prompted dating companies to add video features to their platforms that are likely to remain part of our culture moving forward—like all great accessibility functions, it benefits everyone but has particular appeal for those of us who worry about accessible transportation and budgeting for social events. Ryan, who has CP, said that during the pandemic, he frequently used Zoom to chat with people he'd matched with online. By the time they were able to get together, they had the benefit of a dozen conversations to build on and had gotten some of the potentially sticky stuff out of the way. It's also safe and budget-friendly, and you can pretty quickly figure out whether there's potential (you also avoid the moment where you realize the pictures they posted on their profile were liberally photoshopped).

UNPLUGGED

As outlandish as it may sound, it is possible to meet people in ways other than apps. Bars, schools, clubs, parties, volunteer gigs, religious groups, being set up by friends—all that good old-fashioned stuff that, like Birkenstocks and dirty martinis, seems to never go out of style (or, like Birks, bounces right back if it does).

Some people we talked to mentioned conferences as places where they'd had good luck meeting folks who share similar interests. Daniel, who has CP, said he went out with a woman he met at a ministry gathering. The legendary civil rights matriarch Judy Heumann first encountered her husband, Jorge, at a disability workshop. They didn't speak the same language, but a mutual friend noticed their interest in each other and set up an introduction (and served as translator until they were able to learn enough Spanish and English, respectively, to communicate without a third party). While the odds change when you're hoping to meet someone in a sea of people who may not share a similar goal (for years, my husband was convinced that he was going to meet someone in a coffee shop, which, thankfully for me, never panned out), there's nothing like a shared interest and low-stakes encounter to make the conversation flow.

Meeting someone for the first time in the wild also means that a lot of energy that might be expended on orchestrating that first encounter goes out the window; instead, you can just stifle giggles together while the conference presenter drones on and then hit the free coffee on the way out. Plus, it never hurts to observe someone's interactions with those around them: Are they shy? Always on their phone? Bubbly and inviting? Pompous and prone to mansplaining? Sure, spending a few minutes chatting after a class doesn't mean that either of you is necessarily interested in anything more, but at the very least, it adds to the number of humans with whom we've had happy interactions in the world, and that's nothing to sneeze at.

LOCATION, LOCATION, LOCATION

You remember that time the person I was dating whisked me off on their jet to Ibiza? No? Me neither. Even if I had met a dude who had access to private air travel and a European pied-à-terre, there's little chance I could agree to an attempted whisking situation. Not because I'm disabled: Who can take a week off work at a moment's notice? Who's going to feed the cat or change that dermatology appointment it was impossible to get? We've got lives here, people. We can't just set off at a moment's notice (unless it's to buy those apple-cider donuts that come out only once a year—in that case, forget everything I just said while I reschedule my entire life).

The thing is, so many of our cultural dating stories hold up spontaneity, extravagance, and effortlessness as aspirational. In the cultural soup a lot of us swim in, putting too much work into planning a date is viewed as a buzzkill. We should be able to just float into some impossibly cool, somewhat secret venue we just happen to have stumbled across (not literally stumbled, though) and then, date successfully accomplished, glide back out into the moonlight, cloaked in mystery and desire and definitely not obsessively checking our phone for a "Would love to hang out again + happy face emoji."

While I'm sure there are disabled people out there who were born with some kind of inner navigation system pointing them to hitherto unknown wheelchair-accessible, devastatingly cool speakeasies, the rest of us are planning our dates down to the parking spot. If you find yourself scouting out dating locations with a friend prior to suggesting a place to meet up, you're far from alone: virtually every person we spoke with talked about the process they went through to prep for a date, and it often involved actually going to the place and taking a look around.

So what are they looking for?

First, how do you get there? For a lot of us, transportation is an issue, especially if we don't live in a place with public transportation or reliable paratransit (is any paratransit reliable?). When I first met my husband, I didn't have a driver's license. I lived in the city, so if the spot we were meeting was accessible by bus or cab (this was the primeval era before Uber), it wasn't a big deal. But at one point, I was visiting my parents, who lived close to Kevin's suburban apartment, and we decided to meet up to go to the movies. I either had to ask my mom to drive me, request that this guy I had barely started dating pick me up at my childhood home (prompting a first meeting of the parents way earlier than I would otherwise have wanted), or postpone until I was back in the city. The postponement option seemed a touch over-dramatic, and I was less excited about the parental driving situation, so I asked Kevin to pick me up (he did, and my parents thought he was delightful, so it all worked out).

For a lot of people, having a sense of independence around transportation feels important (that's true in general, but especially when it comes to dating). Disability activist Maria Carlos said she typically isn't comfortable asking a person she just met to pick her up and to assist with getting her wheelchair into the car, nor is she wild about having a relative stranger know exactly where she lives.[2] In that case, finding a few places that are relatively easy to get to that you can suggest for dates is helpful, even if it means you come back to the same places over and over (there are some additional advantages to a "home base" situation, which we talk more about below). One man in his forties who does not drive reflected on his vision of dating versus the reality:

> [I had an] idea in my mind that I'd go and pick up the girl in the car—but it's got to be a place in my neighborhood where I can get by myself: walk there, take an Uber there, because I think . . . the idea that we have to do this like everybody else—throw that out the window. How would a man with cerebral palsy do this? Forget what everybody else does on a date— [think about] what the date looks like for someone like me.[3]

It may well be that both people have requirements around location and transportation. There are plenty of couples where both people are disabled, or where one is but both experience access barriers that impact where and when they can meet. While navigating two people's requirements adds more factors to consider, it also opens up conversations around accessibility and, in some ways, can make communication easier. Kevin was the first disabled guy I had dated, and even though we were then solving for both of us, I felt like the conversations were more open and less draining than I'd experienced in the past because he had an innate understanding of life as a disabled person. At the same time, early in our relationship (and to a lesser extent today), we struggled because one or the other of us was used to pushing through in a situation and expected the other one to suffer along with us. There's no relationship that doesn't bring a set of things to navigate.

But I digress. For those who drive, parking is another consideration. Does the area have accessible parking (and if it does, are there enough spots, and do they tend to be available?). Is the parking on the street, in a well-populated area, or is it in a garage with lots of dark corners? How do you feel about driving, or navigating sidewalks, at night? Again, there are no prizes for people who put themselves in uncomfortable situations while dating.

Depending on what the plans are, questions around transportation aren't resolved on arrival. This is especially significant for those who employ different mobility aids depending on the situation. A young woman planning to go to the movies with a crush wanted to check out the seating in advance to help her decide whether her crutches or a scooter would be better.[4] Those visiting parks or checking out a section of a city thought beforehand about the distance and terrain and made informed choices between walkers, service dogs, and wheelchairs.

One college-aged woman spoke about bringing her dog on a walk around a park: she realized pretty quickly she should have chosen the wheelchair option because she was concentrating so hard on navigating the terrain that she couldn't pay attention to what her date was saying or maintain a conversation.[5] Of course, it's about not only what's safest and easiest for us but also what access limitations exist in the places we're going. If the bar is up a flight of steps and there's no elevator, that may make the case for crutches versus wheelchair. If you think you might be carrying something, like a beer or an ice-cream cone, that would be unwieldy with crutches, a scooter could make moving around easier. In any case, a lot of people felt less anxious about their upcoming date once they had a sense of which equipment they'd be using.

So here's a thing: when it comes to dating, there are some who point out the obvious. For many disabled people, our homes are the places where we have the greatest comfort and freedom of movement.[6] Inviting someone to our place means that we don't have to worry about transportation or choosing the right mobility aid or knowing that we can get to the bathroom when we need to. There's truth to that, and the inherent safety of being in a place set up for our bodies shouldn't be minimized. At the same time, asking someone over brings its own set of risks and assumptions (Netflix and chill, anyone?). If this is the option that, all things being equal, works best for you and the person you're meeting up with, call a friend before and after, establish some guidelines ahead of time ("For real—I actually do mean Netflix"), and keep your phone close by. The only sticky situation you should be in is one you consent to.

But let's say you're meeting up outside your home: What do people look for then? Personally, I'm a big seating scouter. Nothing drives me more bananas than bar sections of restaurants that only have high-top tables. I cannot get myself up onto most stools, and if I do manage the ascent, I spend every ounce of strength balancing my booty and trying not to stiffen up or fall right off. You can imagine how pleasant that must be for all involved. I always felt a little awkward going into a restaurant with a guy I intended just to have a drink with and being like, "Actually—there are no low tables in the bar—are you cool if we sit in the restaurant and order something?" I would do that because it's better than a head injury, but it also put out a sort of "I kind of want your babies" vibe I wasn't trying to project. A casual whiskey at a (low) bar table would have been just fine had that been available.

While I have the mic, I'll add that I'm also a big believer in railings that are more than decorative. I am not clear why entire eras of human existence seemed to have gone by without a person designing functional ways to mount steps (we can manage the Taj Mahal, but the porch railing continues to elude us), but, especially in older buildings, banisters are not a given. The ones that are there are too often twisted behind plants, stop in the middle (cruel!), or are so wide that one must place a hand delicately upon the top while struggling not to tumble to one's demise. The absence of a railing, or curb cut, or any other basic access point means that those of us who have mobility-related disabilities are often in positions where we must ask for assistance from someone we've only recently met. And while on a grand scale, we should all be holding doors open for one another, letting another person have our bus seat, or whatever one might do to be a courteous member of society, many of us feel vulnerable asking for assistance soon after meeting someone.

As one woman we interviewed reflected, asking for an arm is a level of familiarity that may be out of step with the relationship itself. You might not have held hands or hugged yet, but here you are in this very intimate act of holding on to another person and trusting them with your body.[7] People also worry that asking for help places a burden on the person they're requesting it from or sets a vibe for the relationship that they're reluctant to put out: if, as one person said, "I already need help, is this what it's going to be like forever?"[8]

THE MEANING OF LIFE. AND ALSO BATHROOMS.

While I totally get the reluctance to open a relationship with vulnerability, which can feel like the polar opposite of confidence, there is a quiet power in doing so as well. As my sister's fall and subsequent foray into child-rearing (as well as my own experience in those areas) attest, there is a sense in which all relationships have components of physical and emotional vulnerability to varying degrees. Every intimate connection involves a level of exposure to the messiness and changeability of bodies if we're fortunate enough to live long enough. When we are able to ask for what we need without apology, and with the trust that the person is capable of honoring that vulnerability with kindness and respect, it absolutely sets a tone for what will come after.

However, the tone isn't "Oh, look how broken and needy I am— welcome to life as my uncomplaining caregiver" but rather "Oh, look how comfortable I am with myself and my needs. The fact that I am open to my vulnerability is one of the qualities that will make me open to and respectful of yours as well." Seen in that light, asking for a hand is actually one of the more powerful things that we are invited to do and a way in which disability is a path to a much more universal facet of human experience.

OK, now that I've gotten a moment to get all philosophical about the meaning of love and human connection (FYI, that can all be true *and* falling sucks and asking for help is often embarrassing), let's take a minute to talk about bathrooms (I never thought I'd work a bathroom section into every part of this book, but apparently I get uneasy if there isn't a distinct toileting reference every few pages). So there's the obvious: Does the place have them, and if so, can you get into them? (Surprising how often the answer to the second one is no.) Beyond the having of the bathroom and whether it has bars and all of that good stuff, many folks consider catheter or diaper changes when planning dates.

We spoke with a guy with a spinal-cord injury who self-caths; he shared that if he has to change his catheter during a date, he likes to give the person he's with a heads-up because he gets self-conscious if he takes what he feels is too long in the bathroom. He doesn't want his date thinking he's miserable and hiding out or that he got food poisoning. He also said that outdoor dates are tougher because he has to think through how to navigate the cath process without a bathroom close by. He found that his catheter situation is one of the harder elements to introduce with new people because it is so personal, it's inescapably about his penis, and women have questions about the relationship between catheters and sex. He tends to hold off on talking about it until they've reached a level of trust and investment in the relationship.

Thinking carefully beforehand about what one will eat and drink during a date is common for all kinds of reasons. Many people have food allergy needs that require avoiding certain restaurants; one woman we interviewed said her celiac was often a factor when choosing a spot to meet someone and that her dates never seemed to mind. Others avoided beverages in the hope of avoiding a diaper or cath change (or even a trip to a moderately accessible restroom). In the same vein, some people feel self-conscious about how they consume food.

A guy we chatted with who has CP said that he typically uses assistance when eating and cannot chew with his mouth closed or avoid getting food on the table. He shared that for that reason, he likes to wait until he knows people well before eating in front of them.[9] He prefers to start with coffee and build a relationship before sharing that part of his life, which is totally valid—we all have parts of our lives that we don't want to lead with, and starting out with a shared activity in which you feel confident is always a good move. At the same time, the things that we feel most self-conscious about are the parts that those we care about love most. My husband's fine-motor skills aren't the best, and when I first saw him hold a spoon in his giant hands with this very unique-to-him death grip, I fell in love a little. It is something that is so perfectly him, so tied to this person whom I adore.

Besides what we put into our bodies on a date, there's the basic matter of the space itself. In addition to checking out the seating arrangements, people noted whether there was loud music playing or the room made it difficult to filter surrounding noise. This was particularly true for folks with autism spectrum disorder (ASD) or hearing loss. Those subject to migraines took note of lighting and how busy a place was. And obviously, cost is always an issue—we have to meet in places that fit our (often way too limited) budgets.

Another factor may be unique to those of us with mobility-related disabilities: the false presumption of drunkenness. A little earlier, I said we'd circle back to why it can be helpful to have a few dating locations where, as the song goes, everyone knows your name. Because there is nothing fun about being on a date and having either a fellow bar patron or a member of the staff thinking you're drunk.

One woman we spoke with said that in college, bouncers would try to keep her out of bars thinking she was already wasted, which prompted defiant conversations on the street where she had to announce her disability in front of everyone trying to get inside. I walked out of a restaurant with Kevin one night, and a woman gave him the look of death, muttering something about how shameful it is for someone to go around drunk like that. Kevin was not drunk. He had had one beer, and at that moment, I was too surprised at her presumption to wipe that pompous look off her face (actually, I don't think I've ever wiped a pompous look off someone's face, but I do think about it).

This assumption is, unfortunately, quite common, especially when people don't have the visual cue of mobility equipment. Until our species has evolved a bit more, we may not be able to do much about presumptuous fellow bargoers, but at least if the staff at a place knows us, we're less likely to run into a potentially awkward situation (side note: putting the onus on disabled people to avoid awkward situations based on prejudice is one of the most pernicious parts of ableism).

If there's any theme to all of this, it's that at the end of the day, we're all just humans trying to figure this dating stuff out. No one is an expert (even the people who write books about it), but from our collective experience, we do know that being authentic, honest, and hopeful is a really good place to start any relationship.

CHAPTER 6
SEX

JESSICA

My sexual partners would often say . . . this is the best sex that I ever had.

—*Carson Tueller, a disabled man*[1]

BEFORE I TALK MORE ABOUT THE INS AND OUTS OF CONSENSUAL DIS-*abled sex, it's important to pause and acknowledge that many (argu-ably, most) disabled people have experienced sexual trauma. In chapter 8, we discuss sexual assault and rape and the role those awful experiences play in dating as a disabled person.*

IN 2014, MY CARDIOLOGIST WAS EXPERIMENTING WITH DIFFERENT MEDICA-tion combinations with the aim of regulating my heart rate and blood pressure—she was concerned that years of unchecked tachycardia may have damaged my heart muscle. While we waited for the regimen to work and on the results of an echocardiogram and heart monitor, she suggested that I refrain from any strenuous activity.

I rarely left my tiny apartment and spent most of the day in bed, so I agreed to the limitations without hesitation.

And then I met Christopher.

I lived across from a wine bar in Durham, NC, but was too exhausted to walk across the parking lot on our first date, so I asked him to meet me in the courtyard of my converted tobacco-warehouse apartment building. He parked his bike inside the gate, and I waved him over to where I stayed seated (standing up and immediately starting to faint was not how I wanted to start my date). On the patio table, I had arranged what I considered to be a very romantic evening: two cappuccinos and my favorite strategy tile game—Hive.

Christopher was adorable. Shy and frazzled and with the most beautiful hands and shoulders. He loved motorcycles, Almodóvar, Sweden, and unnecessarily expensive T-shirts. The decade he had spent living in Brooklyn radiated off him in our small North Carolina city. I was already swooning, and when I first noticed his blue eyes, I thought, *OK, this is too much. He cannot be this beautiful.*

I won the first game of Hive, and he won the second. After about an hour, I needed to rest on my sofa, but I didn't want to say goodbye. I broke my own safety rules and invited him upstairs but first asked for his last name and texted it to my sister. In my small railroad-style apartment facing the train tracks, he looked around my kitchen and made himself a snack while I reclined on my thrifted yellow sofa.

After eating, he joined me on the bird-and-seashell-patterned couch, and I told him about my illness—POTS. Not long after, with attraction fizzing, he kissed me. Soon I was on his lap, straddling him, his hands were inside my gray T-shirt (I guess I wear gray T-shirts and play bug games on first dates?), and things were becoming, as my cardiologist might say . . .

Strenuous.

"Stop," I told him, and he did. I explained my medications and cardiology testing and said that I would need to get my doctor's approval before we took it any further.

To my delight, this limitation felt kind of hot. The ultimate turn-on: forbidden sex.

After that first date, we quickly fell in love, and every time we saw each other, our attraction became more insistent. We made out in the large window seat facing the train tracks. He brought over ingredients for risotto, and I asked if he would cook shirtless. Lying on the bird sofa facing the kitchen, I catcalled and admired his deltoids. On his lunch breaks, he biked across town and brought me molasses cappuccinos from my favorite coffee shop. He built (while shirtless, again) shelves for my record player.

A few weeks after meeting, impatient and, frankly, sexually frustrated, I emailed my cardiologist,

May I please have sex?

Her response (verbatim):

As long as you can keep sexual activity as a "recumbent exercise" that is not prolonged or overly strenuous, I think you can consider it as physical therapy. Keep tabs on the heart rate and blood pressure to see how your body responds.

I forwarded her reply to Christopher, and he replied,

You certainly don't need to worry about it being prolonged.

ba-dum

Christopher and I became, shall I say, *committed* to my "recumbent physical therapy." I wore my heart monitor during sex and kept my blood-pressure cuff nearby. He would watch my face, and if my cheeks grew too pink, he would pause, both proud and cautious.

A year and a half after our first date, we broke up. But for the duration of our relationship—through moving in together and navigating my evolving health—our sex life was strong and exciting, built around and with my fragile body. I learned with Christopher that boundaries and consent and limitations can be hot. That they can invite a special kind of openness and deeper communication.

I learned what the disability community has been saying for a long time: disabled people (can) have really great sex.

DEFINING SEX

Sex, for nearly every person (disabled or not), is tricky. No one reaches adulthood without some shame or confusion around their sexual impulses or experiences. Most people are exposed in media to only a few examples of what sexual connection looks like (white, hetero, thin, male pleasure focused, penetrative, abled). We expect our bodies and minds to fit within a narrow window of sexual normativity, and those constraints can limit what we want, with whom we want it, and how often.

Even the most common definition of sex is restrictive: a penis inside a vagina or anus. For the sake of this chapter, and based on our conversations about sex with disabled people, we are rejecting that definition and instead define sex as *a consensual act with the goal of giving one another sexual pleasure*. Sex does not require an orgasm and certainly doesn't need a penis inside a vagina to count. For some, sex doesn't even involve touching! Clothes can be on during sex or clothes can be off during sex; it depends only on what the people involved want or need. Expanding our definition of sex gives us space to consider exactly what we like and do not like.

Nondisabled people, particularly those who aren't queer, often try to contort themselves to fit what we expect to be "normal," falling easily into roles and performative sex. Contortion (in this context!) is not sexy. For some disabled people, the limitations of our bodies and minds invite a level of creativity, communication, and openness that helps free us from ill-fitting expectations. When Carson Tueller, who is paralyzed from the chest down, was interviewed by Glennon Doyle for her podcast in 2022, he described his experience having sex as a gay man who became disabled in his twenties:

> I just didn't come in with any ideas of sex. So then I'm here in this body; I don't know what it does. . . . And so I would just set up situations with people that I trusted, where we could just start trying things out. And it was just this slow experimentation of starting very small, and with kissing and with touching, and a lot of foreplay-esque kind of things, I started to have moments of like, "Oh, whoa, that felt very special. That was a treat. Let's go there." And slowly, I found all of these really incredible ways to experience pleasure and orgasm in ways that weren't available to me before. . . . This was different. The orgasm was like, I could repeat it, it could be so powerful that I almost couldn't stand it, and I'd have to stop things. And my sexual partners would often say . . . "This is the best sex that I ever had."

Carson found that his disability invites his partners to explore with him, and that kind of exploration allows for intensely pleasurable and connected experiences. Later in the interview, he clarified that he does not start a sexual activity with the goal of orgasming. Releasing that focus helps move sex away from a success-or-failure mindset toward something more mindful.

Many of the people we interviewed echoed Carson's sentiments. D'Arcee—whom we met in chapter 4 on apps and continue to check in with throughout the book—grew up in small towns in North Carolina and Pennsylvania and had limited sexual experience until studying abroad in Germany while in college. Gay men constantly propositioned D'Arcee when they were abroad, starting on their flight over! This onslaught of sexual interest transformed how he viewed his body and his sexuality. Looking back, he realized that there was some fetishization of his disability and his Blackness at the root of their interest, but regardless, he left Europe feeling happier and more confident than he had ever felt before.

Nearly two decades later, D'Arcee still enjoys an empowered and active sex life. I asked how he defines sex, and he said, "I changed my definition a couple of years ago. A lot of people think of it as a penetrative act, someone 'fucking' someone else. I actually realized that's not, at least for me, how I view it. If I have an orgasm, and he had an orgasm, we had sex. There are many different types of sex."

D'Arcee exclusively has sex with men, and they frequently ask him while messaging on apps, "Top or bottom?" D'Arcee finds that question restrictive and limiting. He answers, "Neither." Past sexual assault and his body's needs influence his response. They were raped by a professor in college, and being penetrated continues to feel traumatic for them outside long-term trusting relationships. He is clear about this boundary and insists that partners honor it.

Most of my multihour conversation with D'Arcee was about sex. Sex has been a way for him to explore his wants and needs. In his professional and advocacy life, he is "type A and organized," and he has found that he enjoys exploring submission sexually. In general, he loves the creativity of sex.

Recently, after attending an out-of-town conference, he posted on the local Craigslist looking for a hookup and ended up spending the evening with a guy with "blueberry moonshine in the bathtub and dolls on the ceiling." When the man pulled out rope cuffs, D'Arcee realized that allowing himself to be cuffed made him vulnerable, but he thought, *Screw it. If nondisabled people can have fun, I can do it too.*

As much as he wants to, it can be hard to let go during sex. He worries about sexually transmitted illnesses (STIs) and sexual assault. Even in the middle of an act, he sometimes tells himself, "You really shouldn't be doing this." But even that ambivalence, to D'Arcee, is a reclamation and rejection of the good and orderly behavior he feels society expects from him. Sexual experimentation and pleasure are empowering, joyful, and creative parts of D'Arcee's life. He is certain that "nondisabled people could learn a lot about sex from disabled people if they would only listen."

CRIPPING UP SEX

A chapter about disabled sex that doesn't talk about Eva Sweeney would be incomplete. Eva, who runs the website *Cripping Up Sex with Eva*, is a queer and disabled sex educator whose resources, innovations, and expertise have changed the landscape of disabled sex. Eva has CP, uses a wheelchair, and has full-time PAs. She communicates using an augmentative and alternative communication (AAC) device.

For those who use AAC devices to communicate in daily life, incorporating them into sexual encounters can sometimes be difficult.[2] According to research, accessing the device while having sex is awkward or impossible. A 2020 Australian study showed that many AAC device users innovate other communication methods during sex, including facial expressions, nodding, smiling, and finger biting.

On Eva's website (https://www.crippingupsexwitheva.com/), she provides pages of Q&As in which disabled people have sent specific questions about sex, and she has done her best to provide clear, kind, and supportive advice. Questions range from strap-on advice for people with limited dexterity to position options for those with hip pain. Elsewhere on her site, she offers consultations and classes in which she explores disabled sexuality, shame, and creativity. Her resources are a gift. Eva has created sex toys for those with limited mobility and reviews sex toys currently on the market through a disabled lens. Her merch page is a total delight. One T-shirt with a drawing of a vibrator features the text "The wand chooses the wizard," and another says, "Sex toys are assistive tech." Eva focuses on inclusion, accessibility, joy, and communication. For her, disabled sex is a civil rights issue.

DISABLED SEX IS A CIVIL RIGHT

The more I researched disabled sex, the more I realized that the right to sexual pleasure and sexual autonomy is, in fact, a civil rights issue. We deserve what scholars and activists call "sexual citizenship."[3] Disabled people have the right to learn about our bodies and explore our sexuality. We deserve access to information and independence. Not only is sex (if we desire it) part of the experience of being human, but when we aren't included in sex education and conversations about consent, we are more likely to be sexually assaulted.

As we discussed in earlier chapters, sex education that acknowledges disabled people and accounts for a variety of bodies and minds is rare and insufficient. Many disabled people are assumed to be asexual and viewed as permanently childlike. There are also some dangerous tropes about hypersexualized disabled people. Embracing healthy sexuality is a rejection of these oppressive systems and discrimination. When we learn what we want to say yes to, we also learn how to say no.

Of course, the desire to be sexual falls on a spectrum, and there are times when a disability intersects with a lack of sexual desire for other people. Sexual desire ebbs and flows for most people, but for some, the desire to have sex with other people is consistently low. Sometimes these people identify as asexual. As Angela Chen explored in *Ace: What Asexuality Reveals About Desire, Society, and the Meaning of Sex*, we should not assume that a disabled person is asexual, but we should believe someone who says they are.[4] In chapter 10, when we look at the intersection of sexual identity and disability, we talk more about the asexuality spectrum.

As I learned more about disabled sexuality as a civil rights issue, I found myself annoyed. Why does everything about disability have to be so *serious*? Why can't sex just be fun? What if we don't want it to be *a thing*?

I think my reaction is valid. It can be tiring to have so many parts of our bodies and lived experiences analyzed and controlled and restricted. It's exhausting to have to constantly prove and perform. So if you don't want to think about sex as part of a larger story, feel free. You deserve a break.

MASTURBATION

For all people, disabled and not, masturbation is an essential part of sexual discovery. Sex without a partner or partners provides the opportunity to explore and experiment without self-consciousness.[5] Depending on the culture you grew up in, you may have been told that masturbation is gross or wrong. It can be hard to move past those feelings.

Or, if you grew up disabled, you may still feel so infantilized that it's hard to imagine yourself as sexually autonomous. If this is the case for you, I encourage you to explore some of the sex resources we've included at the end of the book. You aren't the only one who feels this way. In general, as a disabled person it can be helpful to expand your definition of masturbation beyond genital play for the purpose of orgasm and include all sexual sensation in your conception. Also, depending on your sensory and mobility needs, tools may be essential. You can find a list of masturbation tools and resources at the end of the book.

SAFER SEX

You have the right to protect yourself from STIs and unintended pregnancies. As in all areas of disabled dating, it's crucial to keep in mind that being disabled doesn't mean you should demand or expect less from your partners.

With the exception of condoms and diaphragms, which do both, contraception—which reduces the risk of pregnancy—is different from safer sex. Safer sex involves the use of barriers and other practices to reduce the risk of STIs.

On the other hand, birth-control pills, implants, rings, IUDs, and sterilization exclusively prevent pregnancy. For all methods, accessibility must be considered. If your doctor lacks the training to advise on acceptable birth-control methods, disabled sex educators like Eva Sweeney and websites like Scarleteen offer workshops and consultations that can guide you.

It's crucial to remember that you have the right to refuse to engage sexually with someone who won't use whatever protection is appropriate for your activities: condoms, dental dams, nitrile gloves, and so on. We have the right to insist on safety.

HURDLES

It would be impossible to cover the full spectrum of logistical hurdles that can accompany disabled sex. This topic deserves its own book and an actual sex therapist or intimacy coach to give advice. But I will cover some of the common scenarios that people described to us during our interviews and offer a few solutions. At the end of the book is a collection of sex resources that you might find helpful if you want more technical advice.

PAIN

I hadn't fully grasped the reality of EDS during my delayed *rumspringa* in 2015. From the ages of fourteen to thirty-one, I had been in a string of long-term monogamous relationships. I had also grown up in the South in a fairly repressed sexual culture. I had never really explored my own sexuality. But in the time after Christopher broke up with me and before I met David, I sowed my sexual wild oats. After having spent my twenties in a relationship that was not sexually fulfilling, I had been thrilled to discover, with Christopher, that I really enjoyed having sex. Single and sexually curious, I moved to Berkeley.

Christopher and I were naturally compatible in bed, and I was able to communicate my limits clearly. Early in our relationship, his hugs could be too forceful or his grip too tight for my fragile joints, but it didn't take long to learn what the other needed. Once we broke up and I started having more casual sex, I learned that for my disabled body, new partners brought not only new shapes and textures and pacing but also, to my disappointment, new ways to be injured.

I met a kind and attentive math professor on Hinge, and after only one date, I invited Kyle and his CrossFit-sculpted body back to my tiny rental house. He knew about my POTS and EDS, but I hadn't learned to express (or to even know) what my injury-prone body needed during sex. After our second night together, my right hip started throbbing. It kept me awake, and I couldn't find a comfortable position for a week afterward. Visiting my doctor, I learned that it had been partially dislocated, and the surrounding tissues were inflamed as a result. Something about the positioning of Kyle's legs and mine had popped my hip out, which I had failed to notice during the act. He was communicative and generous during sex and knew that I had to keep my heart rate under control, but neither of us had accounted for joint dislocations.

As the year went on and I met new sexual partners, I found that being on top could injure my shoulders and that sleeping with someone's arm wrapped around my chest would dislodge a rib. I started to learn the delicate balance of letting go in the moment while remembering not to *totally* let go. I tracked which kind of presex pain felt better after sex and which was worse (a slight migraine = better, hip pain = worse) and practiced expressing my needs.

Disabled people aren't the only people who experience pain during sex, but chronic pain is part of daily life for many of us. D'Arcee, who loves and prioritizes a vibrant sex life, often finds orgasms painful. The spasticity in their legs can make the contraction of an orgasm unpleasant. I relate. When my lower back is in pain, the clenching of orgasm feels almost masochistic (and not in a good way). D'Arcee has found ways to make his sexual enjoyment not entirely orgasm-dependent.

I think there are a few requirements for figuring out the balance between pain and sex. First, if you can afford a consultation with an intimacy coach who has experience with disabled people, you might be thrilled to learn about the depth and breadth of tools, positions, and techniques to minimize pain during sex. It's absolutely critical that we have sexual partners who are willing and able to pay attention to our needs. The upside is that having a partner who cares about our needs stands to make sex itself much better too! Finally, I think expanding our perspective of what sex means is the most powerful tool for those of us who experience pain during and after sex. For some people with chronic pain that's so severe that even a light touch burns, sex without touching may be the best option.

SENSATION

Many disabilities impact sensation. Some autistic people find types of touching painful that a neurotypical person might enjoy (more on neurodivergence and sex later in the chapter), and some people with spinal-cord injuries experience different or decreased sensations in their genitals. When I am undergoing certain pain exacerbations, I experience what feels like electrical shocks in my labia. Sex would feel awful on those days.

The people we interviewed for the book expressed frustration that the sensations of their bodies differ from the narrow view of sex that we are exposed to in sex education and media. It can feel daunting to figure out what works without a template.

Again, I recommend finding disabled sex educators online and reading books such as A. Andrews's *A Quick and Easy Guide to Sex and Disability*.[6] While Andrews didn't address every version of disabled sex (no one can, and for that matter, no book could include all types of non-disabled sex either!), they help shift a reader's thinking away from nondisabled-focused sex. Spending time on Eva Sweeney's website can also serve to usher in creativity and acceptance. The solutions to many disability-related hurdles come from increased representation and decreased shame. It's also, as always, important to remember that most disabled people feel some worry that their sensations and needs aren't normal or OK. Shiny movie sex helps no one.

INCONTINENCE

As A. Andrews addressed in *A Quick and Easy Guide to Sex and Disability*, incontinence is more common among disabled and nondisabled people than many realize. Those who experience bladder and/or bowel incontinence may feel anxious about bringing up their related needs with new sexual partners, particularly because sexual arousal and positioning can trigger leaks. That said, sex, in general, is messy and individualized, and planning, humor, and honesty can help ease the awkwardness.

There are pads and other options to help contain any incontinence-related fluid. Many people already use these pads when having sex because all sorts of fluids (ejaculate, lubricant, saliva) can stain sheets or whatever surface you use for sex. If your partner makes you feel ashamed about your body's functions and needs, they aren't the right partner for you.

POSITIONING

Spasticity, pain, paralysis, and body size can impact the positions in which a disabled person can have sex. Again, if our minds hold one (abled, sexist, *blah blah blah*) view of sex, then coming up with other solutions can feel tricky. But trust me when I say disabled people are inventing new and pleasurable options inside and outside the bedroom.

The people we interviewed utilize benches and chairs and special pillows. Finding a way for two bodies to be satisfyingly together requires openness, communication, creativity, and a sense of humor. Many disabled people have accessed their own creativity by spending time learning from disabled sex consultants and engaging with kink culture. Step one: expand what sex means. Step two: try some things!

INTENSITY OR FREQUENCY OF DESIRE

Many of the people we interviewed for this book commented that low sexual desire interferes with having a satisfying sex life. Concern about one's level of sexual desire is not limited to disabled people. As Emily Nagoski explained in *Come As You Are: The New Science That Will Transform Your Sex Life*, low desire impacts all people at some point in their lives.[7] She spent a great deal of her groundbreaking book explaining that what we think is average sexually isn't. That said, certain aspects of living with disabled bodies or minds can interfere with libido.

To me, the tricky part of low desire is that it's often real or perceived judgments about sexual frequency that are the problem, not the actual level of desire. If you just don't want sex all that often, and so you don't have sex all that often, there really isn't a problem. But if you feel that you *should* want sex more or you are comparing yourself to how you imagine others feel sexually, that same level of sexual interest can feel like a problem. Also, if you are in a sexually monogamous partnership and you and your partner have wildly different levels of desire, your mismatched sex drives can be a challenge. But even here, there are solutions. Before deciding that we aren't happy with how much and how often we want sex, we should first consider whether we are feeling our own unhappiness or responding to what we assume is normal.

If you do decide that you want to want sex more, there are a few approaches that you can take. For almost all of them, you'll want to learn from an expert. Before you do, consider where you are getting your advice. Disabled people can smell ableism, and if you are getting the vibe from a sexual therapist that they are centering nondisabled bodies and minds, steer clear. Fortunately, there are many sex coaches and therapists who celebrate a full range of human experiences. See the Resources list at the end of this book.

I also encourage you to be deeply kind to yourself during any examination of your level of desire for sex. Very few disabled people make it to adulthood without having some sort of sexually traumatic experience. We live with bodies and minds that are objectified, othered, and excluded. Even disabled people who have not experienced sexual assault have usually felt disempowered in medical settings and may have body-related trauma. Often the only available solution in traumatic medical situations is dissociation.

The reasons that our desire for sex might wane or be less than we expect are vast and often bound up in the specific ways that disabled people are mistreated. If you wish to explore and expand your sexual desire, there are brilliant disabled sex educators (again, see the Resources section at the end of the book) who can provide guidance and solidarity.

I would also consider reading or listening to *Come As You Are*. When I first read it, I learned a lot about how desire starts and stops and is modulated. Though it's not disabled-centric, it is a good primer on what starts and stops arousal and encourages open acceptance of our bodies and minds.

TRAUMA

The relationship between trauma and sex deserves its own book. In the disabled community, the rates of sexual and medical trauma are staggering. Our bodies hold on to these experiences, and it can be hard to move past them and into pleasure. If this is where you find yourself, I am so sorry for the ways that you have been hurt. Finding a therapist who specializes in somatic trauma work is ideal, but as we are writing this book in 2023, mental health resources are in short supply.

While it may be difficult to find a trauma and disability–literate therapist, there are free resources that may help you find the support you need.

Sexual trauma resources:

The Anti-Violence Project, 212-714-1141
Darkness to Light, 1-866-FOR-LIGHT
Love Is Respect, 1-866-331-9474
RAINN, 800-656-HOPE
Safe Horizon, 1-800-621-HOPE
Abused Deaf Women's Advocacy Services, https://www.thedeaf hotline.org/
Sisters of Color Ending Sexual Assault (SCESA), https://sisters lead.org/
The Breathe Network (a network of affordable therapists)

Know that you aren't alone, and please be gentle with yourself. It's not wrong or bad to have a complicated relationship with your body and sex.

SEX TOOLS

Just as my wheelchair allows me to visit museums, specific benches, beds, and cushions can help disabled people have more fulfilling sexual experiences. In late 2021, when dozens of disabled people were interviewed by Buzzfeed about their sex lives, many mentioned adaptive equipment.[8] "Sex furniture," such as the IntimateRider, developed by a disabled person, can facilitate thrusting and other sexual movements for those with reduced mobility. Other adaptive sex equipment includes the Body Bouncer, which does exactly what it sounds like, and Liberator Shapes—pillows that help with positioning. Some disabled people find the Thigh Sling to be helpful for holding their thighs in specific positions.

Finding and assembling the right equipment can require time and planning, but, as A. Andrews said, disabled people are expert planners![9]

As with nearly every aspect of disabled sex, the first step is acceptance of our bodies and minds, the next is openness to perceiving our needs, and finally, the fun part—creativity.

KINK

D'Arcee wasn't the only person who brought up kink during our interviews. In fact, the majority of disabled people who talked with us about their sex lives talked about kink! For the uninitiated, "kink is defined as a sexual activity that falls outside of sex that society traditionally considers 'acceptable.'"[10]

On paper, kink culture prioritizes consent, communication, and compromise. It embraces nontraditional sexual exploration. It's not surprising, then, that for disabled people whose bodies or minds need sexual adaptation, kink is appealing. The most basic and heteronormative notions of sex include endless assumptions. Kink requires a beginner's mind. Some people with chronic pain are drawn to bondage, discipline, dominance, submission, and sadism (BDSM) because it can give them a sense of control over their pain.[11]

For those who are not familiar with BDSM, which falls under the kink umbrella, it often involves a defined power dynamic and experimenting with control. For disabled people who find normative sex inaccessible, BDSM offers a different structure from which to explore sensations and desires. Sometimes it involves pain experienced as or intended for pleasure.[12]

To be honest, a whole book could be written about the intersection of disability and kink culture. If my brief descriptions elicit something in you, I encourage you to do your own research and reach out to organizations such as Advocating for Sex Positive Education and Consent Culture (ASPECC) and National Center for Sexual Freedom (NCSF), which provide resources for exploring kink safely. You can also listen to Tina Horn's podcast, *Why Are People into That?*

SEXUAL SURROGACY

Another topic that I wish I could read an entire book about is the relationship between sex surrogates and disabled people. Some sex surrogates call themselves sex workers, and some do not. But the goal for all (ethical) sex surrogates is to assist disabled people in finding sexual pleasure and satisfaction. Sometimes a surrogate works one-on-one with a disabled person, and sometimes a couple invites them in to help discover new ways of connecting sexually.

In 2017, Spencer Williams, who has CP, wrote a piece for *Vice* about his choice to use a sexual surrogate. Spencer wrote that immediately after his sessions with his surrogate, he feels confident, but later, he is often plagued by self-doubt and worries that the only sex he will have is the sex he pays for. But he also reminds himself that the knowledge he's gaining from his surrogate can help him as a sexual partner down the road.

Mark O'Brien, who was paralyzed after contracting polio, wrote an essay for the *Sun* in 1990 about his experience with a sex surrogate.[13] The essay was later turned into the 2012 movie *The Sessions*, with Helen Hunt. In his essay, Mark explained that prior to meeting his surrogate, he had a complicated relationship with his sexuality, in part because he had always felt so dependent on his parents. That very close relationship had created a dynamic in which he believed they could always sense his thoughts and feelings. Consequently, he didn't feel the freedom to experiment sexually, even in his own mind.

He was living in Berkeley and watched his friends—many of whom were disabled—learn about and explore their sexuality. As he entered his thirties, he had not found someone with whom he connected sexually and started to consider hiring someone.

When Mark brought up using a surrogate in counseling, his therapist was open to the idea and provided him with the contact information of a group in California that could match him. He was ambivalent about the step but eventually decided that he would try it. His experience was complicated. There were beautiful moments with his therapist, Cheryl, but when they finished their work together, he felt let down and discouraged. He wrote his famous essay four years after their sessions ended, and at that time, he was despondent and lacked hope about his future sexual prospects.

However, a few years later, he reconnected with Susan Fernbach, whom he had met during the process of finding a surrogate, and they fell in love. They were together until he died in 1999. There are endless ways to have a meaningful and transformative personal connection. For many disabled people, sexual surrogacy has opened up new possibilities.

SEX AND PERSONAL ASSISTANTS

Some disabled people have sex with the support of PAs. The Australian study that I mentioned earlier in the chapter also asked participants about their experience with PAs and sex. The disabled people said that while some PAs see sexual facilitation as part of their job, others have boundaries and biases that make it impossible.[14] Eva Sweeney has written about her experience finding a PA whom she could trust with sexual facilitation.

Some disabled people utilize a PA for masturbation, called assisted masturbation. A PA will help with setup, leave the room, and return afterward to help clean up. According to Eva, it's essential in this dynamic to be clear about your expectations and to ensure that a PA is comfortable with the task before hiring.[15]

Madison Parrotta wrote an article on Scarleteen about caregivers and sexuality, and the piece includes helpful practical tips (link in Resources).[16] She explained that there are steps to cultivating a healthy sex life, even with a caregiver, and that the first step is communication. If bringing up sexual needs feels tricky, she encourages finding a therapist or social worker who can serve as a facilitator for that conversation. The tasks that a caregiver may need to perform before and after sexual experiences include dressing, undressing, cleaning, positioning, and providing equipment. As with every facet of disabled sex, agency is crucial. She also clearly delineates the difference between sexual assistance and sexual abuse or incest. These conversations are supremely important.

SEX AND AUTISM

Many neurodivergent people don't identify as disabled, and the range of experiences that fall under the umbrella of neurodivergence is extremely broad (autism, attention-deficit/hyperactivity disorder [ADHD], dysgraphia, dyslexia, social anxiety, Tourette syndrome, etc.). No book, much less a section of a chapter, could encompass sexuality and neurodivergence. For the sake of this chapter, I will refer most frequently to autism, but obviously, not all (or even most) neurodivergent people are autistic, and being autistic covers a huge range of experiences.

Amy Gravino, thirty-nine, is an autistic sex educator. When we spoke, I asked Amy what she would want other autistic people to know about sex. The first lesson is that autistic people deserve to have good sex and deserve to be loved. She said that for too long, she believed that she should accept whatever scraps were offered and that the measure of her sex life was how satisfied her partners were. She couldn't imagine telling someone no.

In fact, when she first started to have sex, she created a questionnaire for partners to fill out after sex. She asked what they had enjoyed, what they hoped to see more of next time, and whether there was anything that they had not enjoyed. She had partners rate, on a scale of 1–5, her vocalizations, presex attire, and oral technique. While postsex communication is crucial, she now realizes that all of her energy was oriented around her partner's pleasure, and she hardly stopped to consider her own.

Now, she feels confident in her abilities to please a partner, but more importantly, she believes she has the right to say no. She will engage in a sexual activity only if she feels an "enthusiastic yes." She no longer worries that this will be her last chance to be loved. Her wish is for every autistic person to feel the same.

We interviewed many autistic people, and their interest in and experience with sex varied. Some viewed autism as a sexual enhancement. For example, Suzannah Weiss, who wrote an essay in *Vice* in 2022, strongly believes that her autism makes her better at sex because of the intensity of her sensory experiences.[17] That said, self-understanding has been essential for giving her a satisfying sex life. Until she was diagnosed with autism in her thirties, she didn't understand why certain light touches brought on intense rage. It took spending time learning about herself and her needs as well as finding a community of other autistic people to have the sex she craved.

In her piece, Suzannah offered advice to other autistic people who wish to make sex more enjoyable. First, she said it's important to consider your sensory experience status in the hours before having sex and to express your needs. For example, if you are overwhelmed with sensory input before having sex, you can say that you need a few minutes alone beforehand to feel more regulated. It's also critical to say what kind of touch feels good and what doesn't.

Suzannah also said that for autistic people, the balance between planning and going with the flow can feel fraught during sex. Some autistic people experience cognitive rigidity, and sex with a partner (or partners) often requires a certain degree of flexibility. In her interviews, she found that some autistic people make cognitive rigidity work for them by setting timers or setting specific sex-related goals (i.e., we must finish in ten minutes).

Kink can be a positive part of sex for autistic people too. The sensory input of ropes or other BDSM tools can focus anxiety and sensory over-/understimulation. Also, the scripts inherent in some BDSM activities can help autistic people navigate vague and nebulous (and unhelpful) social scripts. Finally, as is the case with all disabled sex, it's critical to communicate as much as possible in whatever ways are accessible.

DISABLED SEX IS GOOD SEX, PERIOD

The lessons of disabled sex could (and should) be applied to all sex: judging our own sex lives against the impossible and very narrow version of sex that we see in media will almost always be dissatisfying. Bodies and desires and capacities vary, and holding ourselves to an unattainable standard will subtract all pleasure from what can be deeply satisfying. In fact, everyone could benefit from normalizing the almost universal need for *some* accommodation. All sex, for every person, should be bespoke.

We all deserve to have the resources to address and heal our trauma so that sexual satisfaction is available. We can all take the space to consider what we want and how often we want it. We control our own bodies, and sometimes that autonomy involves assistants and surrogates. Some people like intercourse, but that is just one way to experience sexual fulfillment. Bodies can feel good and connected in many ways, and what a gift it is to be able to explore those ways alone or with a partner or partners.

CHAPTER 7
BREAKUPS

JESSICA

Content note: Sexual abuse and assault.

WHILE RESEARCHING THIS CHAPTER, I WAS DISAPPOINTED TO FIND that most articles about disability and breakups were instructions for or ethical analyses of breaking up with your disabled partner. A whole category of think pieces centered around the assumption that dating disabled people is hard and wanting to leave is natural and appropriate.

I kept searching for the articles *for* disabled people with signs and indicators that we should break up with our partners. While I have been broken up with multiple times because of my illness, I wish I had felt empowered to be the one to end things. I share some of my breakup stories here as well as a few of the stories we were told during interviews. Sometimes the clearest message can be found in the details of another person's life.

"Long story. We are broken up currently. I've decided a life with her would be too limited because of her illness."

Smith and I dated for about six months. It was my first exclusive relationship after getting sick at twenty-eight and divorced at thirty. I had dated a few people, including a guy who, unrequested, licked the front of my teeth like a lollipop during our first kiss. Smith and I developed something that had potential.

When we first met at a bar near my apartment, I had been acutely ill for two years and did not have a diagnosis. Dozens of doctors had failed to find a reason for my nausea, weight loss, constant dizziness, fatigue, fracturing bones, and yellowing skin. Many of them mentioned that perhaps I was anxious. "It's amazing what our minds can do," they warned.

A few weeks before meeting Smith, I had visited a psychiatrist and begged for answers. "If my mind makes me think I'm sick, can you fix my mind?" I pleaded. He listened carefully and asked detailed questions about my symptoms and their timing. At the end of our sixty minutes, he said that he thought my disease was physical, not psychological, and that it actually reminded him of someone he had worked with years before. He referred me to a cardiologist for a tilt-table test, which would monitor my body's response to upright postures.

That appointment was in late September, a few weeks after I had met Smith. A college friend drove me to a medical office where I had my tilt-table test. It revealed a diagnosis: a form of dysautonomia called POTS. The test showed that when I was in an upright position, my heart was unable to direct adequate blood to my brain; my painful symptoms were downstream compensatory effects of constant oxygen deprivation. After two terrifying and excruciating years, I had answers.

When I got my diagnosis, my relationship with Smith was new and casual, so while I told him about the POTS, he was not my primary source of support. But we continued to date and learned about my new diagnosis together over that autumn. For the two years that I had been looking for answers, I had hoped that every day's symptoms were a fluke—that any moment, I would feel like myself again. Every morning, I thought I might wake up, go for a run, and start working full-time.

But as I established care with a POTS specialist, I learned that the course of my illness was likely to be long and complicated. It involved medication trials, grueling cardiac rehab, and significant activity limitations. Failing to heed her advice would put my heart muscle at risk. There was hope for improvement, though—research at that time indicated that 50 percent of POTS patients without underlying (primary) conditions recover.

I think that if you've never experienced a dramatic shift in your body's functioning, it can be hard to understand how long it takes to accept and integrate changes. Every activity and invitation should have gone through the filter of my new reality, but it was easier and more natural to make choices as if I had my old body.

My new body was quite assertive, though. For years, including the time after my POTS diagnosis, I continued to attempt activities that I could not tolerate, and my body reminded me, with fading vision, overwhelming nausea, and severe migraines, that I simply could not push through. Smith witnessed those painful reckonings.

Once, at his family's catered Christmas dinner, I had to excuse myself to lie on the bathroom floor for forty-five minutes because my vision kept tunneling. A few weeks later, he was with me at my own birthday dinner, where dozens of my friends gathered, and I again, due to dizziness and confusion, spent much of it on the bathroom floor. Early in our relationship, we went to the symphony with his mom, and he didn't hesitate to share her review of me: "Jessica's elegant and kind, but I think you can do better than a sick divorcée."

Smith and I were together for six months, and toward the end, I was more consistently aligning the activities I attempted with my new body's abilities. I was having fewer emergencies, but this change also illustrated to Smith that my life might be smaller than he had imagined.

We visited a small, car-free island off the North Carolina coast on our final weekend together, and I, for the first time in years, listened to my body. I didn't try to walk on the beach. When I became faint at a dinner out, I asked to return to the hotel to rest. We spent the chilly weekend in a golf cart, watching birds, the sunset, and the waves. I read in bed.

On the drive home, Smith broke up with me. He said he didn't think we could really love each other, and honestly, that may have been true. I was never fully invested in the relationship. Little things about him annoyed me, and I had to be a smaller version of myself to fit into his life. I didn't want to break up with him, though, because he was consistent and kind, and we had good sex.

And, if I'm honest, his affluence made me feel safe. When we were dating, I was too sick to work but had not yet been approved for disability insurance—my living expenses were depleting my limited savings. I didn't know what I would do after that. I had already borrowed money to pay for POTS testing. Obviously, our finances were completely separate, but the prospect of a long-term partner with a financial cushion made me feel safe—I imagined a future in which I could pay for the medication and treatments that I needed.

I cried for hours the evening after Smith broke up with me, not so much about him as out of fear. Now that I knew why I was so sick, I had to acknowledge that future relationships would include navigating my physical needs. Would anyone else be willing to take that on? I hadn't yet fully accepted taking it on myself. And then, speaking directly to my worries, Smith accidentally texted me when he meant to text his best friend: *I've decided a life with her would be too limited because of her illness.*

I didn't know that Smith would not be the last person to say that.

A few months after Smith and I broke up, Christopher and I met. As I mentioned in chapter 5, we fell in love quickly and enthusiastically. Whereas Smith's flaws were never far from my mind, every new thing

I learned about Christopher made me love him more. I told him about POTS on our first date, and my physical needs were always part of our dynamic.

That said, after the hormones of the first months faded, my limitations became more stressful for both of us. Christopher felt the most alive in settings that I simply could not tolerate: house parties at 3 a.m., bike trips around remote Swedish islands, riding a motorcycle.

A few months after Christopher and I started dating, I learned that my POTS was secondary to EDS, a genetic connective tissue disorder. While the rate of POTS remission for those without an underlying condition is 50 percent, for those with EDS, recovery is exceedingly unlikely. I would not be getting better.

The day that a geneticist diagnosed me with EDS, Christopher called to hear about the appointment. I was crying so hard that I could barely speak. He offered to come over, and I said he didn't need to. Twenty minutes later, he was at my door. I asked what he knew about EDS, and he admitted that he had been researching. "What did you read?" I asked. "All of it," he answered.

He held me as I cried on my sofa. My life had changed. After my tears subsided a bit, he pushed me in my wheelchair to a record store and then to a bar. We laughed so easily together. He cared about me. But both of us knew that the future of our relationship was now more uncertain than ever. Fortunately, I had been approved for SSDI and was now making enough to live on if I was careful. We moved into a tiny and poorly maintained century-old mill house a few months after my diagnosis. I loved that wobbly house.

Christopher wanted to be able to make our relationship work despite nagging worries about his ability to be happy with someone with a limiting chronic illness. One of his concerns was kids—Christopher wanted to be a father to children genetically linked to him. I did not have the same pull. I wanted to parent but didn't feel particularly attached to pregnancy.

I wanted Christopher to be happy, so for the sake of our relationship, I visited a high-risk ob-gyn. She entered the appointment with a stack of medical journal articles, which explained that while pregnancy would be possible for me, it had a high risk of life-threatening complications. "You could try," she said, "but if it's not important to you, it's probably not worth it."

Christopher was deflated and, from what I could tell, felt very guilty about his disappointment. Still, we pushed through.

About a year after we started dating and a few months after moving in together, I was doing daily cardiac rehab to try to increase my ability to be upright. Some days, I met with a physical therapist at a cardiac rehab center, and other days, I did the exercises on my own. It was excruciating. The idea was that I could exercise a tiny bit more every time (thirty seconds to forty seconds to fifty seconds, etc.) and eventually train my body to tolerate walking. I made a little progress, but inevitably, my body would rebel, and I would end up back where I had started. My relentlessness is typically unmatched, but the physiology of my body is stronger than my will.

One morning, I decided to do my rehab a five-minute drive from the house that Christopher and I shared in downtown Durham. A minute or so into my exercises, I found myself losing consciousness—the ground swayed and my hearing and vision faded. I called Christopher, a software engineer at a Brooklyn company, who was working from home. "I'm stuck on the ground," I explained. "Can you come help?" Christopher sighed, annoyed. "I asked you not to bother me while I'm working. It's important that I be able to concentrate."

I hung up and looked at the sky. An architect leaving a meeting nearby and carrying a giant portfolio spotted me and asked what I needed. I said I was dizzy and trying to get in touch with a friend who could help. He sat on the ground next to me and offered some water while I called my friend Maggie, who was working nearby.

She flipped the sign on her business door to "Closed" and drove to me in minutes. Maggie and the architect got me home and inside my house. Christopher stayed at his desk. I know how this story sounds. Christopher sounds like a real asshole, and I sound like a pushover. And maybe in the moment, both of those things were true. But it was more complicated. Christopher never stopped wrestling his worries about whether he was up to the task of being a caregiver. At that point, I never stopped feeling like a burden.

What I wish I had known then and what I would have told that version of myself a decade ago is this:

You will need a partner who can care for you. But what you don't see yet is that you will also care for them. You are wise and thoughtful and loyal. In some ways, the life you offer to a partner is small, but in others, it's beautiful and expansive. If you find someone who cannot recognize that, it's not because you aren't enough; it's because they don't yet understand. It's not your job to stick around until they do.

Later that year, we planned a summer of adventure. I would be in Berkeley, California, where I could take classes at UC Berkeley and enjoy more temperate weather. He would join me for a few weeks before leaving for seven weeks in Europe—attending music festivals in Berlin and camping on small Swedish islands with friends.

While apart that summer, I counted the hours until I would see him again. Our relationship wasn't perfect, and from my perspective now, I realize that I could never have been happy with someone who saw my body as fundamentally deficient, but I did love him. I loved how beautiful he could make an ordinary evening. I loved his innocence and grumpiness.

We reunited at the Raleigh-Durham airport, where he pushed me in my wheelchair to my car. I wore a new linen dress with a deep V in the back. When we got to our shared house, he asked me to sit on our bed— a queen mattress on our slanted floor—and he spoke clearly: "I love you and I'm sorry. We need to break up."

He explained that while apart, he had realized that the life he wanted just couldn't work with my needs. He couldn't be happy with the life I needed. We both wept. Two serious relationships since becoming sick, and both over because of my illness. I wanted a partner, but could a partner want me?

WHEN EVERYONE IS WATCHING

Most of the disabled people we interviewed shared heart-rending and complicated breakup stories. Harriet's story is hers alone, but the themes are common in disabled relationships. Harriet lives in LA, where she is a well-known and highly sought-after disability fashion influencer. She didn't make it to the end of her first date with her former partner, Kyle, before she sensed the first red flag: self-loathing. But despite her bold and confident public persona, her internalized ableism prompted her to override her initial concerns. Harriet is visibly disabled, and Kyle, who has a learning disability, presents as nondisabled.

Harriet is a wheelchair user, and without the chair, her mobility is quite limited. Kyle was large, and so the first time they had sex, she was acutely aware of her physical vulnerability. And that was when the second red flag started waving: Kyle was turned on by physical domination and sexual assault fantasies.

Her fear intensified when, after a few months together, Kyle's anger issues began to emerge. Harriet tried to break things off, but he convinced her to stay, and in the months that followed, they solidified a dynamic that many disabled people find familiar—Kyle treated Harriet like a burden.

Harriet admits that in public and on social media, she loved having a partner who did not publicly identify as disabled. She felt like it offered proof of her worthiness and reinforced her social posts about disabled people being sexually desirable.

But when they were alone, the relationship was corrosive. Kyle's anger and insecurities festered, and Harriet always knew that they couldn't be together long-term. He blamed her for not being able to stay in his (inaccessible) apartment. She was often afraid. Sometimes he was kind, but inevitably he would hold those moments over her head. Because Kyle's relationship with his own identity was so fraught, he resented Harriet's disability advocacy.

She knew she should leave him but admits now that she didn't want to because of her own internalized ableism. While she publicly shares messages about disabled worth, internally, she worried she would never find someone else. She also knew she wanted a partner and didn't want to endure another round of dating app humiliation. In her head, she repeated, "I'll put up with this because he is putting up with me."

Harriet and Kyle met in 2017, and in 2022, she finally insisted on some time apart. During their break, she started to be honest with her parents and closest friends about how she had been treated. Understandably, the people who loved her encouraged her to end things for good, which she did. She is thankful to be single now and feels committed to never again sticking around and accepting unsafe treatment and abuse.

When asked what she would tell other disabled people about dating and breakups, she said, "Never cheapen yourself because of your disability. Don't override your own needs to prove something to people on the outside. Being in an unhealthy relationship just to prove you can be in a relationship isn't worth it."

CAREGIVING AND BREAKUPS

In chapter 12, we discuss caregiver dynamics, which can be complex. In our interviews, we found that failure to navigate that part of disabled relationships often precipitates a breakup.

There is real stress associated with both being a caregiver and needing a caregiver. Also, for many disabled people who rely on a partner for tasks of daily living, the prospect of ending the relationship brings valid safety concerns. Risking a critical component of one's daily survival is not an easy decision.

Disabled people not only sometimes rely on partners for practical help but also are often financially reliant on them. Disabled people are systemically underemployed and underpaid. Federal disability income in the United States is below the poverty line. In many cases, a financial barrier traps us in unhealthy relationships.

For Jack, a man in his forties with paraplegia, living with his mother led to a few breakups. He would refrain from mentioning it on early dates, and when people found out, they cast judgments. Jack's mother needs his help, and he needs her help. Their care for each other is sustainable and works well for both of them. He refuses to be ashamed because of the stigma about living with one's parents. Now he simply tells women about his living situation on the first date—this weeds out those with limited perspectives.

James, who lives in Washington, DC, is a renowned photographer with a physical disability. They married their (now ex-)husband, Nathan, less than two years after starting to date, and reflecting on it now, they disclosed that they would not have married him if they hadn't needed a caregiver and financial support. Nathan enjoyed the recognition that he received caring for a disabled person, and James needed care. This brand of codependence wasn't an adequate substitution for a real partnership, and James knew early on that it wouldn't last.

One evening, a year after getting married, while James was unable to consent or protest due to medications, Nathan sexually assaulted them. James wanted to leave but couldn't find a way to support themselves financially or coordinate the care they needed on a daily basis. It took two more years to leave.

They are now financially insecure but have some consistent financial support because they were granted alimony. Finding caregivers continues to be a challenge. If the social safety net for disabled people were adequate, they could have left years earlier. James isn't unusual. The real story of disabled breakups is that because policies keep disabled people impoverished, we are often forced to choose between two dangerous alternatives. As we discuss in chapter 8, disabled people experience high rates of abuse. In those relationships, we often have to choose between staying with an abuser who will keep us housed and fed or face homelessness, inadequate medical care, and food insecurity.

For disabled or chronically ill people who do not rely on partners for health care and housing, the disruption of a breakup can still exacerbate symptoms and initiate additional health complications. For those of us with bodies that are sensitive to stressors, a shift in our primary attachment dynamic can set us back months or years. The risk of that change is significant and, again, can make it harder to leave. The freedom to leave unhealthy relationships is one of many reasons why we should continue fighting for adequate social support and disability income: disabled mutual aid can save our lives.

KNOWING WHEN TO FOLD 'EM

Quinn, in Edinburgh, knew he needed to end his relationship when his mental health symptoms became worse and he found himself overly reliant on his partner. His dependence on his partner was not his own shortcoming but, again, a failure of the social safety net. There is a delicate balance of self-care and caregiving, and Quinn was able to observe that the balance had shifted and that this dynamic could not last. He reconciled with his partner a few months later, having established outside structural support.

Sometimes we are broken up with because of the structures or functions of our bodies and minds. Sometimes we know we need to leave and fear the very real repercussions. In either case, ending a relationship as a disabled person is fraught.

It's also important to mention that many disabled people end relationships because of issues that have nothing to do with disability. I broke off casual flings for all sorts of reasons—a lack of conversational spark, a difference in life priorities, sexual incompatibility, the ICK. This chapter focuses on disability-specific breakup scenarios, but that should not give the impression that all disabled people are broken up with or end relationships for disability-related reasons. This chapter is meant to fill a gap that other breakup texts have left open.

To be equipped to manage the pain of a breakup, it's important that we enter relationships only after we have done the initial work of embracing our own worth and value. If we feel like a burden, we will accept less than we deserve.

When you are dating and disabled, it can feel like someone is doing you a favor by being in a relationship with you. And then, if that relationship ends, it's easy to wonder if anyone else will make that "sacrifice." If you take nothing else from this chapter, I want it to be this: those beliefs are society's conditioning and not based on truth. We internalize the ableism that we swim in, and it clouds our sense of self-worth. Society's power structure of bodies and minds is false, and the scaffolding is held up by fear.

Finding a way to believe in your own value is crucial. For me, that took identifying as disabled and learning about disability culture. It was there that I began to see the creativity and joy of my disabled identity. I see not just my needs but also my resilience and wisdom.

Unfortunately, even if we love ourselves, we will still be dating in a world that consistently mistreats disabled people. We can love ourselves fully and still be hurt. If you find yourself in relationships that devalue you because of your disability, I encourage you to move on. You always deserve better. A partner would be lucky to have you. I promise.

THE EASIEST WAY TO GET OVER SOMEONE . . . IS WHATEVER WORKS FOR YOU

And what about those long weeks and months after a breakup? How do we heal, particularly when many of the avenues for blowing off steam (dancing all night at a bar) aren't available to all of us? My approach to healing varied by relationship. With Smith, I found that my ego was bruised, but I didn't actually miss him all that much. My biggest worry was that I would never find someone else.

The easiest way to heal from that breakup was to have some casual flings on dating apps. The adage of "getting over by getting under" doesn't work for every person in every situation, but for me, a few casual hookups worked wonders.

With Christopher, healing was much more painful. I had loved him so much. He moved out the day after we broke up, and I asked him not to contact me until I had time to recover. I planned a move to California, and he planned to return to Brooklyn, but in the meantime, we orbited each other in tiny Durham, NC. One night, at a rooftop bar with two friends, I noticed him a few barstools away. We made a quick escape before Christopher spotted us.

During the months that we weren't in touch, I grieved. A small part of me knew that I deserved a relationship that valued every part of me, but I couldn't stop playing our best moments over in my head—sitting on our porch eating guacamole as the sun set, lounging in the swimming hole just outside town, our terrible temporary apartment in Bed-Stuy with a toilet in the bookcase and a shower in the kitchen, watching him cook dinner over a campfire in the North Carolina mountains, late nights playing board games in Brooklyn.

As I write this, nearly eight years after our breakup, I can see how unhappy we would have been long-term. Christopher needs a level of freedom and spontaneity that I can never offer a partner. I need someone I can rely on, always. But I did love him in a way that I had never loved, and I am thankful to have discovered that capacity in myself.

WHAT STORY DO WE TELL?

If you find being angry at your exes to help the process of healing, go ahead! There is plenty to be angry about. Be as mad as you need to be! But also know that ableism is the water we all swim in. I have certainly internalized the false belief that a person's value is tied to how their body and mind functions. Everyone has.

We and our partners are responsible for examining what we actually believe without allowing the poison of ableism to cloud our perspective. Disability culture has shown me that being disabled isn't inherently worse than being nondisabled. My disability brings patience, perspective, and ease. But it's not a matter of weighing the good parts of my body against the bad. My value isn't calculated on a ledger of pros and cons. My disabled body has taught me that life is more complicated and more magical than I had realized.

I came to terms with my disability while in a relationship with David, so I've never had the experience of meeting new people while embracing my disabled identity. I don't know what my years with Christopher would have been like if we had met after I started to identify as disabled and connected with the disability community. I don't know what that would have changed, but I have to believe that when he expressed concern that life with me would be too small, I would have known he was wrong.

DAVID

My next serious relationship after Christopher was with David, my now husband. My disability never threatened our relationship. From the beginning, I felt confident that navigating the world with my body was something we were doing together. I know there are activities that he would like to do and I cannot (for some reason, he always cites visiting Japan as an example), but those seem like minor hurdles. After all, he can always go to Japan without me.

It's been a decade since I met Smith, and my perspective on what makes a life good and full has changed significantly during that time. For one, my identity has changed. When I met Smith, I didn't know why I felt so sick; when I met Christopher, I thought it was temporary; and when I met David, I thought I was permanently ill. Now I identify as disabled, and for me, that identity brings connection to a culture and community with tremendous beauty and strength.

Identifying as disabled has led me to reconsider what I want from life and how I measure my own worth. I no longer think of my body as deficient; rather, I see it as a natural variation. Bodies and minds are not all the same, and we are all better for it. Being disabled has brought pain, but it has also brought creativity and resilience and a sense of true and enduring joy.

I don't think that I would be drawn to people who see a particular kind of adventure as crucial for their own happiness. That perspective feels small to me now. I know that before I was sick, I hung my hopes on ephemeral goals and felt a persistent hum of dissatisfaction. Disability culture has helped me move away from that kind of orientation. My joy lives somewhere deeper now.

MY OWN BREAKUP LESSONS

I wish I hadn't felt so alone when I was dating and recovering from breakups in 2014 and 2015. I wish someone had told me the following:

1. *Don't feel grateful just to be chosen—leave when it's not right.* As Harriet experienced, ableism and misconceptions about disability can send the message that if you are disabled, you are lucky to have any partner at all. That false narrative can make it hard to leave. I wish I had known that my partners were lucky to have me too. I should not accept any treatment I wouldn't want for a close friend. Don't be afraid to walk away.

2. *Don't try to convince someone to love you.* You are loveable exactly how you are, with the body and mind you have. You don't have to minimize your lived experience or overcompensate with qualities you think are more desirable. If you don't feel adored, it's not the right relationship for you. Being single is better than being lonely while in a relationship.

3. *When you are grieving the end of the relationship, pay attention to how ableism is compounding your sadness.* Breaking up is awful. Taking the time to grieve is important for everyone. Don't rush it. But if you hear internal echoes of ableist lies in the process, notice them. There are plenty of strong disabled people who can help you recognize and move past those damaging beliefs. You won't always be alone. You are worthy of love.

CHAPTER 8
SAFETY

CAROLINE

Content warning: This chapter directly addresses issues of physical, sexual, emotional, and caregiver abuse. If these topics are too sensitive, please care for yourself and skip this chapter, take it in small doses, or save it for another season of life. No matter how your body or mind works, no one deserves to be controlled, hurt, or made to feel worthless. If you are in a situation where you are currently unsafe, here are some resources.

For people who speak on the phone:
- Call the National Sexual Assault Hotline at 800-656-4673
- Call the National Domestic Violence Hotline at 800-799-SAFE or 866-331-9474

For people who communicate by text:
- Use the Crisis Text Line at www.crisistextline.org/text-us
- Text the Scarleteen Hotline at 206-866-2279
- Chat with a representative of the National Sexual Assault Hotline at https://hotline.rainn.org/online
- Text or chat with a dating violence specialist at https://www.loveisrespect.org/

For people who communicate using ASL:

- Call the Deaf Services Hotline at 855-812-1001

If you are in immediate danger, call or text 911.

SAFETY. UGH. A CHAPTER WE WISH DIDN'T BELONG IN ANY DATING book, but a topic that we, unfortunately, have to cover, especially as disabled writers and readers. Each of the sections below has a heading, so skip around as you need to. This is tough stuff, and even if you feel like you're in a healthy place, reading about people being hurt can bring up all kinds of emotions. At the end of this chapter is a list of resources for those who want more information on how to help themselves, a friend, or our disabled community through advocacy, so no matter what, check those out and share them broadly.

It's enraging that no amount of knowledge or self-care can entirely protect a person from abuse. Just as even the most skilled and cautious drivers can be hit by another motorist or be caught off guard by an icy patch in the road, people who cultivate every relationship safety skill can still get hurt. The information in this chapter is a general set of practices aimed at reducing the risk of abuse, but we are all too aware that the possibility exists no matter what (and that there is a particularly high risk for disabled people, whether we're dating or not). If you have been hurt, it's not your fault.

With that said, here we go.

THE SCOPE OF THE PROBLEM

It's ironic that while disabled people are so often desexualized, we're also far more likely to be victims of abuse than our nondisabled peers. The statistics are staggering: according to the US Department of Justice, disabled people are three times more likely than nondisabled people to experience sexual abuse.[1] For those with intellectual or developmental disabilities, the abuse rate may be five times more than for those without, though it is also estimated that only 3 percent of cases are ever reported. Women with disabilities are twice as likely to have undesired sex with an intimate partner than nondisabled women, and the rates of childhood sexual abuse are similarly staggering.[2] If we assume that sexual violence against disabled people is even more vastly underreported than sexual abuse generally is, then the rates are guaranteed to be much higher still. It is significant that far more than half of the people we interviewed for this book shared that they were survivors of sexual assault.

WTF is going on? Well, a few things. First, people with disabilities tend to receive a lot less reproductive education than our nondisabled peers.[3] Evidence-based sex ed is woefully lacking across the United States; as of this writing, only 60 percent of states require that it be taught at all, and even where it is provided, the information may not be accessible to disabled students or reflect our specific concerns.[4] Few obstetricians report receiving any academic preparation or formal training in caring for patients with disabilities and so may not initiate conversations with them about sexual health or screen for violence.[5] Thankfully, things are shifting in this area (the American Academy of Pediatrics is finally recommending that all children, specifically disabled kids, receive tools related to sexual health, including information about coercion and abuse).[6] These shifts will hopefully benefit future generations, but if you're like us and grew up on *Dawson's Creek* and Backstreet Boys, you may have had to figure out a lot of this stuff on your own (or with the oft-conflicting, sometimes terrifying health care guidance provided by Dr. Google). Lack of access to accurate health information not only means that we miss out on information about how our bodies work and stay healthy but also results in not getting critical info about consent, decision-making, and how to recognize abuse. If we don't understand basic information about sexual, relational, and emotional health, we become far more likely to experience (or perpetrate) violence in intimate relationships.[7]

While we often talk about the accommodations that those of us with disabilities require to learn, move, and work, what's talked about a lot less is the way that disabled people are constantly accommodating the people around us. As a kid using a wheelchair, I was often turned in the opposite direction from everyone else in elevators so that it would be easier for the pusher to get me in and out. That always felt awkward and dehumanizing—like, can I just face the same way as everyone else, even if it's less efficient? We accommodate when we hold our noses while navigating the accessible restaurant entrance hidden back by the dumpster, when we wake up or go to bed based on the schedule of PAs, or all those times we miss out on something because it's just too much effort to be included. Now, accommodation is a part of life—no one gets to do whatever they want whenever they want to (I say as someone staring at my husband's discarded sock that I've asked him to pick up a dozen times). But when we're raised to unquestioningly accommodate everyone else, particularly those on whom we depend for basic needs, that can easily morph into dangerous territory.

An occupational therapist friend told me that one of the first things she teaches little kids with mobility-related disabilities is how to instruct caretakers on where to put their hands. Sure, it might be quicker for a parent or aide to handle a situation like XYZ, but kids need to learn their own preferences, how to communicate them, and their right to hold others accountable for the ways others touch their bodies.[8] If they learn all this from an early age, they'll be far less vulnerable to abuse later. Even if we missed out on this learning as children, we can make up for lost ground today by thinking through our preferences. We can affirm that disabled bodies are no less deserving of autonomy and dignity than any other kind.

Disabled people are also at risk of being abused due to physical or emotional vulnerability. There have been some terrifying situations in my life where someone was following me or forcing me to do something and I wasn't quick or strong enough to get away without assistance. Disabled people report being forcibly masturbated by assistants, raped by intimate partners, or having mobility aids and medication withheld as a form of control. People who abuse may exploit emotional vulnerability or an intellectual disability by feigning romantic interest to get money or sex. They may assume that a disabled person would not or could not report abuse or leave the relationship.[9] If we grow up thinking that there's something wrong with us, that as disabled people we aren't desirable or attractive and should just be grateful for any person who shows an interest, then we risk accepting a lot of crap we wouldn't expect anyone else to deal with. Thinking we're broken makes us magnets for folks who seek partnerships based on control.

WHAT DO WE MEAN BY ABUSE?

Before we speak about preventing violence, let's get specific about what we mean by abuse. Broadly, abuse is any unwanted act that is intended to cause fear or harm.[10] It may be helpful to think about abuse as a spectrum.

At one end are acts that are absolutely, unequivocally criminal, such as

- Forcing a person to engage in a sexual act, including rape, oral sex, or sexual touching;
- Making a person view explicit content or witness a sexual or explicit act;
- Initiating a sex act with a person who is unable to provide consent either at that moment or more broadly;

- Becoming violent with a partner to force sex or engaging in rough sex without consent; or
- Preventing a person's access to birth control or protection against sexually transmitted diseases.[11]

Abuse against disabled people might also take the following forms:

- Preventing someone from accessing mobility equipment;
- Forcibly over/undermedicating a person in order to control them;
- Withholding or threatening to withhold care;
- Taking advantage of a person's lack of education or experience to coerce them into a sexual relationship (for example, lying to a person about being their boyfriend); or
- Intimidating, name-calling, or belittling someone with the goal of causing pain or increasing control. This may also take the form of trying to convince the victim that the abuser is the only person who would be attracted to or care for them.[12]

Within those categories and beyond them, there are varying levels of harm that can be caused in family, intimate, and caregiving relationships. It can be tempting to make abuse black-and-white, but in the real world, it's often murky. The images of intimate partner violence that we receive are usually oversimplified: a (white, attractive) woman is routinely abused by her (big, macho) male partner, walks out the door into the arms of a waiting friend or well-resourced agency, and never turns back.

However, we know that people of all genders and sexual orientations experience abuse, that partners can be in relationships where they each inflict harm on the other, that folks return to abusive relationships after having left, and that people choose to stay with violent partners for all kinds of reasons. One disabled woman we spoke with stayed with a partner because although she was being sexually assaulted, she also loved being in a partnership of any kind—the social capital we receive as partnered disabled people is a powerful draw toward staying in awful relationships.

Others may choose to stay because they perceive that the alternatives, like living in an institutional setting or losing medical insurance coverage, are worse than the harm they're experiencing in the relationship. They may consider what they're going through not bad enough to leave. Later in this chapter, we share some resources with guidance on how to leave an abusive relationship, but ultimately, the decision to stay or go is yours. However, we do say with complete certainty that there is absolutely no one anywhere with any kind of body or mind who deserves to be hurt. There is no lower limit for "enough" abuse to leave: if a relationship makes you feel bad about yourself, scared, or hopeless, get out. You deserve better, even if better means being single and safe.

INVESTMENT IN HEALTH AND PREVENTION

While we can't entirely prevent other people from hurting us, we can put energy into making ourselves less vulnerable to abuse. You can start these things anytime, but bonus points if you invest in them while you're single. That way, you're headed into dating with the greatest number of tools.

Take some time to get to know yourself. Emotionally, temperamentally, sexually, you name it. While we all evolve over the years, and life can be enriched by new experiences, having a degree of self-understanding will help you better articulate what kind of partner will enhance your life and what kind will detract from it.

For example, let's say you really feed off the energy of being connected to many people: you like maintaining friendships and sharing what's happening in your world. While you may date a more introverted person and choose to accommodate their need for quiet time by mixing social situations with more low-key dates at home, anyone good for you will support the social side of your personality and encourage your connections with friends. Big red flags would be putting down your social circle, forcing you to choose between friends and a romantic partner, or trying to cut you off from your support structure. Feeling a little lost about how to start? There are many ways to approach this. The most obvious is with a counselor, but other avenues are journaling, talking with a trusted friend, or making a practice of thinking about what parts of your life bring you joy.

And about sex . . . You are your own first and most important partner. Sure, we can learn about sexual preferences through experimentation, both alone and with others. Trial and error can enhance our understanding of what we like and what's out of bounds. You may try something once and be like, "OK—that [position, act, location] was an experience to remember. Unsubscribe." Even in loving, safe relationships, we may choose to have sex when we're not totally in the mood because a partner wants to (and for some, desire comes once you start kissing or touching, not before). All cool, as long as that decision is freely made and builds up the overall quality of the relationship. That's very different from being hurt physically or emotionally, made to feel small, misled, or coerced into sex that makes you feel awful.

Hone your instincts. As the saying goes, an ounce of prevention is worth a pound of cure. If we apply that proverb to dating, we might say that an ounce of trusting your own instincts about jackasses is worth a pound of recovery from the emotional, physical, and spiritual repercussions of extricating yourself from a harmful relationship.

People we spoke with for this book advised checking out potential dates on Google and social media before meeting up: "You can learn a lot about a person's values by gauging their social circle," one commented. There are also background-check reporting systems that you can subscribe to (and you could share a subscription with a friend!). That being said, even the most persistent interweb sleuths aren't immune to being snookered. One need only turn to Netflix to see that the most prolific criminals are usually devoted family men who coach the soccer team and volunteer at food pantries. If you've been on the receiving end of a creep who wormed their way into your life before you realized they were trouble, I'm sorry, and (again) it's not your fault.

However, if I may toot our collective disability community horn for a moment, I am totally convinced that disabled people are singularly talented (differently abled, as it were) at spotting assholes. Let me explain: as you well know, having an apparent disability makes you a magnet for attention. We get it all, from the street-corner preachers who yell out that if we *just prayed harder* we'd be healed to the person who grabs our arm to "help" and nearly (or actually) knocks us over.

We know when someone is engaging us out of a true desire to connect or just to make themselves look good. We view depictions of disabled people in the media and can intuit what's inspiration porn and which stories are respectful and nuanced. In sticky situations, our spidey sense kicks in, giving us clues about whom to approach for assistance and whom to avoid, even if we can't quite articulate why we chose one person over another. If there's gaydar, there's also "cripdar" (OK, still working on a name for that). But whatever it is, we have it, and we can hone our superpowers when it comes to dating. If a person strikes you as off (maybe too intrusive, too interested in your disability, too ready to tell you what you need), don't second-guess yourself. As one interviewee put it, "If you don't like them or they creep you out, haul ass."

A note about parents and friends. Common enough to be a cliché, many people who date have experienced a parental figure's disapproval of their choice of partner. Every teen movie has someone sneaking out a bedroom window to canoodle with the forbidden object of their affections, their love triumphantly winning the day (or at least hanging on until the end of the movie). Unless you're in a culture where marriages are arranged (or, like me, your husband and father hit it off immediately and turned you into the third wheel of their bromance), there's a good chance that along the way you've dated someone your family is less than thrilled about.

For disabled people who are dating, that parental approval dynamic may be even more pronounced. First, for a lot of us who grew up with disabilities, our parents or guardians were a much bigger presence in our lives than they were for our nondisabled siblings. They drove (or drive) us places, were present for a zillion doctor's appointments, helped with toileting and all kinds of intimate acts, and advocated for us ad nauseam.

That level of investment would lead otherwise reasonable people to deduce that they have more of a say in our lives than the average bear. A parent who's been so highly involved might have difficulty stepping back to allow the risk that's an inherent part of dating. Plus, even the most evolved parents can have some ableist biases. They could be uncomfortable about their now-adult child having a romantic relationship or feel that, on some level, there's an inherent deviance in anyone who is attracted to a disabled person. One woman who has a growth condition that gives her the appearance of a young child talked about her parents' concern that anyone attracted to her would likely have some form of pedophilia.[13]

Parents may warn against even trying to date. However, by definition, a parent has been on this earth longer than we have. Even the prickliest may have picked up some of their own spidey sense along the way. We can be so overwhelmed by excitement or lust or whatever it is that we really do miss warning signs that those around us—parents, friends, counselors, whoever—see. Given that, here are a few things to think about when it comes to navigating conversations with members of our inner circle who have opinions about our love lives:

- *Pay attention.* Does your parent/guardian/sibling/friend tend to pooh-pooh anyone you date, or are they sharing concerns about one individual in particular? Do they bristle when you make any efforts toward autonomy or imply that they always know best? Identify whether this is an isolated situation or part of a larger pattern in your relationship.

- *Ask.* It's easy to get super-frustrated when someone questions our choices. As disabled people, we're often infantilized; having someone poke at a romantic relationship can be humiliating and enraging. If you can, find a quiet moment (not while you're steaming) and ask your loved one for specifics. What concerns them about the words, behaviors, or attitudes of the person you're dating? What changes have they noticed in you since the relationship started? When did they start to become worried? One person we interviewed for this book advised, "Talk to your friends about what's happening. If at any time they take you aside and tell you they don't like your partner for some reason, you listen to them! Your friends love you just as you are, for all your glitter and gaudiness. They embrace who you are and respect you and your boundaries. They want to see you happy and thriving. Your partner should do the same."[14]

- *Educate.* The universe doesn't hand parents a book teaching them how to allow young adults to differentiate. It's hard enough for those of us who are actually in this disability world to find resources about dating; the chances of your nondisabled inner circle having any clue about healthy, consensual sexual relationships involving disability are slim. They may think that the only tool they have is to keep you far from anyone who might hurt you (as in any romantic relationship forever and ever). As hard as it is to educate, it may be on you (or a good therapist if you have one) to give them some additional tools and ways of thinking about disability and dating so that it's not an eternal bone of contention. There's a list at the end of this chapter that you can start with (or, you know, you could always lend them a certain book you are literally reading right now).

- *Make a plan.* Regardless of whether their concerns are justified, make a plan for how to address abuse as it may arise. Maybe you tell them how you would handle a dangerous situation if it came up or establish a code word you could use if needed. You could offer to see a counselor together or separately to bring a nonanxious third party into the mix. For anyone who is dating, it is actually quite helpful to have a broad network of people on whom to rely if something goes wrong. Help this person be part of the solution, giving them a job to do if you do find yourself in trouble. And if all else fails, turn back to your own judgment: Is this a situation where the two of you will never see eye to eye? If so, how do you meet your need for adult relationships without relying on their support?

SAFETY TIPS FOR FIRST (AND FIFTEENTH) DATES

So you've Googled your date, snooped on the socials, chatted over Face-Time, and decided you want to meet up. Hooray! Slap on that lipstick and your sexy undies (a lesson from the French: wear sexy undies even if you have no plans to show them to anyone—it gives that extra *boost de confidence*). Before you head out the door, here are a few simple tips and tricks for staying safe out there:

- Let a few people know where you're going and with whom.
- Have a code that you can quickly and unobtrusively text to someone you trust. Like, if you send a heart emoji, they know to call you to ask if you can hang out later. If you say, "I'd love to," they know you need help ASAP.
- If you're inviting your date to your house, make sure your cell is close by at all times. Know how to access the SOS function.

- Don't rely on your date for transportation. If you need to stick at the restaurant until someone can get you, that's OK.
- Watch your alcohol consumption; try to stay clear-headed. If possible, don't leave your date alone with your food or drink.
- If someone's creeping you out, just leave. You don't have to tell them why; just make an excuse and get out of there.
- Ask for help if you need it, and yell if you have to. This is not a time to be polite and accommodating.

Now that I've thoroughly freaked you out, have fun out there! (And remember . . . sexy undies.)

CONSENT AND DISABILITY

Consent is the ability to communicate whether and how you feel comfortable interacting with other humans. We often use it around sex, but more broadly, consent applies to what we reveal to another, whether we let someone into our space, and how our bodies are touched, receive medical attention, or are moved. It's not a one-time decision you make when entering a relationship or starting a sexual encounter but a series of check-ins at each stage of the game. Just because you agreed to a date doesn't mean you said yes to having sex; just because you said yes to oral doesn't mean you are agreeing to penetration. There are helpful resources at the end of the chapter that explore consent more broadly, but for now, let's chat about some specific issues around consent and disability.

First, think about how you communicate in general. Do you use spoken words, ASL, or another tool like a picture board? Will you have access to what you need to communicate not only leading up to a sexual act but during it? For example, if you use ASL to converse and you want to experiment with bondage, how will you tell your partner to stop or switch things up if you are in a situation where you can't move your arms? If you do use spoken words, are you able to form them spontaneously and under pressure (ahem) so that you can articulate *no* or *stop* (or *yes, keep going*) clearly? You may want to consider which ways of communicating you will have access to, not only when you're in a clear head space but also when you're smack in the middle of whatever earthly delights you've got planned for this weekend. Prior to heading to the sack, think about how you will communicate if you want to slow things down.

Another piece of consent is letting potential partners know about times you may be unable to agree to sex (like after you take a particular medication that really knocks you out) or if you have a condition that makes it challenging to read social cues. This may be true for folks who have certain forms of neurodivergence and anyone who experiences psychosis. When we're in a situation where we're not able to share a sense of reality with the people around us, we're more likely to be hurt or to unwittingly hurt someone else. Together, you and your partner can come up with a communication plan that works for you.

Talking about all of this in advance might sound awkward, but it's important (and can also be really sexy—nothing builds anticipation like talking about what turns you on). You don't want to be hurt, and you don't want your partner to be in a situation where they're hurting you. Plus, if the person is dismissive about consent, mocks you, or refuses to use contraception, you have just gotten the info you needed to peace out.

FETISHISM

Devoteeism, also known as a disability fetish, describes those who are aroused by disabled bodies. Often devotees express an attraction to a particular condition, such as amputation, spinal-cord injury, shortened limbs, or mobility devices like wheelchairs or crutches. People of all genders can be devotees, and, as with pretty much everything else when it comes to attraction, there's a pretty wide spectrum. There are those who are primarily attracted to folks with disabilities and those who are aroused when viewing disabled people performing (or struggling to perform) daily tasks. There are disabled people who describe devoteeism as empowering. They enjoy being an object of fascination and desire and find the sexual attention or financial independence gained from sex work gratifying. These folks characterize their devotee relationships as mutually empowering rather than objectifying.[15]

However, devoteeism can quickly make the leap into abusive territory. Those who fetishize disability typically focus on a single characteristic, not the whole person. They may like the vulnerability that is connected to disability, the idea of dependence, or the possibility of having physical or emotional control over someone. There's a world of difference between "I think you're really sexy" and "I'm the only one who will ever think you're sexy." Devotees may also describe disabled people as innocent and in need of a protection that only they can provide. While there are particular corners of the Internet where devotees like to hang out, they may also slide into your DMs, seek you out on dating apps (particularly those targeting disabled people), or comment on pics you post. Assuming you want to find someone attracted to the whole rock star that is you and not just a particular aspect of your physique, keep an eye out for people who

- Ask persistent or intrusive questions about your disability and don't respect the boundaries you set,
- Request pictures of you that highlight your disability or assistive devices or ask you for videos of yourself doing seemingly ordinary things like transferring from your wheelchair,
- Routinely praise you for having a disability or make assumptions about what kind of person you are because of your disability,
- Steer every conversation back to your body and aren't interested in any other part of your life,
- Focus on their own sexual arousal rather than your desires and needs,

- Make you feel like they're doing you a favor by being attracted to you or express that no one but them will ever think you're sexy, or
- Attempt to distance you from health care providers and make you dependent on their advice.[16]

It may be intoxicating to be the object of desire, but like any other drug, fetishism can leave a bad hangover. If you feel icky, scared, or dehumanized, run the other way. You deserve more.

CAREGIVER ABUSE

Many disabled people experience some degree of dependence on others (scratch that—every human experiences some degree of dependence on others). In healthy relationships, dependence is shared, and we care for one another in complementary ways. One person handles finances and the other transportation; someone cooks dinner, and the other one does the laundry. Disabled people may also rely on family members for more intimate activities like toileting and shaving and might also employ PAs who help with a range of tasks in exchange for a wage. Whether the relationship is personal or professional, it should include mutual respect and dignity.

In healthy caregiving relationships, everyone benefits. Lives are enriched because of the partnership, whether it's personal or professional. But unfortunately, we know that not every relationship is healthy. If you're in a situation where you rely on someone for physical assistance, here are some red flags to watch out for:

- Someone who restricts your access to mobility equipment, communication tools, service animals, or medication either to control your behavior or access to others or to coerce you into sex;

- People who are seemingly kind and attentive in public but whose behavior shifts behind closed doors;
- Someone who hurts or threatens to hurt an animal;
- Anyone who gaslights you or ignores your need for help;
- Those who mock, belittle, or humiliate you; and
- People who keep you from medical care or who over-/under-medicate you.

Tragically, people who utilize professional assistants have been raped or coerced into sex by the people they pay to help them. This line of work can attract assholes who get off on having power over others. They assume (tragically, often correctly) that a disabled person won't be believed if they speak up about abuse. Because so few of these cases are ever reported, and fewer still go to trial, there is lots of room for repeat offenders to rotate through caregiving systems and victimize many people.

While constant paranoia is a tough way to go through life, trust your instincts. Yes, humans, like pandas, are known to crush on each other when put into the same space over any length of time. The intimacy of sharing experiences with a paid assistant may lead either or both of you to desire a different kind of relationship. That being said, if a paid caregiver communicates that they're attracted to you and the feeling's mutual, there are some critical steps to take before going further. Together, you should report the relationship to the person's employer, and they should find other work while you're dating. If the person you employ threatens you, forces you to engage in or witness sexual acts, or makes excuses for why the relationship has to be secret, use the safety tips at the end of this chapter right away.

FINANCIAL ABUSE

While disability too often goes hand in hand with economic insecurity (damn you, structural oppression), there are still creepy types who see disabled people as targets for financial abuse. Some consider a Social Security benefit an easy source of income or feign romantic interest in order to get a disabled person to fork over money. One woman I met sent thousands of dollars to a person she had only ever spoken with on the phone. Phone guy professed love from some faraway city and kept asking for just a little more money so he could fly out to visit (the visit, as far as I know, never materialized). Another young person was literally imprisoned by a family member who stole their monthly checks. Thankfully, this is an evil perpetrated by a small subset of the population, but once you know it happens, you can be on the lookout.

To that end, watch out for anyone who seems overly interested in your financial situation, wants access to your bank accounts, or doesn't have their own reliable source of income. A good rule of thumb is to be automatically wary of anyone who wants you to give them money. Even if the amount is minimal and seems reasonable at first glance, the requests can mount over time. As your emotional entanglement becomes deeper, you may find requests harder to refuse. You deserve someone who is in a relationship not for what you can financially provide for them but for the delightful person you are.

LEAVING ABUSE

Hopefully, you will never experience abuse, and this part of the chapter won't apply to you. We hope that it will become so irrelevant that it will no longer be included in future editions of this book. But until that time, let's talk about how to leave a dangerous situation.

There are huge barriers for all people who seek to escape from intimate partner violence, but (big surprise) for disabled people, those barriers are higher and harder to navigate. There are a number of reasons for this. Isolating a victim is part of an abuser's playbook, and disabled people might have smaller or fewer circles of support than those who aren't living with health challenges.

Disabled people may depend on their abuser to leave the house at all, so escape isn't as simple as getting into the car and driving away (not that it's ever that simple). Perpetrators frequently threaten to harm a pet to keep their victim from moving out; this threat is even more frightening when you're talking about a service animal that the victim depends on to navigate the world. Even if they are able to leave with the service animal, those experiencing abuse may be uncertain whether a shelter can accommodate them along with any mobility or communication needs they may have. Victims might well depend on an abuser for health insurance, personal care, and financial security. If there are children involved, a victim may stay out of concern that a judge would award custody to the abusive parent rather than the disabled one.

However high the barriers, no one deserves to live in fear.

There is some very good guidance about how to get out of a violent relationship when you live with your abuser, and we've shared those resources at the end of this chapter. Also, assume you're being spied on: clear your search history, hide emergency numbers under unassuming contact names, and if you have critical meds, try to save a few pills in a place the abuser won't check. In addition, here are a few general tips:

- Think about whom in your life you trust and who has supported you in the past. If you can, reach out to those people and let them know what's going on.
- If you have access to a medical provider (even a dentist or podiatrist), tell them what's going on and ask for help. You can also alert a PA.
- If the abuse is being perpetrated by a paid caregiver, alert their employment agency (the higher the position of the person you're alerting, the better—call the CEO if possible).
- If you have young children, try to alert their school's guidance counselor as to what's going on. Children should always leave

the house first, and the counselor may be able to help you navigate that.

- If you can safely do so, call local domestic violence organizations and share the specifics of your situation and any accessibility or assistance needs you'd require in a temporary shelter. If the first one cannot help, keep trying.
- Call or text 911.
- Call or chat with one of the organizations listed at the start of this chapter.
- Remember: abuse is never your fault.

BUT ALL THAT BEING SAID . . .

Reading this chapter could have scared the living daylights out of you. You may decide that dating is just too risky. Please know that while every human interaction involves risk, there are literally millions of disabled people across the world in loving, supportive partnerships. Abuse is not inevitable when you are dating with a disability. Everyone deserves love, and knowing what to avoid makes it that much more likely that we'll find the partnership we're looking for.

RESOURCES

We've included these here and at the back of the book for easy reference.

HOTLINES

For people who speak on the phone:
- Call the National Sexual Assault Hotline at 800-656-4673
- Call the National Domestic Violence Hotline at 800-799-SAFE or 866-331-9474

For people who communicate by text:

- Chat with a representative of the National Sexual Assault Hotline at https://hotline.rainn.org/online
- Use the Crisis Text Line at www.crisistextline.org/text-us
- Text the Scarleteen Hotline at 206-866-2279
- Text or chat with a dating violence specialist at https://www .loveisrespect.org/

For people who communicate using ASL:

- Call the Deaf Services Hotline at 855-812-1001

If you are in immediate danger, call or text 911.

CONSENT

An article for disabled people and their sexual partners on navigating consent: "Consent Is Sexy: Sexual Autonomy and Disability," Scarleteen, updated August 22, 2023, https://www.scarleteen.com /consent_is_sexy_sexual_autonomy_and_disability.

Establishing consent practices with a nonverbal partner: "A Brief Guide to Consenting with a Nonverbal Partner," Scarleteen, updated August 22, 2023, https://www.scarleteen.com/article/disability _relationships_sexuality/a_brief_guide_to_consenting_with_a _nonverbal_partner.

DEAF SURVIVORS

Curated resources, including a text-based hotline: "Resources," Dawn, https://deafdawn.org/resources.

LEAVING ABUSE

A general guide to those considering leaving abusive partners: "Safety Plan: When You Live with the Abuse," Scarleteen, updated

August 22, 2023, https://www.scarleteen.com/safety_plan_when _you_live_with_the_abuse.

SERVICE ANIMALS

According to the Americans with Disabilities Act (ADA), service animals cannot be barred from domestic violence shelters. However, individual shelter managers may not be in compliance with these laws, and there may be other issues with general accessibility. If you are contemplating leaving an abusive relationship and will take a service animal with you, call a national hotline or your local domestic violence center for guidance. Make sure you have your service animal's health and training paperwork and contact information for your veterinarian.

CRIME VICTIM SUPPORT

Victim Connect Resource Center—a phone-, chat-, and text-based referral service with an accessible website operated by the National Center for the Victims of Crime: https://victimconnect.org/.

CHAPTER 9
ETHICAL NONMONOGAMY

JESSICA

WHEN WE SET OUT TO WRITE THIS BOOK, WE HAD SOME IDEA OF what we'd be covering. Dating apps? Check. Breaking up? Check. Sex? Definitely. Ethical nonmonogamy (ENM)? Um—twist!

We also knew we wanted to share stories of disabled people's relationships as they actually are, whether that's a married hetero couple with two kids and a dog or someone living in romantic relationships with multiple people at once. Some of the stories that our subjects shared felt familiar, closely matching our own experiences. Others expanded our views of what healthy, life-giving relationships between consenting adults could look like. We learned a lot. We Googled *a lot*. We are very thankful for the people who trusted us enough to share their stories, and we hope that we treated them with respect.

So let's get into it.

Charlotte lives in the UK and considers herself a relationship anarchist. She lives alone and has multiple partners (aka solo polyamory). Each of her partners has multiple partners. Their relationship structure was hard for me to visualize, and after our call, at my request, she sent me a diagram to illustrate the whole dating family tree (it did actually look like a family tree). It was my conversation with Charlotte that made it obvious that ENM needed its own chapter in *Dateable*. She was one of many disabled interviewees who shared that their relationships weren't monogamous, but it was how she talked about relationships that brought home the importance of this topic as it connects to disability.

Charlotte is a thirty-four-year-old autistic lesbian. Her disabilities include hypermobility, fatigue, and sensory issues. She credits her autistic identity with her capacity to think creatively and independently about situations in which other people might be more easily swayed by popular opinion—for example, monogamy. No one has provided Charlotte with a convincing argument for default monogamy, and therefore, she does not see it as the automatic or best option for everybody. "I throw out norms easily," she clarified.

Over the years, she has developed the capacity to acknowledge and respect her own needs. For this reason, she knows that she does not want to live with any of her partners. She requires a great deal of physical space and time alone and is unwilling to sacrifice these fundamental needs because society expects relationships always to move toward cohabitation.

Charlotte is healthiest when living alone, and this dynamic complements a multipartner relationship structure well—if one or more of her partners were to feel best when living with a romantic partner, they could have that need met by other people without sacrificing their connection and relationship with Charlotte. Contradictory needs do not have to threaten the integrity or future of Charlotte's relationships.

When I imagine the person I was before becoming disabled, I cannot imagine that version of myself expressing my desires as Charlotte does. During those years, it was much harder for me to accept that I had physical or mental needs that may, at times, inconvenience other people. My tendencies are understandable—we all live in a society that values, above all, grit, independence, and, contradictorily, compliance. For the first two years with my life-altering illness, I tried each day to override my symptoms. It was my eventual connection with the disability community that helped me start to accept and accommodate what my body needs to survive.

Accepting and caring for one's unique needs, which most disabilities require, is countercultural. Disability culture reminds us that being tough is not the ultimate achievement. This lesson seems to cross over into disabled relationships. Just as I no longer try to walk farther than my body can carry me and instead use a wheelchair, many disabled people have stopped powering through conventional relationship structures and instead take a step back and consider all of their options.

They ask, who am I? What do I need? What does my partner need? What are our options?

In Charlotte's case, she has a partner of eight years, Morgan, who is trans and very extroverted. Charlotte and Morgan met at a kink workshop. Morgan requires much more social and sexual interaction than Charlotte could sustain. About six years ago, Morgan started dating Eunice, who fulfilled some of those needs. Eventually, Eunice and Charlotte developed their own romantic connection. Eunice and Morgan each have four other partners. Eunice, Charlotte, and Morgan do not rely on just one partner to meet all of their primary attachment needs. For them, this arrangement is healthy because it fits everyone's needs.

Disability culture also celebrates mutual aid—the practice of supporting one another in a complex web of practical and emotional support. It's a communal practice of care and a rejection of toxic independence and unsustainable codependence. After talking to many polyamorous disabled people, I started to think that the mutual-aid mindset crosses over into romantic attachments. Charlotte specifically mentioned that

ENM allows for a more sustainable supportive network versus a single partner with whom she might develop an unhealthy and unsustainable codependence.

This may all sound theoretical, or as if I am saying that the only true option for a disabled person is to have multiple partners, but I don't believe that is true at all. I have, however, learned an enormous amount from those I interviewed and the books and articles I read afterward. Writing *Dateable* has been my introduction to polyamory and ENM, and it has been eye-opening. It would be a disservice not to share what I've learned. It's well known that queer culture is more likely to embrace nontraditional and nonmonogamous structures, but through our research, we found that by its nature, disability culture has the same connection.

WHAT IS ETHICAL NONMONOGAMY?

In general, ENM is any relationship structure in which the participants have agreed to have romantic or sexual attachments with more than one person. While monogamy, by definition, can be monolithic, ENM encompasses a broad range of arrangements. Some people have occasional sexual relationships with people other than their primary partner, and some people are in rambling structures of dozens of casual and committed relationships. There are polyamorous relationships involving sexual exclusivity among three people and some in which the primary couple only have sex with other people when their primary partner is present.

ENM refers to values more than relationship composition. Honesty, respect, informed consent, and safety are paramount to ENM practitioners. Just as our research taught us that those who incorporate kink and BDSM into their sex lives are particularly aware of safety and consent, those with nonmonogamous relationship structures are particularly strict about honesty.

In a traditional monogamous relationship, the rule book is pretty clear: two people commit to keeping sex and romantic attachment to just the two of them. The structure is there, and while it can be broken or severed, it's not generally something a couple is crafting day to day, year to year. However, when you don't have those assumptions about structure that come with monogamy, you are forced to communicate far more than you otherwise would.

People who have had both monogamous and nonmonogamous relationships say that what they value about ENM is that all involved have to consider and articulate what they need. For those who never evaluate what they want from monogamy, assumptions can end up being painful for all involved, especially if someone's definition of monogamy is different from their partner's.

Before we go much further, a review of ENM terms might be helpful. I know it took me a bit to learn the vocabulary.

GLOSSARY

It's rare for a conversation about ENM to pass without someone mentioning *The Ethical Slut: A Practical Guide to Polyamory, Open Relationships & Other Adventures* by Janet Hardy and Dossie Easton.[1] The first edition was published in 1997, and the most recent update came out in 2017. Toward the end of the book, the authors include a robust glossary of terms, which you can find in various forms online. For the sake of this chapter, I will highlight a few from their glossary and from other sources.

Compersion: Happiness or erotic feelings that emerge when you see your partner experience pleasure with another person.

Fluid Bonding: A practice in which someone has unprotected sex with a primary partner but sex with barriers with all other partners. Many ENM practices aim to increase sexual safety.

Metamour: The partner of one's partner.

Monogamish: A term originally coined by Dan Savage, referring to a relationship structure in which two people are mostly monogamous but have some sexual encounters with other people.

Munch: A (usually nonsexual) gathering of polyamorous people to meet those who are like-minded.

New Relationship Energy (**NRE**): Intense feelings at the beginning of a relationship.

Open Relationship: A relationship with the freedom to love or have sex with other people to some degree.

Outercourse: Sexual acts that do not involve genitals or that involve keeping clothes on. It is one manner of reducing the risk of STIs.

Polyamory: Definitions are inconsistent, but many people define it as all relationship structures that aren't monogamous.

Polycule: A group of people connected through sexual or romantic connections.

Polyfidelity: An ENM structure in which a group of people stays exclusively committed to one another (for example, three couples).

Primary Partner: Many ENM practitioners have a primary partner and other, secondary partners. There might be agreements governing secondary relationships that aim to prioritize and protect the primary relationship.

Relationship Anarchy: An ENM structure in which relationships aren't ranked and agreements and rules are minimized.

DISABILITY CULTURE AND ETHICAL NONMONOGAMY

As we talked to disabled people for this book, the same themes kept repeating themselves: a sense of creativity, acceptance, and curiosity about individual needs. These features of disabled relationships are what draw many disabled people to kink culture and, relatedly, to nonmonogamy. Disabled people, because our bodies and minds don't behave the way mainstream culture dictates, are often able to consider our relationship structures from a place of openness and without traditional assumptions.

Hardy and Easton articulated the same ideas without mentioning disability. They found that ENM provides an opportunity for "freeing ourselves to enjoy sex and sexual love in as many ways as may fit for each of us." Like many disabled people, Hardy and Easton said that "one of the most valuable things we learn from open sexual lifestyles is that our programming about love, intimacy, and sex can be rewritten. When we begin to question all the ways we have been told we ought to be, we can begin to edit and rewrite our old tapes." That sounds a lot like disability culture.

Many of the disabled people whom I interviewed about sex mentioned that they have an expansive and open definition of sex, including phone sex, erotic talk, and any physical touch that brings erotic pleasure. Hardy and Easton echoed these beliefs: "We think erotic energy is everywhere—in the deep breath that fills our lungs as we step out into a warm spring morning. . . . In our combined three-quarters of a century of work as sex writers and educators, we've found that the more we learn about sex, the less we know about how to define it."

The ENM handbook echoes what disabled people shared with us: mainstream definitions of sex are inadequate. Reading *The Ethical Slut*, I found myself unsurprised that so many of the disabled people we spoke to practice ENM.

SAFETY

Every text I read on ENM reinforced the mandate that each sexual and romantic interaction within polyamory should be safe. Consent is critical. Engaging in an ENM relationship structure requires that you first consider your comfort and needs. You must also be able to express those needs and limits. Just as I learned from those in the kink community, the communication required for ENM can feel like freedom for disabled people, to whom conventional assumptions about sex do not apply.

There are many resources on how to protect yourself and your partners from STIs if you have multiple sexual relationships, and we have included those in the Resources section at the end of the book. Spoiler: barriers are crucial.

HOW IT ACTUALLY WORKS

Since some readers may not know anyone in a polyamorous relationship and/or may be wondering about the whys and hows, here are two other examples of ENM relationships structures.

QUINN

Like Charlotte, Quinn, who lives in Edinburgh, is solo polyamorous. He is autistic, bisexual, and trans and has a history of suicidal ideation, but he wonders how much of his early depression was due to his undiagnosed autism. He didn't receive an official diagnosis until his midtwenties.

In his teens, Quinn was not out as trans and tried to push against his own internal dysphoria by working to be "the perfect girl." This obsessive quest further eroded his mental health, and it wasn't until he became open about his gender identity and learned of his autism diagnosis that he began to feel comfortable in his own skin and life. It was during that time that he first learned about ENM, and he knew instantly that it was the structure that would work best for him.

He identifies proudly as a slut and has kept a sex blog since his late teens. He loves sex and sees himself as his own primary partner, in part because he worries that his history of mental illness would make it too easy to develop unhealthy codependence with another primary partner. As his own number one, he must take ownership of his own care, which, in his case, is critical. Otherwise, he knows he has the tendency to wait until someone comes to rescue him. "I have to be the one to save myself," he told me.

Quinn has had seasons in which he was more sexually active than others. There was one eighteen-month stretch in which he had "quite a lot of sex" at kink clubs, group sex at parties, and casual hookups with friends. Toward the end of that period, he met a person named Quemby at the Edinburgh Fringe, where they both performed onstage as part of the "slut slam." Soon after meeting, they started sleeping together, and after four days of incredible sex, they realized they might want something more serious.

Quinn and Quemby have now been together for three years and have exchanged ear cuffs as a symbol of their mutual commitment. Quemby has three other relationships, including a serious one with a woman named Emily, to whom they recently became engaged. When Quemby and Emily get married, Quinn will be the best man.

Quinn has no other long-term relationships because he prioritizes casual sex. He wants a life of love and partners but not cohabitation and kids. Quinn's ability to build his ideal relationship structure from scratch reflects how he, out of necessity, was forced to carve out his own neurodivergent and gender identity after being raised as a neurotypical girl.

VAYL

Like Quinn, Vayl is autistic but does not consider their neurodivergence a disability. They are also disabled, though, due to progressive spinal degeneration along with autoimmune illnesses and are a wheelchair user. Vayl has three partners: two platonic and one romantic. Unlike Quinn and Charlotte, Vayl lives with one of their partners, Josh, a gender-flexible asexual (ace) man.

Josh and Vayl have been together for sixteen years and have known each other even longer. They met thirty-one years ago as children. Their initial connection was platonic but committed and then developed into a romantic and sexual partnership. The sexual and romantic connection did not work for their relationship, but they realized that they were deeply committed to each other. As I discuss in Chapter 10, many ace people find deep fulfillment in nonsexual committed partnerships.

When Josh purchased a home, Vayl moved in, and Josh became their caregiver. Vayl qualifies for Medicaid-funded assistance with tasks of daily living and was able to direct that reimbursement to Josh, so for the last ten years, he has been their compensated caregiver, which helps the dynamic feel more sustainable for them both. They have considered marriage, but Vayl would lose their Supplemental Security Income (SSI) if they were to marry someone with an income. In order for Vayl to keep SSI and Medicaid, Josh can make only very small financial contributions to Vayl's living expenses.

Josh is fulfilled by their relationship and does not have a need for other romantic attachments. When Vayl and Josh were romantically involved, they were monogamous, but after their relationship became platonic, they shifted to ENM. Because Vayl is not ace, they crave other, more romantic relationships, and Josh supports Vayl in seeking those elsewhere. Vayl has a new (five months) romantic and sexual partner, Andrew, who lives near them and has no other partners.

Vayl also has another platonic partner, Kingston, with whom they are in a committed long-distance relationship. Kingston has a local romantic partner, Thomas, who is also disabled. Vayl is happy with their three relationships and is not looking for a fourth. Like Quinn and Charlotte, Vayl considered their own needs and the needs of those they love and created a relationship structure that worked for all involved.

TELLING OUR OWN POLY STORIES

While I wasn't able to track down a disability-focused ENM book (*ahem*, publishers), a number of essays, articles, and podcasts have addressed the particular intersection between disability and ENM. In 2022, Jillian

Weise wrote an essay for *The Cut* in which she described ENM as the natural extension of freeing herself from a nondisabled narrative of what her life should be.[2]

Plus, she said, why should disabled people try to emulate popular romantic representations when we are excluded anyway? "Polyamory defies every love song, every romantic comedy. But disabled people are rarely in love songs or romantic comedies. Why should I try to make my life look like a traditional romantic story? Why should I limit myself to one identity?"

I loved that perspective. Why should disabled people try to force ourselves into a mold that was made without our inclusion or consent?

For Amanda Van Slyke, who wrote a 2017 piece about ENM for *Thought Catalog*, polyamory gives her the relationship freedom to express her specific needs and not try to mold herself to fit others' assumptions about what her relationship should look like.[3] A polyamorous mindset allowed her to express her need for ample alone time while traveling with her romantic partner, including having her own room. She now identifies as solo polyamorous, an identity that many of the people we interviewed related to.

Van Slyke explained, "It wasn't until looking into solo polyamory I realized I don't have to feel guilty for having separate needs from my partner. Solo polyamory is the idea that people are autonomous beings who have different needs and wants, and alongside good communication and mutual respect between all partners, no one puts rules on each other because no one owns one other. There's this expectation in mainstream society that if you're a couple you should want to be together most of the time—but with solo polyamory, partners respect how much time you can set aside. . . . There's no pressure to converge lives the longer you're dating because with solo polyamory commitment and time together aren't seen as mutually exclusive."[4]

In 2017, Morgan Mac Caisín, who is disabled and asexual, wrote an essay for *The Mighty* about the ENM relationship structure that works best for her—a throuple.[5] She is in a long-term relationship with two other people—one is disabled, and the other isn't. They are a closed triad, so they do not have romantic or sexual relationships with anyone outside the throuple.

Mac Caisín finds that having three people in the relationship provides a more structurally sound caretaking structure. Their physical and mental needs complement one another. They all feel cared for and supported, and as hardships emerge, they are prepared to endure them together.

Importantly, just as many disabled people don't find safety in monogamy, not all disabled people find freedom in ENM. Teighlor McGee, a disability activist, wrote in *Autostraddle* in 2022 that their monogamous relationship with their girlfriend was a radical act. For years, McGee had practiced ENM, but their partners were often white, and they felt diminished sharing their "Black love with white outside parties." Instead of being empowered in nontraditional structures, McGee felt like a not-fully-realized version of themself.[6]

Upon reflection, they realized that their intersecting identities impacted their own perspective of how desirable they were and what they could expect from a partner. After years of practicing ENM, McGee fell in love with a Black trans woman, and it was in that exclusive relationship that they felt the most radical.

"For me—a person living at the intersections of fatness, Blackness, and disability—polyamory was not conducive to my happiness because of the ways desirability politics have burned me. I am not ashamed to admit this. . . . My monogamous relationship still feels radical. It is a radical act for two Black disabled people to find one another in a world that isn't built for our survival. It is radical to have built this monogamous relationship from the scraps we were given. It is radical to recognize that you need to build a new foundation."

Sadly, McGee died on April 2, 2022, a few months after their piece was published. In the days leading up to their death, they wrote about their mistreatment at the hospital and the difficulty they experienced accessing medical care. Their partner was by their side until the end.[7]

OPENING OUR RELATIONSHIPS AND OUR MINDS

I have learned an enormous amount while writing *Dateable*. Disability culture continues to amaze me, and the disabled approach to polyamory is no exception. In all facets, disabled people have considered the ways in which the world is not designed for us and have developed collective and creative solutions. It wasn't until our dozens of interviews that I learned how disabled innovation is applied to the very structure of our romantic attachments.

Learning from other disabled people who have rejected assumptions about what they need and what is normal inspires me to consider my own self-imposed limits. Why should I impose an inaccessible world's rules on my personal life?

I keep visualizing a Venn diagram of kink, queer culture, ENM, and disability that I hope to read a book about one day. This chapter is meant to serve as an introduction, and I hope readers who are new to these concepts have been able to keep an open mind when considering others' experiences, even if monogamy is what's right for you. For those who would like to learn more from ENM experts and practitioners, we have included resources at the end of the book.

CHAPTER 10
QUEER & CRIP

JESSICA

D'ARCEE, WHOM WE GOT TO KNOW IN EARLIER CHAPTERS, HAS become a bit of a main character in this book—their openness and generosity with their stories and time made our writing better. We are thankful for his candor. In some of his pictures on Grindr, he shows his wheelchair. In others, you wouldn't know he has CP. Regularly, men message him, say they like his photos, and then ask who the guy in the wheelchair is.

This is devastating. He feels like an integral part of his identity is being rejected and eliminated. During the writing of this book, D'Arcee and I spoke for over three hours, and the only time he cried was while telling me this. "It's so hurtful that they don't know it's me. They straight up erase me."

Many of the men who notice that he's the one in the wheelchair ask immediately about his penis. They want to know if it "works." When he feels like engaging, he replies, "And if it didn't?" He tries to get them to see their question through.

Disabled people face all sorts of assumptions about our sexuality and sex drives—mainly that we don't have them (more on asexuality later). Our other identities sometimes complicate those stereotypes. Black men, like D'Arcee, are presumed to be hypersexual, and many people hold the same assumption about gay men. With all of these assumptions, there isn't much room left for D'Arcee, the person, with his own individual sexual reality—which, as for all of us, is uniquely his and informed by identity, personality, background, and trauma.

D'Arcee can't remember a time when he didn't view and make decisions about his disability through another's gaze. During his childhood in North Carolina, he used forearm crutches for mobility. When he was fourteen, he decided to switch to a wheelchair because the gait and aesthetics of the crutches didn't match what he envisioned for his future. He pictured himself as an adult, out of North Carolina, and working as a corporate attorney. He imagined his three-piece suit and the courtroom. A wheelchair would be more distinguished, he decided.

He feels some loss now in realizing that his mobility decisions were not based on his own needs. And now, he has no choice but to use a wheelchair. That decision made decades ago has impacted him profoundly, particularly when it comes to dating. He has noticed that gay men are more concerned about the sexual function of a man in a wheelchair than a man on crutches. To compensate, when he's on Grindr, D'Arcee often feels pressure to include nudes, not because he wants to but because he feels an extra burden to prove that he's sexual.

WHERE QUEER AND CRIP MEET

Many authors and thinkers have talked about the intersection of queer culture and crip culture, including Eli Clare and Alison Kafer. In fact, queer activists often expand the definition of queer not just to include sexuality but also as a rejection of the status quo. In that sense, it's logical to say that disability is the queering of our bodies and minds.[1] We are rejecting the dominant narrative of how we "should" be. But when you exit the world of theory, the lived reality of queer disabled people is much more fraught, particularly when dating.

I'm queer, and when I moved to California and started dating, I included all genders as possible matches on the apps I used. I also considered different queer events happening around Berkeley and Oakland. The events I could find were rarely accessible and often included some element of fitness—hikes, bike rides, and dance parties.

To be clear, my experience is specific to me, and I am sure I could have taken other approaches, but I found that as a disabled person, engaging in queer culture in the East Bay was very daunting.

Also—and this is my own baggage as a white cisgender woman raised in the South—I had a much easier time slotting myself into straight culture. I need a lot of help—my partner will always need to be, in part, a caregiver. (More on this in chapter 12.) I grew up in a world that encouraged a version of the frail and dependent white woman.

I could picture that paradigm—I, a pale artifact, reclining on my fainting couch, murmuring requests for water and a fan. My paramour, a strong and confident man, rescuing me. I could be that. I could shoehorn myself into an opposite-sex relationship. There was a category in my mind that I could fit my disability into. Queer people invent and create new roles and spaces, and finding my place there didn't feel obvious. So I mostly just stayed away.

FINDING YOUR IDENTITY

There are as many ways to be queer as there are to be disabled. This chapter cannot possibly cover all the ways that bodies and minds across the full spectrum interact sexually and romantically. It will, instead, serve as an overview while highlighting a few common topics.

Certain queer ideas kept coming up as we interviewed and researched. I'll discuss some here, and we also include a list of writers and creators who explore the intersection of their queerness and disability (see Resources, pages 231). If this chapter wakes something up in you and you want to explore this topic more, you will discover a wealth of brilliant queer and disabled educators.

For those who are just beginning to learn about LGBTQIA+ culture, I've listed some terms below. There are other, more detailed resources at the back of the book. Note that these terms are constantly evolving, and by the time you read this book, they may have shifted.[2]

GENDER VERSUS SEXUAL ORIENTATION

For those who are just exploring their own sexuality or who are learning about queer issues for the first time, the difference between gender identity and sexual orientation can be confusing. In short, your gender identity is how *you* identify, and your sexual orientation references the people you do or do not want to have sexual or romantic relationships *with*. The term "queer" is an umbrella term referring to anyone who isn't straight or cisgender.

TERMS RELATED TO GENDER

Gender Expression: How gender is expressed externally. Includes pronouns, clothing, voice, and more.

Androgynous: A neutral or mixed gender expression.

Cisgender: Identifying with the gender you were assigned at birth.

Femme: A feminine gender expression.

Gender-Affirmative Care: Many who are transgender elect to have surgical or other medical interventions so that their appearance can match their identity.

Gender Identity: A person's internal sense of their own gender.

Masc: A masculine gender expression.

Transgender: Not identifying with the gender you were assigned at birth.

Transition: When a transgender person changes their gender expression to more closely match their gender identity.

They/Them/Their Pronouns: Gender-neutral singular pronouns.

TERMS RELATED TO SEXUAL ORIENTATION

Asexual/Ace: Experiencing low or no sexual attraction.

Bisexual: Being attracted to your own gender and other genders.

Gay: Can refer to men who are attracted to men or to anyone who is attracted to those of the same gender.

Lesbian: Women who are attracted to women (some women prefer "gay woman").

Pansexual: Being attracted to any gender identity.

Straight: People who are primarily attracted to a gender other than their own.

QUESTIONING

To me, something about these terms and definitions can make the experience of gender and sexuality feel contained and discrete—like a truth you can easily find and know about yourself. But learning who you are is a lifelong process. Exploring or questioning your sexual or gender identity is common and natural—for anyone, disabled or not. We never stop evolving.

I talked to Amma, a disabled college student in her twenties. She said that she really wants a partner and has been on dating apps for years.

When I asked about her sexual orientation, our conversation shifted. "I've kissed way more women than men," she said, laughing. "Whenever I'm drunk, I think about having sex with women." I asked if she identifies as queer, and she said no, "but maybe that's just internalized homophobia? I'm way more attracted to women."

She went on, "Growing up in the South, we weren't allowed to think about those things."

I asked if she's ever been truly attracted to men. "Just the unattainable ones . . . or the feminine ones." She remembered her childhood crushes on Louis Tomlinson and Harry Styles: "All of the Harry and Louis girls end up gay."

So what do we do with our questions? To start, I could offer my younger self advice. I wasn't disabled until twenty-eight, but I knew that I might be queer decades before that. I have so much empathy for that younger version of me, growing up in the 1990s in the Evangelical South. I would first tell her that her desires aren't wrong or strange. That it's OK to explore the maze of her budding sexuality. I would remind her over and over that she isn't alone.

When she goes off to college, I'd encourage her to experiment more and judge less. I would say that not knowing is a perfectly safe place to spend time. When she moves to California at thirty to sow her wild oats, I'd tell her that it may be hard to find her place in the queer community but that she shouldn't give up. Even if she ends up in a straight relationship, finding her people is worth the effort.

I am so happy with how my life has evolved, and I love my husband, *and* I wish I hadn't carried shame and alienation for so many years. I wish I had known that it's OK to change and to wonder.

I also know that I was an adolescent in the time before social media. The world is different now, and disabled people everywhere have access to highly specific information and online communities. The disabled creators and writers who are sharing the details of their lived experiences online are lifelines (see Resources on page 231).

So if you are coming to terms with your own queerness and its relationship with your disability, I urge you to find your people online. It's a valuable step on the way to self-acceptance. If you have access to therapy, make sure your therapist is LGBTQIA+ affirming (which they will almost always list on their website or Psychology Today page. If they don't mention it or deflect when you ask directly, red flag). You deserve that. There is nothing wrong with you. You are perfect.

While you bolster your own self-love and acceptance, it might be worth keeping an open mind as you consider what kind of romantic and sexual relationships you want. Pay attention to the social scripts that are getting in the way of your creativity. Ask yourself over and over—what and whom do you want and need?

And then, experiment! It's totally OK to date different genders and people and gender expressions as you learn about yourself and your own sexuality. Be open and observe. But also, be honest about where you are in the process with people you want to experiment with.

What do you like? Whom do you like? Are you romantically attracted to one gender but sexually attracted to another? That's OK! Are you sexually attracted only to someone you have a romantic connection with? That's OK too! Pay attention and learn. And have fun along the way.

And while you are finding whom you want to love, work on building your community, online and in person. There are disabled and queer people who will love and understand you, I promise. It might just take a little digging.

I'm not the only disabled person who was raised female and clung to straight relationships for safety. James, who is trans, knew they were queer but, because they were disabled, thought it would be safer to find a cis man to take care of them. Starting in high school, they entered a series of long and intense relationships with (often older) men. Tragically, despite searching for safety and security, they ended up married to someone who sexually assaulted them.

Now, at thirty, they are divorced and out, and in many ways, they are starting from scratch. They have found a wealth of information and support online. They are also vocal about being autistic and disabled. I asked them what social media and online disability activism have meant to them.

"Social media has been critical in letting me know that people I didn't know existed, existed. Seeing people like me online helped me feel less alone. It gave me permission to be those things and feel those things.

"It gives me permission to thrive and to know that I deserve better. It helps me to start building a future. To know that I am valid and loved and that I deserve to be seen."

ACCESSIBILITY IN QUEER SPACES

The issue that came up most often in our interviews about queerness was the inaccessibility of queer spaces. This topic has been heavily discussed in major publications and in private online communities. I have experienced the same hurdles. It is often very difficult to attend queer events as a disabled person.

I've wondered if it's partly because queer events tend to take place in alternative or underground spaces (literally or figuratively). For so long, LGBTQIA+ people had to hide, and this history of furtive or hidden culture means that there is often a physical barrier to entry.

For example, Flaniel, a trans and disabled man, told me that the gay bars where he grew up were not accessible to people with mobility equipment, and where he lives now, the queer social tap house isn't accessible to wheelchair users.

In 2018, Lynn Zelvin was turned away from the Stonewall Inn because of their service dog, which they need because they are blind.[3] Ace Ratcliff, a queer writer, reflected in 2020 that having places to gather and connect is an integral part of safety for queer people.[4] It's critical that these places are accessible to disabled people.

According to many researchers, one in three queer people is disabled. It's hard to believe, in that case, that the issue of accessibility is so widespread. It's incredibly painful to be ignored and excluded, particularly when homophobia has already led to feelings of isolation. As Raven Ishak wrote in 2021, "Attending events that treat accessibility as an after-thought at best and an inconvenience at worst is utterly soul-destroying. Facing inaccessibility, as a person with disabilities, feels like wearing an irremovable post-it note on my head with the words 'I don't belong here' spelled out in capital letters."[5]

Early in the COVID-19 pandemic, thanks to virtual options, disabled people found that we were able to attend events that had previously been inaccessible to us. And then, when people began gathering in person again, health precautions like masking and ventilation made spaces safer for disabled people at high risk for infectious diseases. But as time went on, nondisabled people began removing safety measures, even though COVID remains dangerous and, as of 2023, twenty-three million people in the United States alone have long COVID.

Queer and disabled people who want to meet and possibly date other queer people are once again being excluded.[6] Activists are baffled. The HIV/AIDS crisis put health and medical care at the forefront of LGBTQIA+ advocacy, and many queer people have experienced medical bias and hardship firsthand. Disabled people cannot understand why collective safety isn't more of a priority. As Oni Blackstock, the founder of Health Justice, said, queer spaces are further marginalizing the disabled within their own community.

Disabled and queer activists have been working hard to make queer events and spaces more accessible.[7] For example, Annie Segarra has been pushing to make sure that events not only include wheelchair access but also incorporate video captions, translators, and audio descriptions. She also reiterates the need for virtual options—not only because of viruses but because some disabled people have trouble leaving their homes at all.[8]

For Alexis Hillyard, the key is to make it so that disabled people don't feel like they need to change who they are to fit into queer culture.[9] Both activists remind organizers that the goal should be dignity, not just checking off boxes and doing the bare minimum. It is my hope that queer culture will move toward a more collective approach to disability access and embrace the wisdom and resources that disabled queer culture offers.

ASEXUALITY

It's easy to get defensive if you're disabled and someone brings up asexuality. Many disabled people have been hurt by the assumption that we are not interested in sex and are not sexually desirable. The truth is, surveys of disabled people show levels of sexual desire similar to those of their nondisabled counterparts.[10] The sexless crip is a tired and painful trope. At the same time, there are people, disabled and not, who do identify as asexual, or ace. It's a sexual orientation as valid as any other.

Those who study asexuality have found that approximately 1 percent of people are ace, though that number may be low due to a lack of awareness and representation.[11] Statistically, it makes sense that there are disabled ace people. According to the Asexual Visibility and Education Network (AVEN), an ace person "does not experience sexual attraction or an intrinsic desire to have sexual relationships."[12] The individual experiences under this umbrella vary. Some asexual people still have sexual relationships, and some do not. Many are in romantic relationships.

In her transformative book on asexuality, *Ace*, Angela Chen described Cara, an asexual wheelchair user. Cara is aware that her sexuality seemingly confirms some people's assumptions about disabled people being sexless. But within her disabled community, she experiences the opposite—so many of her friends have pushed against the stereotypes about disabled people not being sexual that they feel threatened by Cara's ace identity. Cara sometimes feels guilty because she doesn't want to have sex. She also worries that some people think of her identity as some sort of defensive posturing—that it's actually because no one wants to have sex with her. Similarly, the ace community has worked to distance itself from the idea that being asexual is a sickness, and so they are slow to embrace an asexual disabled person.

The disabled community and the asexual communities both have work to do. According to Chen,

> The disabled community must welcome disabled aces because sexual variation exists and disabled people can be ace, and there is nothing wrong with being ace. The ace community must welcome disabled people because sexual variation exists and ace people can be disabled, and there is nothing wrong with being disabled. . . . True sexual liberation means having many choices—no sex forever, sex three times a day, and everything in between—that all feel equally available and accepted.[13]

GAY BEAUTY

One aspect of queerness that came up repeatedly is the specific relationship between gay men and beauty. That's not to say that other subcultures don't have complicated relationships with bodies (hello, trans people!). However, all of the gay men I interviewed mentioned how appearance-focused gay culture is and how deviating from a narrow standard can negatively impact mental health. Ryan O'Connell, a gay man with CP, explored being physically disabled in gay spaces in his Netflix series, *Special*, and in his two books, *I'm Special: And Other Lies We Tell Ourselves* and *Just By Looking at Him*.

Ryan has written openly about how challenging it is to be disabled and gay. In fact, for years, he pretended that he wasn't disabled. He claimed instead that he was recovering from a car accident because he thought other gay men would find that more attractive. In fact, he said that it was much easier to come out as gay than to come out as disabled.[14]

When he did come out on his blog in 2015, he described the feeling of being rejected because of his disability. "You have no idea what it's like to go into a gay bar and feel utterly invisible because the way you walk renders you unfuckable."[15] In 2015, he wrote in *Vice* that he wasn't sure he would even date himself—the pervasive ableism he had encountered had become that internalized.[16]

The gay relationships he was exposed to in his teens and twenties all involved a very specific kind of man, and because his body was different, he couldn't find a spot for himself. He wrote,

> I have cerebral palsy—a group of disorders that affect a person's ability to move and maintain balance and posture—and I'm fucking gay. This combination can feel like a death sentence for your love life.
>
> I blame part of my defeatist attitude on *Queer As Folk*. *Queer As Folk* presented a superficial world, where hot sociopathic guys with nice asses have mind-blowing sex 24/7 while smart, adorable gays hang by the sidelines.... The show's message about the importance of physical perfection came in loud and queer for gimpy ol' me. After coming to the umpteenth shot of washboard abs, I'd look down at my own body, which was undefined and covered in scars from various surgeries. I'd think, *Well, babe, I'm fucked! And not in the literal way.*[17]

But it wasn't only media that showed an unattainable standard for gay men:

> I wish I could tell you the gay world was kind and accepting—nothing like those garbage monsters on Showtime—but, to a large extent, it wasn't. Gay men acted as elitist and judgmental as I feared. Having a nice body meant everything.[18]

The constant rejection later impacted Ryan's ability to form healthy relationships, even with men who were interested:

I stayed celibate partially because no one great wanted to fuck me, but also because I suffered from serious intimacy issues. It was a vicious cycle. I craved physical affection, but the second a guy touched me, I freaked out and felt unworthy. *The gay disabled guy does not get to have amazing sex*, I'd think. *The gay disabled guy does not get to have a relationship.*[19]

Ryan's openness is a gift to other disabled people who have experienced rejection and internalized ableism. Sometimes it's valuable not to try to solve a societal problem and just acknowledge how hard it can be to live it.

AUTISM AND QUEERNESS

Another complicated intersection is that between autism and queerness. As a reminder—some autistic people identify as disabled, and some do not. A 2021 study out of the University of Cambridge put in numbers what many had been saying for a while: autistic people are disproportionately queer.[20] A recent Trevor Project survey found that 35 percent of queer people identify as autistic. Anecdotally, I observed this in my interviews. I also found that autistic people were more likely to be ENM and to explore kink. A British woman whom we mentioned early in the book, Charlotte, explained that her autism helps her consider her own wants and needs apart from society's expectations. She isn't convinced that a tradition or identity has merit just because it's "typical."

This theory is common. But we don't actually know how to explain the statistics. We just know that an autistic person is far less likely to be cis or straight than a nonautistic person (sometimes called allistic). Some people, like Quinn, a trans man also in the UK, know they are queer before realizing they are autistic. For others, the autism identity comes first.

In talking with people for this book, I found a powerful and creative community of disabled autistic people sharing their experiences and

155

advancing conversations on queerness and neurodivergence. A queer and autistic friend sent me down a very informative TikTok rabbit hole in which autistic and queer people share their dating experiences with their largely queer and autistic audiences. One creator explored what it's like when a partner becomes a special interest. Having special interests, which involves a great deal of focus on or attention to a topic, idea, or behavior, is a common experience for autistic people.

I spoke with Christie Faye Collins, the queer and autistic creator of NOMI, the dating app for disabled people, and asked how she sees those facets of her identity intersecting in her love life. She said that she sees a great deal of overlap. For one, she enjoys challenging norms, a capacity for which she credits her queerness and her autism. She likes to complicate systems that society says should be only one way.

When I asked about her experience dating, she said, "Everyone I've dated is autistic. All of my friends have ADHD. There is an understanding, and that's really big." She also said her specific queer community tends to be intentional and communicative. They collectively value deep, intimate, and loving connection. Like many disabled people we interviewed, Christie said that she has also been involved in the kink community. In fact, that was her entry point for meeting other autistic queer people.

James, a trans and autistic person, told me that for most of their life, they felt like they had to hide their sexuality, gender identity, and autism. Masking upon masking, they explained. Taking off all of those masks is complicated and exhausting. But worth it.

Queer autistic people often encounter skepticism when they disclose their LGBTQIA+ identities. Unjustly, neurotypical people make assumptions about autistic people's ability to understand their own experiences. There are also widespread assumptions about autistic people being asexual. All disabled people face this assumption, but for autistic people, it comes with its own specific flavor of infantilization.

DATING WHILE QUEER AND DISABLED. IT'S COMPLICATED.

While I had trouble finding a place for myself in the Bay Area queer scene, other disabled people have had the opposite experience. They have found that the queer community is more accepting of disabled bodies and minds than hetero communities are.

For example, Dayna Troisi, a woman with a limb difference, has been amazed by how the women she has dated have embraced her disability. On Buzzfeed, she shared a story about how removing her bionic arm did nothing to dampen the mood when she was making out with a new partner. She felt attractive and wholly seen.[21]

That said, it's hard to argue that in the United States and Canada, there is one privileged way to be a person and to be in a relationship: the ideal couple is young, white, thin, wealthy, nondisabled, cisgender, and straight. This is, of course, bullshit. Queer relationships, by definition, reject some of those standards. I wonder if it's a relationship to the ideal/privileged relationship that, in part, determines a queer person's or group's response to disability.

For example, if a couple totally rejects the whole system that resulted in one "ideal" type of person, then they will be more likely to embrace disabled people. However, if, to retain access to power, they try to make their queerness as much like the straight ideal as possible, perhaps they will be less likely to accept and embrace body diversity.

Granted, this is a generalized theory, but our interviews and research found a complicated dynamic between queer dating and disabled dating. Some of it can certainly be explained by our relationship with the status quo.

This may be why we found that disabled and queer people were also more likely to embrace nontraditional relationship structures. We've already acknowledged that the system is broken, so we are willing to adapt it to our own needs.

SO WHAT NOW?

OK, I know that's getting a little heady and theoretical. The real question is how do we apply all of this to our lives? If we are queer and disabled, how do we navigate love and sex? With so much of what we discuss in this book, the first step is coming to terms with the reality of our own bodies and minds. We must, as trite as it sounds, be able to love ourselves first. When our identity includes queerness, that adds a layer. If you are disabled, queer, a person of color, or fat, you will navigate additional complications and contradictions. Our identities intersect with one another—in daily life and in romance.

With antitrans and antiqueer legislation increasing, safety is a growing concern. There is no easy answer here. The best I can say is this: find your people and hold one another close.

CHAPTER 11
PARTNERING UP

CAROLINE

I envision a long-term relationship where all parties establish trust with each other. We are open and honest about what we need, want, and expect from each other. We are also open about what we can offer and accept each other's limitations.

We are an interdependent family unit. We work together toward common goals. We share many things while also having our own individual sense of self. We all contribute to the family we create as well as to our home and our communities. We grow together.

I don't know if it's a pipe dream. I see my friends doing it every day despite their own disabilities, both mental and physical. So who knows?

John A.[1]

KEVIN AND I WERE FIRST MATCHED ONLINE, BACK IN THE DAYS WHEN meeting someone that way still felt a little edgy. After a month of chatting back and forth (including one week when I ghosted him while visiting friends in California), he asked if I wanted to go on a date. Our initial conversations had been positive (though I was a little suspicious about whether "internal auditor" was a real job—apparently it is). He seemed kind and funny, and I was excited about getting to know him more. I was living in Philadelphia at the time and he in a nearby suburb, so he offered to take the train into town and meet me at a little tea shop neither of us had been to before.

I arrived a few minutes early to a storefront that definitely had been a tea shop at some point but was now blocked off with a sign that read, "Permanently closed." Maybe not the best omen, but it did mean that I was standing outside the boarded-up building when I caught sight of Kevin for the first time. He walked down the street toward me, tall and lanky, his left toe pointed inward at a 45-degree angle, which gave his gait a slightly halting rhythm. As I watched him make his way down the block, I thought, *Oh, how interesting—I'm going to marry this guy.*

It was an odd feeling because, on the one hand, I was entirely certain that we'd end up together, and at the same time, I had no idea whether he'd call me after our first date. Later he admitted that he almost hadn't—he too had felt something significant happening as we talked for hours over dinner that first night (the closure of the tea place having propelled us into a slightly awkward conversation about whether to upgrade the date to a full-on dinner at a somewhat fancy restaurant down the block). Having CP himself, Kevin was aware of the possible challenges of sharing a life with another disabled person. He wasn't sure it was the best idea. So he hesitated to call those first few days, and I dated a few other people, scared to put all my eggs in the basket of this funny, bespectacled dude with the (totally not fake) tech job. Four days after we met, he finally convinced himself to call (I got his message while hiding out in the bathroom during a super-awkward date with someone else), and fifteen years later, I'm typing this on our kitchen counter surrounded by the Lego-strewn chaos of our shared life.

Monogamous cohabitation is not the goal of every human, nor is it some kind of pinnacle toward which all relationships must evolve. People can be blissfully content in all manner of housing and romantic configurations. At the same time, many of us want a companion to share a life with (or at least we want someone who has a legal obligation to share their toothbrush with us in a pinch). To that end, this chapter explores the wild, wonderful, at times utterly unromantic world of partnering up.

For simplicity's sake, I use language that implies two people sleeping under the same roof, but take whatever is useful and apply it to your own situation. We also know that this chapter could be an entire book (or several). Because we've mostly focused on the beginning parts of dating relationships in this book, we decided to cram Relationship v. 2 (or v. 2–100) into one megachapter.

TOGETHERING

Moving in. Shacking up. Living in sin. U-hauling. Putting a ring on it. Whatever you call it, there's something about sharing a roof that brings out the wonderful, the grueling, and everything in between. The goods are very good: building a home with someone you adore, creating shared memories, having a person who will respond to your frantic yells from the shower when you've forgotten a towel. But moving in also turns up the heat on issues that could have happily simmered on the back burner when you saw each other only on weekends and routinely shaved your legs.

According to smart people everywhere (and confirmed by my family therapist mom), the Big Issues that virtually every couple deals with are pretty standard: money, kids, values, communication, division of labor, and sex. There's a bonus Big Issue for many disabled folks, and that's the role of caregiving, but we're giving that one its own chapter (as we did with sex and will do with finances since there is a lot to say about those areas when it comes to disability).

British rabbi Lionel Blue once joked that "Jews are just like everyone else, only more so." We might say that relationships where one or both people are disabled are just like every other, only more so (and as a disabled Jew, I'm wondering if this makes me just that much extra). More than anything, issues around disability don't put people on some kind of unique relationship plane but rather open up conversations around topics that come up in most committed relationships.

"WHAT DOES COOKING METH SMELL LIKE?"

Before we get to the big topics, let's chat about moving in. Being a traditionalist at heart, I never imagined I'd live with someone before we were married (eek, I know—I'm a dinosaur). After that first date, my relationship with Kevin progressed quickly. He spent more and more time at my Philly apartment and proposed on New Year's Eve, just a few months after we met.

We talked about the future but had no plans to sign a lease together until closer to the wedding. Part of the reason was that I was reluctant to leave my life in the city to move closer to Kevin's work. I also didn't want to give up the cool industrial apartment that served as my sister's and my bachelorette pad. I looked forward to the next stage of life but didn't feel a need to rush into anything. Soon after we got engaged, though, a scary situation with a stalking coworker bubbled back up, and I no longer felt safe in our apartment. Kevin packed a bag to stay with us until things were resolved and just never left. Knowing that my former coworker had my address, we left that apartment as soon as the lease was up and moved in together (now officially) in the 'burbs, which I grudgingly grew to enjoy once I saw the size of the grocery stores.

Jessica and David's moving-in story was similarly practical. As she described it,

I was living alone in this basement in Berkeley, and I loved it! I was surrounded by redwoods and felt like it was a tree house. In retrospect, it was pretty crappy, but I truly didn't mind. As far as I was concerned, the only initial downside was that my landlord upstairs had a 120-pound dog who left giant turds outside my front door.

But within a month, it became clear that the living situation wasn't sustainable. My landlord and her boyfriend seemed to use a lot of . . . substances . . . and were very rowdy all night. On more than one occasion, I Googled, "What does cooking meth smell like?"

David and I had been together a few months at that point (I had lived with roommates before the basement), and I told him about my concerns. He was obviously protective, but I said maybe I was just being dramatic (says every woman when we are not). But one night, my landlord's boyfriend knocked on my door with a frying pan at 1 a.m. I cracked the door, and he said, eyes darting frantically, "Oh! Don't worry! I'm not about to hit you!"

I slammed and locked the door and texted David: I need to move out.

I was living on a disability income and could not afford much of anything in Berkeley or Oakland, but I tried. The basement had been uniquely affordable (red flag!), and as I searched, it became clear that I would need to find roommates again.

David had also been living with roommates and was ready for his own space. So we decided to find a space together to double our budget. To be honest, I think that if housing were more affordable in the East Bay, we would have waited longer!

Not exactly a fairy tale. But also a pretty clear reminder that committed relationships can contain a giant dose of practical. For every Cinderella charmed off her glass slipper, there are millions of us making utterly sensible decisions about safety, down payments, and how much access to a dishwasher is worth to us emotionally.

THE ACCESSIBLE HOUSING DILEMMA

While Kevin and I were excited to move in together, we were also faced with the reality that our apartment options were both expensive and limited. At the time, I wasn't driving, so we needed a place where I could walk no more than a quarter mile to the train to get to my job in the city. We required few steps or an elevator (both rare in the area) and a place that either had its own laundry or machines on the same floor. In an ideal world, indoor parking would have been on that list, but that took us from the realm of the rare to that of the mythical.

Disability author Rebekah Taussig has explored this topic as well. She wrote about the challenges of finding any affordable, accessible home for her family, let alone one that actually fit her sense of style:

> We'd wasted so much time visiting homes that looked at first glance like they could be accessible, but surprised us with inconvenient, sometimes bizarre design choices like compact kitchens not wide enough to fit both a wheelchair and an open oven door, or three entry steps into a bedroom closet. We knew we weren't going to find an accessible dream house; we'd have to put time and money into some DIY accommodations. But the longer we looked, the less likely it seemed we would find a house that was minimally functional, let alone charming.[2]

For many of us with disabilities, finding a place to live isn't just a matter of making a few compromises about carpets versus hardwood or lawn size, *House Hunters*-style. It's literally, "Can I get my body into this bathroom? Do I have access to public transportation, home health aides, and food stores, and can my partner access what they need as well?"

Finding a living space that fits all those criteria and is somewhat afford-able, let alone one you actually *like*, is the rainbow unicorn.

Frugal by nature, Kevin was shocked at the cost of renting an apart-ment that worked for me. He struggled with the idea of sending a huge chunk of our income out the door each month, and I struggled with the idea of making compromises that put my safety at risk. It was rough. We argued and bargained and talked (and talked and talked). And even-tually we found a dear little hole-in-the-wall apartment with its own laundry facilities, no steps, and a shower that was aesthetically unfor-tunate but mutually acceptable. It was hard-won, but it worked for us, and we repeated the process (with less fighting) as we moved again (and again and again). I also recognize that our challenges pale in com-parison to those faced by other disabled and interabled couples. We're college-educated people with families who had the ability to assist us financially. We don't require home health aides at this time in our lives. So if you're reading this and rolling your eyes, I'm with you. Our prob-lems fall firmly into the prosecco category.

That being said, even at the honeymoon stage, the topics we would wrestle with, come together on, and relitigate were being established. And for that reason, I would say that in addition to accepting the prac-tical realities of cohabitation, it's something to undertake only with a person whom you really like and trust. Relationship onboarding can be tough, especially when options for compromise are limited, and as dis-abled people, we face more than our fair share of hurdles. But once you move past orientation and become comfortable with each other's needs and wants, it's a delightful way of moving through the world.

WHEN YOU KNOW, YOU KNOW

One side note about moving in together: it was quite striking how many of the disabled people we interviewed moved in with their partners quickly (and stayed together). There wasn't a lot of "Oh, we dated for five years, then thought about moving in for another three, and then lazily drifted into sharing a houseplant." There is literally a section in my interview notes tagged *When you know, you know*. One woman I spoke with, Katie, was thirty when she met her husband. She described having been "through the wringer" with dating, and those experiences taught her a lot about herself and what kind of person she was looking for. Meeting a guy who was in school to be a physical therapist was a relief; she felt like she could be up-front about having CP and trust that he already had some familiarity with the way that bodies like hers worked. "It was comfortable," she reflected. "We connected."[3]

For some, this confidence comes with a more complicated set of circumstances. In her book *Easy Beauty*, disabled philosopher Chloé Cooper Jones described the moment she and her new boyfriend learned that she was unexpectedly pregnant, after having been told her whole life that she wouldn't be able to conceive: "'I think we can do this,' I said, and the color came back into his face as if he believed this were possible, that we, near strangers, with no money, could take this on."[4] Despite the initial terror, they married and became parents. While not every couple will choose to keep a pregnancy, nor will all relationships last, it can be encouraging to see that many disabled people are in life-giving and sustaining partnerships.

I'm wondering if some of this *When you know, you know* phenomenon has to do with the cripdar that we talked about earlier in the book (I swear I will keep pushing this word *cripdar* until it catches on). We disabled people become so accomplished at reading people and situations that perhaps we're more confident in our relationships than many nondisabled people (or this is a gross oversimplification and self-serving toot of our collective crip horn). There's also the reality that for some of us our expected lifespan may not extend into old age, so we don't want to weigh current happiness against the opportunity cost of settling down. Economics may force our hand as well—we may choose to move in together more quickly because it is cheaper than living solo (though conversely, as we talk about in the finance chapter, moving in can be even more expensive). In any case, if you feel like the quicker-than-usual timeline you're working on is raising eyebrows among your nondisabled friends and family, you are in good company.

BODIES CHANGE

What you have today is not what you may have tomorrow.

—Judy Heumann[5]

When I asked the late Judy Heumann about her marriage to Jorge Pineda, her husband of thirty-plus years, she reflected on the changes they had experienced together (also of note regarding dating time-lines: Judy and Jorge met in August, moved in together in January, and were married in May—*When you know, you know*). Anyway, Judy said that when she and Jorge first met, he used crutches to get around and didn't require any in-home care. As the years progressed, he began using a wheelchair, and they each adjusted to having caregivers as an increasingly present part of their lives. Her point was that all our bodies are changing, to varying degrees and at varying rates, throughout our life-times. Strong relationships are built like skyscrapers made to withstand earthquakes, hurricanes, and shifts in temperature. The advantage that we have as disabled people is that this shift doesn't come as a surprise; we don't have the illusion of eternal ability coloring our perceptions of reality.

And, of course, change means not only adjustment to increasing impairment but also the courage to try new things. I got my driver's license in my early twenties, but I wasn't a confident driver and eventually let it expire. As my life circumstances changed and public transportation became less available, driving became a more attractive option. Still, no matter how much I psyched myself up, I panicked behind the wheel; my spastic legs would seize, and I was terrified that I'd slam on the gas pedal and be unable to stop. Before Kevin (BK), I had always been reluctant to try hand controls. I avoided anything that made me feel more disabled, more dependent on adaptive technology (ah, internalized ableism—the gift that keeps on giving). But being in a supportive relationship gave me a confidence boost, and I signed up for adaptive driving school. It turned out that with hand controls, I was a totally proficient and nonanxious driver, if one who occasionally has to charm her way out of speeding tickets. In the years that followed, I became the primary driver in our family.

A gradual shift in any direction is one thing, but the folks we spoke with also described the challenges that arose from more rapid health changes. When asked how she navigated a long-term relationship with a chronic autoimmune disease, one woman reflected,

My last four years with my partner is actually when my chronic illness has been the worst. He went from it being a nonissue to being overwhelmed by it to being worried about me to shutting down at times when I lose my composure after another bad test result. We live together, and I am coparenting his two teens and a twenty-two-year-old, so it's a heavy load. My mental health is also impacted at times, so I can be difficult or unreasonable, especially on high-pain days.

One way I deal with my overwhelming health issues is laughing and making jokes about the ridiculousness of my situation, and he often tries to chuckle along with it. I put on a "good" face that I am OK, but the truth is I am crumbling inside and do not want to burden him with it. There are days when I burst and there are tears and sobbing and he often tries soothing me and patting me on the back, but he doesn't know how to handle it most days. He is learning every day, though—the fact that I am an activist and it's my job to create disability-inclusive spaces actually helps him understand me better.[6]

Heather, an autistic woman who also lives with a variety of chronic health conditions, shared a similar experience:

> My migraines are debilitating, and sometimes when they hit, I can't move, I can't cook, can't work, can't drive the kids anywhere—I'm just out. I know this adds pressure to [my partner] and his busy schedule, but for the most part, he understands. I think at the end of the day, we navigate our relationship with constant communication, honesty, and hard work—like any relationship, but we have the added issue of how to do all that when one person has no control over their pain and body shutting down, so it's all of that plus educating your partner on ableism and access, on the intersections of disability and other identities—how being a woman means my pain is dismissed more often than men.[7]

NEVER STOP TALKING. UNLESS YOU NEED TO.

The unpredictable nature of some disabilities can make each day a guessing game, a puzzle to navigate. The couples that thrive are the ones who communicate their physical and emotional needs candidly and respectfully. In an article on interabled relationships (a relationship where one partner is nondisabled or the degree of disability is different between partners), Dan Digmann, who both has and is married to someone with multiple sclerosis (MS), counseled, "Always be truthful with each other. . . . Honest but not hurtful."[8]

Disability not only invites discussion on topics about needs and vulnerabilities but also may impact how one communicates in general. My communication style as a disabled woman with a nonconfrontational personality had always been grounded in putting the person in front of me at ease. Was I too confident? I'd be gentler. Too smart? I'd be self-deprecating. Did I have a preference on apartments? I'd meet you at

80 percent. Kevin, on the other hand, grew up in a family where affection was displayed in the boisterous exchange of ideas. His parents, siblings, and assorted friends would spend hours over Thanksgiving dinner arguing heatedly over hypothetical situations or the correct English translation of *tiramisu*. For Kevin, love meant treating me as a person who can hold her own in the world. For me, it meant giving in to what I thought he wanted. It took us months to figure out that I was expecting him to guess my preferences, and he was waiting for me to say what I needed. Gradually he became a little softer and I became tougher, better versions of the people we had been at the beginning (and to finally settle this, *tiramisu* means "pick me up").

One of the advantages of being in a relationship where authentic communication is part of your operating manual is that it doesn't just cover disability. Reflecting on her way of communicating with her partner, Heather shared,

> We are also lucky that we talk about societal issues and injustice often with the children and as a family—my partner is Korean American, and the last few years (on top of decades of racism) have not been easy for Asian Americans—so our dialogues on disability have been part of a broader conversation, which may make it a bit easier. We have a good foundation.[9]

And I'll add my constant therapy refrain: if you feel like your relationship could benefit from some fine-tuning around communication and you have the financial resources to do so, book a few sessions with a counselor (if you can get one in your area—if not, virtual therapy is a good option). Though it's tempting to see one's own relationship as a special snowflake, most communication issues are fairly standard; a session or two with your local therapist doesn't mean you're signing up for analysis for the next three decades and may well give you some helpful skills to make life more pleasant.

TAKIN' CARE OF BUSINESS

I see the coffee wasn't made.

—My house, every third morning

If communication is one side of the coin, the other is its pesky little sister, the all-important division of labor. That is not a government organization but rather one of the relationship dams that either keeps your household running smoothly or plunges it into a seething hellscape of rage and overflowing passive aggression. At the most overarching level, folks will probably agree that each person in a partnership should contribute in a meaningful way. It gets tougher when you start parsing out what that contribution actually looks like (ahem, coffee). There are as many acceptable ways of divvying up household labor as there are partnered humans (and much to say about the intersections of household labor with gender and culture), but for now, I'll focus on some of the specific issues around disability.

The thing about disability is that it often (but not always) either creates more work in a relationship or makes it unrealistic for one or both people to participate in some of the work of the household. When the skills are complementary, it doesn't necessarily lead to strain: Kevin brings the heavy grocery bags in, and I cook dinner. We both like our half of that equation. It's also not too bad when there's a task that we both agree is frustrating or hard; it sucks that the kid is throwing up and throws our work days into disarray, or one of us gets a flat tire and we have to spend the weekend trying to fix it. Then we're united in our mutual complaining about the unfairness of life and can drown our sorrows in Netflix.

The big struggles happen when the dividing line is not mutually acceptable and one person feels taken advantage of or like they routinely get the raw end of the deal (that is, not during a specific time of particular struggle but when that unacceptable dividing line is baked into the relationship). One man whom we spoke with said, "My autism can make me focus on special projects . . . sometimes [my wife] will feel like a single parent to our six-year-old." His attempts to point out the things he does do, like providing financially for the family, are of limited effectiveness, he admitted: "I feel more satisfied with my role than she does with hers."[10]

After Kevin and I had a baby, I was scared all the time. I worried that I'd drop him, that Kevin would drop him, that I'd trip and crush him, that Kevin, holding him, would suddenly leap twenty yards to the right and plummet over a railing. I was a joy to be around. While Kevin was (and is) an amazing dad and 100 percent pulled his weight, my fear became a big factor in our relationship during that time. I was asking him to take on jobs that I could technically do by myself but believed it was safer for him to do (like interrupting a meeting to trek down to our apartment's garage and move our kid from the car seat into the stroller). We had conversations like "How could you [*monster*] not prioritize the safety of your innocent child?" to which he'd counter, "How are you going to build confidence if you refuse to do the things you can actually do well?" In the end, he came downstairs when he could, I restarted Lexapro, and we made it through, but those were some tough months.

For better or worse, division of labor isn't something I believe any couple has figured out once and for all (unless you're lucky enough to have a full team of household staff at your disposal, and even then, there's probably some management to divide up). It's a constant renegotiation as your circumstances and bodies change. The complexity of life means that an exact and sustained fifty-fifty split is probably never going to happen, and trying to make that split perfect is one way to guarantee misery for everyone. The good news is that relationships tend to work when both people want them to and when each approaches the other person with respect, kindness, and a healthy dose of humor (when my mother-in-law was asked how she's remained happily married for fifty years, her response was "Low expectations").

BUILDING YOUR TEAM

We need to put that on the job application. Are you funny? Please submit a five-minute reel of your best humor.

—*Shane and Hannah Burcaw*[11]

A big part of being in a relationship is figuring out how to make decisions together. I'm not one of those "two bodies, one soul" types: we don't suddenly fuse when we enter a partnership; you're going to retain your individual opinions, values, and ironclad commitment to the correct way of hanging a roll of toilet paper. At the same time, in healthy relationships, people make decisions together and those relationships are porous: we continue to support, and be supported by, a whole network of connections outside the relationship itself. Those connections differ depending on the individuals involved, their needs, resources, and season of life. They can be personal—family, friends, religious groups—or professional—paid caregivers, educators, therapists, cleaning services. When we live with another person, we may choose to share tasks that we previously outsourced or, conversely, find that we have the resources to outsource tasks we no longer want to do (one woman I interviewed said she and her husband both didn't like laundry and had the resources to pay someone else to do it, so they gleefully took that option).[12]

For some disabled people, the first connection we need to navigate when entering into a partnership is the one we have with our parents (assuming those parents have been present and generally healthy fixtures in our lives). My parents were the ones who helped me navigate the world. They were my advocates and the only people I felt like I could be completely myself with. In turn, I was their miracle child, the one who defied expectations and aligned my aspirations with theirs.

And then I got married, and all of that had to shift. It does for everyone, but for me, that change felt strange and abrupt because I hadn't had a lot of practice—at home, I was myself; in the world, I was who I thought people wanted me to be; and the family I was creating with my husband didn't yet feel like home. Though my parents loved Kevin and supported our relationship, I think letting go was tough for them too. It took a lot of talking, some crying, and a few blowups, but in a few years, the lines were redrawn and everyone settled into a healthier and more sustainable set of new roles.

Working with professional aides is an area that couples may have to navigate (and indeed that most people, disabled or not, will wrestle with as they age). Help at home can range from getting assistance with yard work to having a person prepare and position your body for sexual activity. Financial resources and eligibility for benefits play a huge part in what assistance people can access, as does a shared sense of values around what kind of help is desired. In his book on interabled partnerships, author Ben Mattlin talked about the competing values of privacy and convenience/safety: he and his wife prefer not to have outside people in their home all the time but also recognize that some tasks, for physical or emotional reasons, are best performed by professionals.[13] Disability YouTubers Shane and Hannah Burcaw have spoken publicly about their deliberations leading up to hiring a caregiver and desire for one person (their "golden unicorn") versus working with an agency or hiring different people depending on the need.[14] During one stage of life you may need fewer sources of outside help, and during others (particularly if you go down the kid path, have surgery, or age), you might need more. The two key words here are "knowledge" and "communication": What are the care options you can access given your resources and circumstances, and how do you talk about them with your partner? It may also be helpful to remind ourselves and each other that humans are herd animals—self-sufficiency is a recent cultural construct and illusion that serves none of us well. Disabled or not, we're all part of a web of interdependent relationships.

PARENTING

Ah, parenting. Just when you think you have the whole communication and division of labor thing figured out, when you're cooking along with your families of origin and you've had a meeting of the minds around values, religious practices, finances, and whether to get a cat, you utter the P-word, and suddenly you're right back at the starting gate.

Not really, actually—parenting is just a larger, poopier version of all that stuff listed above. If you want to turn up the heat on a relationship, talk about having a kid. Things that you thought were totally not a big deal now become *the most important deal ever*, and all of the worry and insecurity that were tucked nicely back into the corners of our psyches come roaring back out.

Not everyone reading this will want to become a biological parent or to have kids at all. Some of you may have experienced infertility or know that getting pregnant will take some combination of medical intervention and reproductive support. Others will stepparent, foster parent, or adopt children. Many will be curious about parenting but uncertain whether it is something they wish to take on with a disability or given other commitments and values. Judy Heumann said that by the time she married her husband, they were in their forties with active careers and decided not to parent,[15] but she maintained deep supportive connections with many younger people in and outside her family.

When Kevin and I first got together, he wasn't sure about having a kid (as opposed to me, who was always 100 percent sure I wanted to be a mom). He had never seen disabled people parenting. He eventually opened up to the idea, and after decades of my body not behaving how I wanted it to, it suddenly shifted course, and my pregnancy was utterly routine. Nine months and one scheduled C-section later, we were handed an eight-pound meatball who changed our lives forever. Rebekah Taussig experienced something like this as well, reflecting, "My body's deficiencies had been drilled so deeply into my mind that I could not fathom it being able to grow and protect a whole baby human. But it did—with very little drama."[16] Jessica and her husband became parents the first time through adoption and the second through surrogacy.

Parenting as disabled people is a huge subject that deserves its own book (actually, Jessica has written that book, and it's totally worth checking out if the subject intrigues you at all). We can't do justice to the breadth, challenges, or beauty of disabled parenting here but want to at least acknowledge that for many people in partnerships, the subject will come up, and (some, not all) disabled people do want to raise kids. We also understand that for some of us, not wanting to parent comes with its own doubts. One person I spoke with wondered whether his desire to be child-free was his own internalized ableism or would have been the case had he not been disabled. His parents encourage him all the time to have kids, and he sometimes feels that their urging is, paradoxically, a way of dismissing his bodily autonomy in the same way that it would be if they discouraged him from having kids. The good news is that if you do choose to make parenting part of your relationship, the same skills that you use around communication, division of labor, and acquiring resources will serve you well in that endeavor.

NO SHAME IN YOUR GAME

Growing up, I never thought I'd have a family of my own—there was a blank space where a relationship and children were. I didn't know anyone who looked like me who had a partner, a kid, and a rescue goldfish. No matter how chaotic or messy or entirely unremarkable my life is, I'm glad I didn't let my uncertainty or the lack of representation have the last word. And I hope that's true for you as well: whether your view of the good life is one that's happily single and surrounded by great friends, partnered with one or more people, child-free or captain of the preschool car line, you have every right to own those hopes and work toward a life that reflects them (and, when life inevitably shifts away from what we expect, to grieve and rage and find some joy and surprises in what we end up with, because life is messy like that). Being disabled doesn't mean that we have to shift our hopes to reflect the limited adult roles we've been exposed to. Whatever it is you want, own it.

CHAPTER 12
CAREGIVING

JESSICA

THESE ARE THE THINGS THAT I NEED: SIX OF THE SMALL FROZEN CIR-
cles, my cloth bag of rice and lavender heated for one minute and
forty seconds, and my big cup filled with water. Sometimes, if it's a bad
night and I'm feeling particularly wobbly, I need David to sit outside
the bathroom while I pee in case I fall.

I now have a fridge near the bed with a small coffee maker on top.
That helps. I also have an adjustable bed, so I don't need help arranging
my pillows. We moved the thermostat to my nightstand so that I can
reach it. I have a caddy nearby with a blood-pressure cuff, gingers for
nausea, my books, and a cozy scarf.

Before we go somewhere as a family, David attaches my wheelchair
trailer to our car. He loads my wheelchair. He cools down or warms up
the car since I don't thermoregulate well.

If I wake up very sick, which I sometimes do, he wakes with me. He holds my hand and reminds me that it will pass. He knows when it's an emergency and when it's just agony.

When I arrive at a doctor's appointment, he opens the trailer, unloads my wheelchair, and brings it to my side of the car. He walks in with me to make sure that the building doesn't have stairs and that the buttons that open the doors are actually working. Sometimes, on a hot day, he reconnoiters to make sure the establishment's air conditioning is working so that I don't get heat exhaustion, which I'm prone to.

David is my caregiver.

ROMANCE AND CAREGIVING

In 2019, Dr. Phil aired an episode called "I Swiped Right on My Quadriplegic Boyfriend," which aimed to explore caregiving dynamics in interabled relationships. The episode featured a disabled man, Bailey, and his girlfriend, Harley.

Bailey and Harley were deeply unhappy in their relationship. Harley wanted help caring for Bailey, but in their rural location, they were unable to access the support they needed. Bailey carried a great deal of insecurity and resentment about his disability and took those feelings out on Harley. Their reliance and dissatisfaction were, from all accounts, closer to codependence than interdependence.

That said they loved each other and wanted to make things work. Unfortunately, they sought help from Dr. Phil, who brought with him into the episode truckloads of ableism and ignorance. To start, he made the assumption that being with a disabled person is inherently worse than being with a nondisabled person. Early on, he said to Harley, "You're a young, single, attractive female. Out of all the people that you can choose, why choose someone in a wheelchair?"

The implication is that only a person with limited prospects would date a disabled person. It's worth noting that, *oh, just maybe*, one reason for Bailey's dissatisfaction with his body was bullshit comments like this.

Later in the episode, after Dr. Phil had explored their particular dynamics, he made the comment that caused disabled people globally to erupt with outrage. Referencing caregiving in intimate relationships, he decreed, "This won't work. One hundred out of one hundred times, this won't work." He went on, "There are a lot of people that can be his caretaker, but there are not a lot of people who can be his girlfriend and his lover. It's not your job. You're either going to be his lover or his caretaker."

Dr. Phil had concluded that the source of their dysfunction was that Harley was helping Bailey with tasks of daily living. If she could only revert to a "lover-only" role, they would be OK. He also implied that her desire to be with a disabled man indicated some sort of pathology. Before we consider caregiving relationships further, we should note a few things.

First, Bailey and Harley *wanted* more help, but there was none available. So even if Harley was not suited to be a caregiver but did want to be in a relationship with Bailey, she had no other options! The problem wasn't their relationship but the fact that disabled people are often unable to access adequate social support.

Second, Dr. Phil assumed that it was the act of caregiving that was destroying their relationship, not the fact that society treats disabled people as a burden. From the sound of the interview, Bailey's insecurities erupted as anger. If Harley had stopped being a caregiver, it's likely that Bailey would still have had episodes of anger.

Third, Dr. Phil failed to consider what Bailey might have offered Harley in the relationship. He adopted a simplistic and binary framing of their relationship: Harley as the giver and Bailey as the receiver. People aren't that simple. Perhaps a reframing of each person's value and contributions could have done wonders.

Toward the end of the episode, Dr. Phil insisted that Harley make a choice: she needed to be a lover or a caregiver. In tears, she answered, "A lover."

But was that the solution? Who would provide Bailey's care? Was he suddenly not going to be overcome by internalized ableism? Were they going to be able to access the social safety net they needed to survive?[1]

SHANE AND HANNAH BURCAW SPEAK ABOUT THE CAREGIVING DYNAMIC IN their marriage with humor and candor. They have millions of subscribers and followers on YouTube and Instagram. They were actually contacted to be on that *Dr. Phil* episode and turned it down because they were afraid they wouldn't have enough control over how disability was presented.

Once the episode aired, they were relieved to have turned it down and shared a video explaining their history with the episode. They also started a social media hashtag: #100outof100, in which interabled couples shared photos and described their relationships. Within days, thousands of couples were posting their happy caregiving stories and how long they had been together.

Since then, Shane and Hannah have opened up even more about the details of their relationship. Shane, who has spinal muscular atrophy (SMA), relies on Hannah for many of his tasks of daily living. She gets him out of bed in the morning and helps him with toileting, eating, brushing his teeth, medications, etc. She is a caregiver by any definition. They also have a hilarious and flirtatious dynamic. By their accounts, their sex life is active and satisfying. And just as in my marriage, the care doesn't only go one way. Shane is the coordinator of the couple and takes the lead on travel planning and business ventures. He also provides a great deal of practical and emotional support.

In 2020, they offered the following tips for success in caregiving relationships to BraunAbility, a company that makes accessible vehicles:[2]

1. *Communicate:* they shared the importance of addressing possible schedule- or task-related conflicts well in advance, for example, if one person needs to wake up early for an

event or the other would like to have something particular for dinner.

2. *Remember that romance and caregiving don't have to be mutually exclusive:* they explained that while some people prefer to have professional caregivers, other couples find that caregiving and romance are "seamlessly intertwined":

It's pretty simple. The moments when Hannah is performing "care" for me . . . are just another opportunity for us to be together and enjoy each other's company. It's not like we flip a switch and turn off our passion for each other just because Hannah happens to be doing my care. In fact, we often find that our romance and caregiving go hand in hand. We laugh and tell stories to each other while she's showering me. We make fun of each other while she's shaving my face. We use the time spent caregiving as any two people in love spend their time together: laughing and play-arguing and loving.[3]

3. *Laugh:* they say that this sounds cheesy but is actually crucial for their relationship. They credit their compatibility to being able to laugh in adversity:

For example, a few weeks ago, I woke up at 3 a.m. with a horrible stomach virus requiring Hannah to emergency carry me from our bed to the bathroom. It was almost a very messy catastrophe, but instead of getting annoyed or angry about this difficult moment, we found ourselves laughing uncontrollably.[4]

Shane and Hannah acknowledge that their dynamic doesn't work for everyone, and duh, of course. Relationships are all unique, regardless of whether disability is a factor. What's crucial is that a couple has the ability to carve out their own structure apart from ableism and inadequate social safety nets.

THE EARLY DAYS

When entering a new relationship, every disabled person has the right to introduce the topic of caregiving however they like. In most healthy and trusting relationships, conversations about care will evolve naturally. Logistics will be addressed and PAs introduced. If someone needs help dressing or eating, there may be days during which a romantic partner asks to take over those responsibilities to facilitate privacy.

As a relationship shifts from new to established, it is a good idea to have a frank discussion about what each person imagines with respect to caregiving in the short- and long-term. A discussion is warranted regardless of whether the couple is interabled or both people are disabled. Of course, our lives will change over time. Bodies always change. Our needs at the beginning of a relationship are not predictive of our needs ten years in. This is true even if neither person is disabled. Caregiving needs and responsibilities will always evolve.

STRUCTURES

There are countless ways to organize our care. When I was in a serious relationship with Christopher, it was clear that he was not comfortable as a caregiver. He valued his autonomy and independence too much.

Even though we lived together and led intertwined lives, I did not rely on Christopher for my care. I paid a PA to do my grocery shopping. A friend took the garbage out. When I needed rides to cardiac rehab, a group of friends divided up the days. As I discussed in chapter 7, his reluctance to involve himself in my care was an indicator that he was not suited to a relationship with a disabled person. But I imagine there are sustainable ways to structure a healthy relationship in which caregiving is almost entirely outsourced.

With David, we are constantly tweaking our lives to help me feel independent (which I value) and to give him the time and rest he needs. In California, we had a PA visit for a few hours per week to help me with doctor's appointments and errands. When I had frequent physical therapy in California, friends stepped in.

As I mentioned, we put that fridge and coffee maker near the bed where I spend my days. This allows me to access food without asking David to bring me something from the kitchen. I do our grocery shopping online and signed up for a service that allows me to have packages picked up, so David doesn't have to visit the post office. Of course, some of these solutions involve money, but others don't. I think a crucial component for us is that we can openly communicate our capacities and needs. The division of care is never static.

Vayl, whom we met earlier in chapter 9, lives with their caregiver in a platonic partnership; Vayl also has other romantic partnerships. Their caregiver receives some government funding to use toward Vayl's care and appreciates cohabitating with a committed partner (see chapter 13 for more detailed money talk). Regardless, there are countless ways to structure relationships and care.

GRATITUDE AND ABLEISM

Once I was visiting a friend who was able to move only her head. She relied on full-time assistants. Despite the omnipresent helpers in her home, she still needed to ask her husband and daughter for help. "Can you nudge my tea closer?" "Can you put the straw closer to my hand?" "Can you cover my knees with my skirt?"

One day, when we were in her family room alone, the other members of our families running around with her dog in the backyard, she whispered to me, "Don't you get so fucking tired of saying thank you?" The question was a breath of fresh air. "God, yes," I said.

And what is that? I mean, I *am* thankful. Thankful that when I text "Heat and circles," David knows I mean six tiny ice packs and my heat pack warmed for one minute and forty seconds. Thankful that he unloaded my wheelchair yesterday at the eye doctor's and, when it was too warm in the lobby, took care of my paperwork. But something about always being the one who is thankful can really wear on a person.

Because the truth is, while I am proud to be disabled and wouldn't switch my body for another, I wish I didn't have to inconvenience other people. I wish I could hop in my car and go for a drive. I wish I could make my own lunch on hard health days. I wish I could shower when I'm home alone without sending a safety text first: "If I don't say I'm out in 15 minutes, send help."

I believe both of these things can be true. I can, ultimately, love my life and still crave autonomy. And it makes sense that saying thank you for a thing I don't want to have to ask for feels like adding insult to injury. "You think I want to be lifted onto my toilet swing?" my friend said. "You think I'm thankful to need another person to scratch my nose?"

While some of the gratitude exhaustion comes from the fact that having disabled bodies and minds is literally exhausting, I have to believe another part stems from ableism. We are all, disabled or not, fed the lie that an independent life is the best kind of life. Our society (at least in the United States and Canada) maintains a toxic obsession with capacity as the measure of merit.

In this paradigm, it makes sense that a constant reminder of our weaknesses feels demoralizing. Interdependence is, quite literally, counter to our culture's morals. So then, as disabled people, every time we need help, there is a little voice that whispers, "You are less worthy."

No wonder saying thank you sucks.

When you take the dependence quagmire and insert it into romance, it all becomes more tricky. It's easy to imagine how corrosive it is in a relationship for one person to be constantly reminded that they are fundamentally less useful. The caregiver's sense of goodness naturally inflates, while the care receiver's diminishes. If you bring in martyrdom and identity, it can easily turn into poison soup.

Caregiving does not have to be that way. If we can, alongside our disabled community, acknowledge and address our internalized ableism, the meaning of caregiving can shift. Because the truth is that every person needs care.

Take, for example, my dynamic with David.

David is also disabled. He is mostly blind in one eye and has autism. Fine-motor activities are tricky for him, and he frequently delivers tasks to me in bed—shoelaces to untangle, zippers to unstick, liners to insert into boots.

Years ago, he wrote about his thoughts on the word "caregiving":

Here is something that lies beyond the boundary of caregiving: My wife and I laugh. We laugh a lot, especially at the nonsense that our kid says day in, day out. We read books together and watch shows together. Terrible shows. And we laugh.

Here is something else: She takes care of me. She pays our bills. She orders healthy, delicious food for us. She reads the instructions for our wallpaper because I can't bear to do it, and she tells me how to cut it and how to use a level. When I say that her requests for soup upend my trains of thought, she says that she will email soup requests to me, so that I can receive them when I'm at a good stopping point. She slows down for me.

More than that: She finds books on parenting, on transracial adoption. She creates communities for our family. She learns to care for our kid's hair. By engaging online, she learns how to keep our kid safe. I have trouble even broaching these topics, and yet she does the emotional work and caregiving to bring them into my everyday dialect. Often she does this work in the morning, from our bed.

Even more than that: I didn't take care of myself before I met her. I worked too hard. I ate and drank too much. I had a coating of black mold in my shower. It was impossible to have people over at my apartment. Now I live in a home that could double as a charming bed and breakfast.

Not all caregivers will find their care reciprocated in these ways or to these degrees, but all caregivers will be given a lesson. We learn how to be patient. We learn, through confronting the needs of another, that there can be space between our desires and our actions. We find this patience modeled, notably, in the behavior of those for whom we care. They are often waiting. They are often struggling. But they wait.

Pema Chödrön has an essay about the value of waiting, of refraining from whatever habitual response we might ordinarily have in a certain situation. The result of being able to refrain, she says, is that "anything can come up, anything can walk into our house; we can find anything sitting on our living-room couch, and we don't freak out."[5] This is caregiving. If we have trouble seeing its inherent value when it comes to partners or potential partners, or if we have trouble distinguishing the care from the person receiving it, then we should stop to reflect—for surely we are not so confused when it comes to our children. Surely we can see that a child is not the same thing as a dirty diaper, much less the sum of its dirty diapers, even as changing that diaper is an act of love, a necessity, and a chance to venture beyond our own needs.

CHORES

Sex and adoration aside, as Caroline addressed in chapter 11, at some points a long-term relationship can be mostly a division of labor. Particularly once kids are involved, a great deal of time and energy must be devoted to keeping the family system functioning. I am not the only disabled person who has noticed that in straight/cis relationships, disability can serve to shift common gender roles.

In fact, recently, someone on a TV show said the word "housewife," and our six-year-old asked what it meant. I get that the term is problematic, but I still tried to explain the origin and concept succinctly. After I finished, our daughter thought for a second and then declared, "Daddy is our housewife!"

And, in many ways, it's true. David does the dishes and cooks our daughter's meals. David wipes down the kitchen at the end of the day. I am in charge of taxes, finances, and general higher-level coordination. I meet with financial planners and attorneys. I file insurance claims.

David washes the laundry, and I fold it, weeding out items with holes. I patch ripped jeans and toss shredded socks. Every few months, I sort our daugher's clothes and make sure everything fits. To be honest, I think our labor division is actually quite even. But, as an impatient perfectionist raised in the South, were I not disabled, most responsibilities would be mine. I'd insist on it. Caregiving and disability invite a thoughtfulness into labor and home management that is otherwise hard to find.

THE BURDEN AND THE SAINT

When Dr. Sarah Rainey, a feminist scholar, met Max online in 2003, she worried about what his diagnosis of MS would mean for their relationship. She read all she could about his illness and, with questions still unanswered, took a leap and entered into a relationship with him.[6] He died five years later, but during that time, she was struck by the intensity and inaccuracy of outsiders' assumptions. She felt that despite their protests, they couldn't escape the assumption that Max was a burden and she was a saint.

In 2011, Rainey published *Love, Sex, and Disability: The Pleasures of Care*, which explored the caregiving dynamics in the relationships of seven interabled couples, including her own. Her primary objective was to use evidence to discount the common framing of caregiving as a physical and burdensome task. She expanded the definition to include emotional and intellectual support. She also looked at the emotional intimacy that caregiving facilitates and cited it as a factor in relationship resilience.

It's incredible that over a decade later, the tropes of the disabled person as a burden and the caregiver as a hero still prevail. I think it's in part because the idea that disabled people are fundamentally deficient is still pervasive. Until we can loosen ableism's grip, its impacts are unlikely to shift.

But I understand that you aren't reading this book for a college course on theory. So what does Rainey's work mean for your actual relationship? I find it helpful to remind myself, when I question my own value as a partner, that my beliefs aren't formed in a vacuum. Ableism is the water we swim in, and my own interpretation of my value is not always reliable.

AUTONOMY/RESPECT

When I watch Hannah and Shane's videos or listen to their podcast, I am often struck by how they prioritize autonomy. They were talking about alcohol recently, and Shane joked about drinking five beers in a short amount of time. They laughed because his body would have trouble processing that amount of alcohol, and it would end poorly. Shane asked, "What would you do if I wanted to drink five beers?"

"I'd tell you that it was a bad idea. I'd act annoyed. And then I'd pour you the beer."

The conversation was light and funny, but I thought Hannah's response was profound. At no point does she use her physical capacities to exert power over Shane. In a recent podcast episode, he said that maybe he would start dyeing his hair. She said she thought he'd regret it but then said, "If you choose to do this, I'll help you."

These small moments drove home to me how important it is to find a way for both people to have control of their bodies in a relationship. Otherwise, it's not intimacy—it's abuse. During our interviews for this book, we spoke to a few people whose partners in caregiving roles withheld care in order to exert control. That is never, ever OK.

MUTUAL AID

For some people, caregiving in a romantic partnership feels unsustainable. They may find themselves suffering from caregiver burnout or observe that their own capacities are not a match for what their partner needs. It's important to note that a relationship with a disabled person does not inherently involve caregiving. There are other structures.

In addition to health insurance– or government-funded assistants— or, for those who are independently wealthy, those paid out of pocket— there is mutual aid. In disability culture, mutual aid is a system of collective care in which there is no distinction between the care *giver* and the care *receiver*.

Leah Lakshmi Piepzna-Samarasinha, a disabled Canadian activist, has published two books on disabled mutual aid: *The Future Is Disabled: Prophecies, Love Notes and Mourning Songs* and *Care Work: Dreaming Disability Justice*. They described a messy web of disabled interdependence as a revolution. Disabled people are experts at finding creative ways to survive, and we support and protect each other.

Of course, if you need constant help with tasks of daily living, it's unlikely that your local or global community of other disabled people will be able to take that on, but it is likely that they will be able to help reduce some of your partner's responsibility. Here are some ways I have benefited from mutual aid:

A disabled friend often sends me links to products that will help me perform tasks of daily living without help.

Another sends me links to government programs in Canada that will provide our family with disability-related financial assistance.

One of my disabled friends lets me share the daily details of my pain and physical discomfort, which means that David doesn't have to carry it all.

A local disabled friend who doesn't use a wheelchair frequently updates me on which stores and restaurants have ramps and accessible bathrooms.

And in each of these cases, I care for them too. We have woven our own net.

CAREGIVING IS INEVITABLE

The topic of caregiving is real, daily, and practical. Also, there is a false binary of people who need care and those who do not. The truth is, we *all* need care, disabled or not. Caring for one another's needs is part of every single healthy, loving relationship. We cook for each other. We debrief about bad days. We offer career advice. The space between disabled care and nondisabled care is partially an ableism-created illusion.

And, critically, every single person who lives long enough will one day be disabled. Nearly every romantic relationship that lasts long enough will involve caregiving and care receiving. Navigating our capacities and our needs is a skill that most people will eventually need. It's crucial that the discussion shift away from blaming disabled people for being burdens to considering what structures could help support what is essential about being human: bodies change.

CHAPTER 13
MONEY

CAROLINE

TWO THINGS.

First, I've had the Destiny's Child song "Bills, Bills, Bills" running through my head the whole time I've been working through this chapter . . . "When times get hard, I need someone to help me out / Instead of a scrub like you who don't know what a man's about" (On a related note, there is apparently no subject that lacks connection to the immortal wisdom of Beyoncé).

Second, when it comes to the subject of money, I've been thinking a lot about my first job. After grad school, I worked as a chaplain in a physical rehabilitation hospital. It was a setting where congenital disabilities were a rarity; the majority of the folks who found themselves there had experienced a sudden spinal cord or traumatic brain injury.

This meant that most days, my role was simply to listen as people shared the circumstances of their injuries, navigated emotional and physical healing, and started to gain comfort with a new way of being embodied in the world (other duties included refereeing wheelchair drag races and feigning ignorance re: the dudes trying to plant weed in the therapeutic horticulture area). People being people, the range of responses to sudden impairment varied from person to person and day to day. There was no one path that people took to acceptance, no straight line to something a psychologist or spiritual adviser could define as healing. But there was shared experience, mutual support, and (apparently) a quick toke in the greenhouse from time to time.

While universals are elusive when it comes to disability, for the folks I met, money was generally at or near the top of the stress list. A woman would be tossed off her surfboard and the next thing she knew, she had to take leave from her job or resign entirely and was plunged into the whirlwind of navigating medical assistance programs, employing home health aides, figuring out how to finance expensive renovations, and purchasing medical equipment that cost as much as a fancy vacation home. To make matters worse, it typically takes over two years to be approved for disability benefits under Social Security; during the waiting period, the cost of care is borne by the individual and their family. To be approved for certain forms of assistance also means that a household must exhaust other sources of income or move assets into specialized accounts designed for disabled people (*adios*, nest egg). In an instant, everyone in a household can go from being financially stable to living with crushing debt.

Financial worries are not limited to those who acquire an impairment during adulthood. There are plenty of statistics showing that disabled people are less likely to attend college than those without disabilities. We are more likely to be unemployed, sporadically employed, or underemployed. One person I spoke with, Shoshanna, described her experience this way:

> My disabilities have affected my financial life. Finding a "regular" job is not easy for me, as I require a lot of accessibility. I am Deaf, which means

I require an ASL interpreter where I work. I use a power chair, so I need physical accessibility. I have eleven degrees, including four doctorates, and I'm fluent in two languages and have intermediate/advanced skills in five other languages. But finding a job in my field where the location is nearby that I can get to, as well as the accessibility to work there, has not come my way. This means that I am on government support, which is not a lot of money per month.[1]

Shoshanna's experience seems more common than not; in an informal review of disabled folks I know, I'm struck by how many people (even those with advanced degrees) are not working consistently or are not employed in their chosen fields. Most cases of underemployment are because there are no accessible jobs or because a paid job would disqualify them from medical assistance.

DISABLED AND BROKE

In the United States, poverty is baked into the system of life-sustaining care. As many of you can attest, if you have a disability that requires expensive equipment, transportation, or in-home assistance, Medicaid is virtually the only provider that will cover these services, and to get Medicaid, your household must have an income of less than $3,000 per month (varying a bit depending on which state you live in). That means that for millions of people, accessing life-sustaining care requires them to live under the poverty line; any income over a low threshold you (or your partner) make stands to boot you out of the program and eliminate your access to essential services.

Disabled attorney Gabriella Garbero estimated that to pay out of pocket for the home health aides and nurses she needs, she would be looking at spending $100,000–200,000 a year; these figures do not include any other essential health care equipment or medications. Even for a lawyer, those are astronomical figures.

For those of us whose bodies don't require obscenely expensive health care or technology, it's still costly to live with a disability in the United States. My husband and I fall into the cluster of disabled people who had sufficient financial resources to attend college, along with bodies and brains that conform closely enough to what our society considers employable to function in white-collar professions. If we were in positions where our minds couldn't fit themselves to the requirements of corporate life or tolerate the narrow bands of what are currently considered social norms, we'd struggle (neither of us could function in a job where physical strength or stamina is necessary). When it comes to finances, we recognize our incredible privilege.

And yet, even with the resources we have, disability adds a financial component to our lives that our nondisabled friends and family do not face. When we were first searching for an apartment and later looking to buy a house, we found that apartments were generally affordable but inaccessible or accessible and wildly expensive. Apartments that cost about what we could afford often had basement laundry facilities and no elevator. Spending extra on rent limited how much we could save for a down payment on a house, and when we did finally enter the home-buying realm, the same pattern repeated itself: houses were either accessible and expensive or affordable but completely unworkable for me. And it's not just housing: crutches that don't destroy my shoulders aren't cheap, our dragging feet require more frequent shoe purchases, and my hand controls add well over a grand to any car purchase.

For me as a disabled woman, pregnancy and parenting were both more expensive than they would have been otherwise: all those extra medical and therapy appointments with their $45 copays plus limited choices for strollers, bassinets, and bouncy seats meant there was essentially a disability surcharge on having a kid. Again, even as I'm writing this, I know that to call these challenges is insulting, or at the very least ridiculous, to those who are literally choosing between medication and rent or working and health care. By accident of birth, Kevin and I are obscenely fortunate. I use these examples only to show that unless you are in the realm of Elton John and money is so abundant as to be an almost abstract consideration in your life, disability adds layers of financial complication for pretty much every household.

I'll also add the caveat that all of this is a distinctly American problem. The government of the good old US of A has decided that this nightmare of a system is the best that *We the People* can do for those of us with disabilities (and we haven't even gotten to the marriage penalty yet!). I'm grateful for the amazing medical options that exist in much of the United States, but our strategy for providing life-sustaining care for disabled people is pretty rotten.

DATING AND FINANCES

But forget for a moment about mortgages, durable medical equipment, and national embarrassment—what about dating and finances? The folks we spoke with had a lot to say on this subject. From first swipe to happily ever after, money plays an outsized role in the romantic lives of disabled people. For example, if you're among those with SSI-limited income, a martini or two, let alone dinner and a movie, can be prohibitively expensive. If you gross $2,000 a month (minus taxes), spending $30 on a simple night out is an actual calculable percentage of your income (not being a math person, I will not attempt to bungle through figuring out the actual percentage it represents, but it's not negligible).

I read one advice column for people living with income-reducing health conditions in which the author counseled disabled folks to spend exclusively on food and housing: if it's not absolutely necessary to sustain biological processes, give it up. That might be bleakly logical guidance, but it's hardly an appealing way to live (let alone an existence that many of us would feel a ton of confidence inviting another person to share).

Now, obviously, not every romantic encounter has to be an extravagant display of material wealth. People are endlessly creative at coming up with budget-friendly date ideas (Explore a park! Walk around town! Watch a sunset! Make out in the car!). But when you combine safety concerns (maybe a stroll in a park with a stranger isn't the most appealing option when you can't run away from a creeper), accessibility (that dive bar up a steep flight of stairs), and the fact that we're all a little more like peacocks than we'd like to admit (fancy restaurants and promposals being things we tend to chatter on about), it's just tougher to date when your income's limited. Shoshanna reflected on the impact of finances on her relationships, saying, "I don't have the resources to just do whatever I want."[2] Starting dating relationships is tough enough—add financial worries, and there's yet another layer of complication to navigate.

Gilead, a man in his forties with CP with whom we spoke in Chapter 3, also noted that in his experience even casual dating is more expensive with a disability. As an example, he described a connection he made with a woman at a regional professional event. The two hit it off, and though they lived a great distance from each other, the attraction was strong enough that they wanted to see where it might lead. Gilead doesn't drive, so seeing this woman IRL meant booking a flight and hotel and investing in a weekend's worth of together time with a person whom he barely knew.

He also noted that had his dating apps yielded a bunch of local matches, traveling a few states away for a meetup may have been less appealing. However, given the slim pickings locally, he felt that following through on the connection was worth the effort and expense. Gilead explained,

When you finally meet someone and they're not local—now I have to spend more money to go and see them and they have to spend money to come and see me, and that [is] awful. You don't have a lot of money, and how can I spend all of this money to go on three dates with you somewhere because I'm still on a fixed income and it makes it a lot more difficult.

Gilead also worried about the impact finances would have on their future relationship. Voicing these concerns, he wondered, "How would two people make it in [a super-expensive city], let alone two people with disabilities? Are we going to have a hard time making it because of how much we have going against us?" On the other hand, he reflected that there's something pretty cool about investing all that time in a person—it's impossible to treat someone as an object, a simple swipe to the right or left, due to all the sacrifice and effort to be with them. In that way, disabled dating is an appealing antidote to our instant-attraction, overly option-filled culture. It forces a person to slow down and think from the very beginning about how to connect.[3]

Jack, a divorced man in his fifties with paraplegia, had also seen the impact of financial status on his dating relationships. He said that many of the women he dates ask pointed questions about his financial situation right off the bat. Behind their grilling, he hears concern about whether he will be able to provide for them and what kind of life they would have together. Jack said that he can almost visualize the mental checklist being marked off as his date goes down the list: housing, transportation, medical expenses, and so on—all of the financial outlays that make nonessential expenditures that much harder to cover.

Forget about upward mobility and saving for a comfortable retirement; his income will always be limited by Medicaid guidelines. He also wondered whether some of this emphasis on stability and security may just be part of dating in midlife, especially in a more religiously conservative culture where fewer women work outside the home. He said, "When you're twenty, you can kind of fake things . . . when you're older, the risk management piece eclipses rich connection and intimacy." Jack's candor about dating made me realize how many complex layers there are to relationships: we are all swimming in a soup of cultural expectations, economic systems, physical realities, personal history, and biological attraction. I bet an anthropologist could spend their whole career studying a single relationship, maybe even a single date. And yet, as Jack said, even in the midst of all of that, dating is still, somehow, wonderful: "I am living the wild frontiers of this dating scene midlife which every day pushes the weirdest buttons, creates awkwardness, discovers the craziest adventures and releases that in an abundance of laughter. How is this all going to work out for me? Only God knows! But I am thankful for the journey."[4]

MORE THAN A NUMBER

Up to this point, we've been looking at finances largely from a very literal, *how many dollars are in your checking account* kind of way. And that's important because those dollars buy us stuff we need to live (and, at the risk of pissing off the advice columnist I referred to earlier, even a few things we just want), but that's hardly the whole story. My mother is a psychotherapist and has always said that conflicts over religion and finances keep her in business. Money is one of those overloaded concepts that stands for far more than numbers on a bank statement: in relationships, how people earn, spend, and make decisions about money has everything to do with power, communication, and self-worth.

At the risk of making too universal a statement, a couple that is well aligned around money is likely strong in their relationship overall, and if a couple thinks about money in vastly different ways, then there may be more general areas of conflict: there are too many unhappy couples where one person uses their status as wage earner to gain an unfair advantage in the relationship, and people may stay in unhealthy partnerships for financial reasons, either for security or because they can't afford to live on their own.

Now, that is not to say that to have a balanced partnership, two people need to both be wage earners or make roughly the same amount of money (or have exactly the same priorities when it comes to money, because no two human beings do). If that were true, among the billions of people who ever lived, there would be maybe three satisfying relationships ever, and that defies common sense. There are cultures throughout the planet that promote the ideal of one person in the family working for money and the other contributing unpaid labor. I'm also aware you may be sitting there going, *Um, lady, I'm just looking to meet up for a cocktail, not an anthropological essay on economics and culture.*

If you're in the cocktail stage, or casual dating is what you're after, feel free to disregard this section. But for disabled folks who could envision themselves in partnerships where finances are blended, it's worth noting that there is a different level of vulnerability when one person cannot obtain a consistent, income-generating job and the entire responsibility for keeping the household financially afloat rests on a single individual. That is the kind of vulnerability that some people with disabilities spoke about around their relationships—the critical difference between "choose not to" and "can't." One woman, Rachel, debating whether to move in with her girlfriend, noted that if they were to do so, Rachel would become financially dependent on her girlfriend due to Medicaid rules, and she thought that was a tough way to begin a relationship: "I worry that my girlfriend will resent working that much and earning that much and never having any money." Rachel was concerned that her financial reliance on her girlfriend would eventually doom their relationship.[5]

Jessica once had some of these same worries: "I had another serious relationship before David in which he earned a good salary and I was living on minimal savings (I was not able to work and did not have disability insurance income). We were not very open about money, and it felt like a background tension and point of sensitivity for me. I was insecure about not being able to earn money and didn't like that my financial situation impacted what he might need to pay for or what we could do."

Even though Kevin and I both work, I connect to these feelings of vulnerability and self-doubt when it comes to money. Due in part to our different professions, I make less than half what Kevin does. And yet

I'm the one whose body requires a lot more when it comes to expensive equipment and accessible housing. Kevin's kind and supportive and all those vitally important things, but I do look at some of the tools I need and recognize that it's his income that's covering them (and that having enough of an income to cover these needs is, in itself, a ridiculous privilege given what a huge number of disabled people face in this whacked-out, unfair system we live in). There are times I resent my disability and wish that I could change out of it like a torn pair of socks that no longer keep me warm.

Plus the reason that Kevin and I are able to be married at all is that, for now, neither of us currently requires in-home care, expensive medication, or complex mobility aids that, without vast personal wealth, in the United States can be paid for only through public assistance. Had either of those two things not been the case, we would face what millions of disabled Americans encounter: the marriage penalty.

THE MARRIAGE PENALTY

Simply put, the marriage penalty is the partial or total loss of life-sustaining benefits due to relationship status. To paraphrase the childhood rhyme, *First comes love, then comes marriage* . . . then comes catastrophic financial ruin (if you're disabled). So here's how it works: let's say Taylor has a spinal-cord injury and receives Social Security payments of $1,000 a month to (barely) cover housing, food, and shelter (though in reality, most SSI payments top out at $850). As a disabled person with a low income, Taylor is also eligible for Medicaid, which provides personal care aids, transportation, durable medical equipment, and lots of other things that aren't covered by private insurance. Now, let's say Taylor meets Alex. Alex has SMA, is enrolled in Medicaid, and also receives an SSI payment of $1,000 per month. Taylor and Alex fall in love (#blessed) and get married. The second those rings are exchanged, each automatically loses 25 percent of their

SSI income. Instead of a combined $2,000 per month, they now have to figure out how to live on $1,500.

The theory behind the payment reduction is that two people can live together less expensively than they can apart. This sounds well and good when you have two people who are both earning large salaries— if Taylor and Alex made $100,000 a year and didn't rely on Medicaid, they could share the costs of a mortgage, utilities, property taxes, and so on. But to receive SSI, one has to have virtually no other sources of income, and the payments cover only the absolute bare minimum (if that). Sharing a house doesn't mean eating 25 percent less food, wearing 25 percent less clothing, brushing with 25 percent less toothpaste, or changing your incontinence aids only 75 percent as much as you did pre–shacking up. Those are fixed costs no matter what your living situation. To add insult to injury, the increase in income that comes from combining finances may also trigger recalculation of the amount a person contributes toward a housing voucher or reduce their Supplemental Nutrition Assistance Program (SNAP) benefits, so overall household expenses may go up rather than down. Plenty of couples look at that level of income reduction and realize that they simply can't afford to get married.

But let's switch it up and say that Alex isn't disabled or on SSDI but rather is a teacher with private health insurance making $120,000 a year (both because it makes for easy math and is what teachers deserve!). So now Alex and Taylor fall in love and get married, but doing so bumps their combined income to $14,000 per month. That is way above the $3,000 household limit for SSI and would automatically stop Taylor's participation in the program. Now, not only is Taylor prohibited from contributing to their family financially, but he also has the terrifying prospect of losing eligibility for Medicaid.

As disabled activist Dominick Evans said, without Medicaid, "I would lose home health care services, which pay for personal care attendants to come into my home and get me out of bed, get me dressed, help me to take a bath, give me my medication, eat my meals, and pretty much any other activity of daily living. Without these services, I would end up stuck in bed."[6] If it's like most private insurance plans, Alex's employer-sponsored health insurance would not cover the in-home care, equipment, or transportation costs that Taylor needs. This means that as a couple, they either need to figure out a way to pay out of pocket for hundreds of thousands of dollars' worth of care, or Alex must lower his income to $3,000 per month (or $2,000 if Taylor retains his $1,000 SSI payment) to maintain Taylor's Medicaid enrollment. In a situation like this, which is playing out every day, the price of marrying is poverty or, potentially, death due to lack of health care.

In her blog *The Girl Who Sits*, disabled lawyer and activist Gabriella Garbero speaks about the financial impact of marrying her fiancé, Juan:

Juan and I can't set a date for our wedding because if we get married . . . I will lose the Medicaid benefits that keep me alive. So until those laws change, or until one of us wins the lottery or starts making half a million dollars a year, there won't be a wedding.

She elaborates on the additional issues that would jeopardize her Medicaid eligibility:

So if [Juan's] salary is above the federal poverty line (it is) or if our combined income adds up to more than 83% of the federal poverty line (it would), I would no longer qualify. If our combined assets add up to more than $3,000 (they would), I would no longer qualify. If we share more than one vehicle (he has three), I would no longer qualify. If either one of us has a life insurance policy worth more than $1,500 (he does), I would no longer qualify.[7]

This is utterly bananas, especially given how much focus there has been over the past decades on marriage as a fundamental human right. In the course of hearing the landmark case *Obergefell versus Hodges*, which ultimately granted LGBTQ Americans the legal right to marry, Supreme Court Justice Anthony Kennedy stated, "Rising from the most basic human needs, marriage is essential to our most profound hopes and aspirations." Let's say that one more time—*profound hopes and aspirations* (obviously not for everyone, but for many of us, it is; why else would we revise our OkCupid bios a gazillion times?). The United Nations recognizes marriage between adults as a universal human right. And yet disabled folks are often forced to choose between creating a family and accessing the tools that we need to survive.

The thing is, our government wants to make the cost of what is essentially a blank check for health care resources so high that no one would voluntarily choose it. If the monetary cost to taxpayers is going to be high, then the cost to the one receiving the care will also be high. Which would maybe make sense if this were some kind of punishment for bad behavior, but disabled people aren't criminals (or some of us are, but not for needing health care).

Now, I don't imagine that there's a group of sinister bureaucrats sitting in an office somewhere plotting to keep disabled people from marrying. I believe these injustices are more likely evidence of the lingering ableism that's built into the structures of our government systems. When entitlement programs were set up, the assumption was that disabled people wouldn't get married; we'd be under our parents' care or living in institutions. As attorney Ayesha Elaine Lewis commented, "The complex bureaucracies that provide essential services and supports for people with disabilities were created piecemeal, and were based on outdated assumptions about marriage, paternalism and a limited understanding of the full and vibrant lives possible for people with disabilities."[8] The legislation hasn't caught up to the reality that disabled people do have relationships that, without these barriers, would lead to marriage: we have the same desires and aspirations as our nondisabled friends and family.

HOLDING OUT

So you thought you were reading a lighthearted book about disabled dating and ended up in the middle of an overly long rant about social safety nets (I'm not exactly Marvin Gaye over here). But seriously, if you're facing a situation like this, what options are available? The obvious way of getting around the marriage penalty is to forgo legal marriage. Throw a party, get a clergyperson or friend to bless your relationship, and move in together, but don't actually apply for a marriage license. Simple, right? Not so much: the Social Security Administration has a concept called "holding out" that is designed to hold couples accountable in that exact situation. For the purposes of SSI, an unwed couple can be counted as married if they do any of the following:

- Introduce themselves as a married couple to friends, relatives, or their community;
- Use the same last name socially, even if a legal name change was never completed;
- Receive mail, including bills, invitations, or magazines, addressed to the couple; or
- Live in a home rented or owned by both people.

If a couple is suspected of holding out, a Social Security representative can interview relatives, friends, and acquaintances to investigate how the couple presents themselves in public. If witnesses even perceive the couple to be married, that may be enough to eliminate eligibility for federal assistance. As Gabby Garbero wrote, "My benefits are so precarious that they can be taken away by something as simple as a misinformed neighbor, incorrectly addressed mail, or an SSA employee who makes a bad judgment call."[9] Given the life-or-death risks associated with losing benefits, it's no surprise that plenty of disabled couples forgo living together or even acknowledging that they are in a relationship. The other side to this awful situation is that there are happily married couples who are forced to divorce in order to receive life-sustaining benefits.

Thankfully, there is proposed legislation at both the state and federal levels that is seeking to do away with the marriage penalty for those with disabilities (see H.R. 6405, which was introduced in 2022).[10] Such legislation would keep the SSI benefit rate for couples at two times the individual rate and increase the amount of earnings and assets that individuals and couples can retain without losing eligibility for aid. But until that legislation winds its way through our lawmaking bodies, what's a couple to do?

In addition to voting and calling your elected representatives, if you're thinking of moving in with your partner, get thee to an attorney and a financial planner pronto. This is especially true if you're planning a wedding (legal or not) and may be receiving cash gifts, which, if not handled in specific ways, could impact SSI eligibility. Eligibility criteria are mind-numbingly complicated. There are significant differences between SSDI, SSI, and DAC (Disabled Adult Child eligibility) when it comes to marriage and allowable assets. There are also differences depending on which state you live in (and if you're Canadian, there are entirely different sets of criteria).

A competent financial planner can help you figure out how to hold assets in ways that can't be included in SSA calculations around benefit eligibility. Lawyers may be able to set up trusts that will protect you as individuals and as a couple as well as protect any inheritance for your children. The Internet can help with framing some of the questions and issues to address, but I wouldn't rely on it for definitive guidance because what is allowed is so dependent on where you live, and even general advice on the web is contradictory.

I'm also mindful of the irony of advising a couple who are living below the poverty line to shell out money for lawyers and financial planners. A conversation like that might cost a few hundred bucks. If you need guidance but don't have the money to spend on it, start with a local legal aid society or call a reputable law or accounting firm to ask for recommendations. There may be a nonprofit organization that provides services at little or no cost to those who are eligible (and while registering for a legal consultation is hardly a fun wedding present, it may end up being more useful than that set of holiday china!).

While you're at it, if you're in an interabled relationship, you may want to ask a financial planner about options for being paid for the personal assistance that the nondisabled partner is providing. This is a bit of a sticky issue; it depends on a lot of factors, including where you live, your eligibility for benefits, and whether the person receiving home health care is a veteran. There are also all of the relationship dynamics around a spouse caring for their partner as Jessica discussed in the previous chapter.

In the worst-case scenarios, relying on income from one spouse to cover physical assistance for the other can lead to burnout, injury, neglect, or abuse. But for some couples, particularly those in rural areas where reliable and trustworthy paid assistance is hard to come by, this kind of arrangement can be a total game changer. One couple reflected, "When it comes down to it, having [my husband] as both a [paid] caregiver and partner gives us a bond that is stronger than any other." Rather than paying a stranger to come in and provide assistance, a family can earn income and retain more control over how care is provided.

You may read all of this and wonder how any disabled couples make it at all. There are barriers to our relationships at every level: social, financial, and bureaucratic. Legislation isn't moving fast enough to allow many people to enjoy the basic human rights of marriage and family. And so it bears repeating that in spite of it all, couples do make this work. There are millions of disabled people out there who are married, raising kids, living in the community, and going about their lives. We're disabled: we're nothing if not clever when it comes to navigating inaccessible situations. Demand the financial and legal advice you need as a couple, and go live happily ever after (or whatever the real-life equivalent of that is!).

CHAPTER 14
S*?! (AHEM, STUFF) PEOPLE SAY

CAROLINE

Ryan Honick, a wheelchair user, and his nondisabled girlfriend flew across the country to attend his friend's wedding. Soon after they arrived, Ryan felt terrible, and he and his date made their way to urgent care. The doctor, seeing them holding hands, looked slowly from one to the other before finally asking, "So, um, how do you two know each other?"

Ryan looked the doctor dead in the eye and replied, "Biblically."[1]

Ryan is fine now (RIP, appendix), but when he told me about that interaction, I vowed I'd either find a way to include it in this book or get some reference to it tattooed on my person. I don't know about you, but my brilliant responses to ridiculous comments tend to come in the middle of the night and hang there in the dark like sad, lonely little penguins. The fact that someone landed the perfect retort midconvo (in the midst of a bursting appendix, no less) feels like a triumph for disabled people everywhere (#inspiring).

There are a thousand different definitions of what it means to be part of the disability community, but one pretty strong marker of inclusion is that you've been on the receiving end of some ridiculous comments. From the moment my devout little Presbyterian Sunday School–attending self was informed by a passerby that if I *just believed in Jesus*, I'd walk again (again?), I realized, *Oh . . . this is going to be a thing*. I don't believe I ever consciously thought that being partnered would insulate me against ridiculous comments, but I harbored a sense that being in a relationship was a ticket into some elite circle, a way of passing in a society where physical ability and being desired are inherent markers of status and worth. There are many wonderful things about going through life with another person, but being partnered doesn't stop the peanut gallery from chiming in.

PRESUMPTION OF INNOCENCE

Able-bodied people always assume that I don't know what I'm doing [in a relationship]. Like immediately they explain things to me even if they've been divorced three times. I didn't even ask you about dating. I didn't say, "How do you date?" I just tell you that I'm in a relationship, and you're now telling me how I can do it. Ableism [is the presumption that] you don't know what you're doing. Let me figure it out on my own. I hit back a couple of times—I stopped telling people about being in a relationship. Me and her are the only people who matter in a relationship. It doesn't matter what you say. I learned to keep all of my able-bodied friends in the dark when it came to relationships. My family is fine. They know not to tell me what to do because I'm not going to do it anyway.

—*Gilead*[2]

Back when I worked in the trauma unit of a hospital, my security guard colleagues used to whisper, "No one hits the chaplain" before pushing me into the room to meet with a distraught family. While at first I felt nervous meeting with people going through violent grief or in the throes of a psychotic episode, I soon learned that my physical vulnerability was actually an advantage in those situations. A person who had been lashing out in rage or fear would see my bent body and crutches and, more often than not, calm down almost instantaneously. It was not unusual for a giant, aggressive dude to stop throwing punches and chivalrously offer me a chair. When I spoke with my aunt, a psychiatric nurse, about this phenomenon, she confirmed that this paradox is well-known in hospitals and law enforcement: where there is violence, the seemingly vulnerable person holds the most power. The last thing you want to do in a fraught situation is send in your biggest, burliest security guard. There's something primal in us humans that softens and releases when we come into contact with obvious vulnerability.

What does this have to do with disability, dating, and relationships? As the man we interviewed earlier observed, there is often a presumption of far-ranging innocence or incapacity when it comes to disability. Depending on the situation, we can use that presumption to our and other vulnerable people's advantage, as in helping to defuse a tense interaction. However, a physical or intellectual impairment can also create the impression that we are innocent or clueless in every area of life, just longing for advice from anyone with a pair of working legs, eyes, or ears (even if they have no actual expertise on the subject in question).

This can be enraging. It drives me up the wall every time I use the stairs and a passerby stops me to point out the (very obvious) ramp with the assumption that I haven't seen it or am not a competent judge of what would be easiest for me. Their well-meaning comments can feel like a major diss of my ability to determine my way of moving through the world. I also recognize that guarding myself against offers of assistance can create its own ridiculousness. Recently I was making my way down some steps and heard a man I know ask, "Do you need any help?"

I whipped around and answered, "I'm fine." He replied, "I know *you're* fine—I was talking to the small child behind you." Oops.

On my best days, I try to remember that we're all making false assumptions about one another and that, just as I hope others will deal graciously with my mistakes, I'll do my best to extend that same grace to them. And then there are the days I just groan and try to ignore it (preferably in close proximity to a glass of wine).

ASSUMING INCOMPETENCE

But in any case, when Gilead described his annoyance with utterly unqualified people giving him relationship advice, I related to his frustration. It is absolutely legit to hold back from sharing information about our lives with people who have a history of responding in patronizing ways. We can also choose to share things with those people but be clear about boundaries—*I'm telling you this, but I'm not asking for your opinion or for guidance—I just want to share something in my life that I'm excited about.* Sometimes being frank about what we're looking for is helpful (in all areas of life, not just dating and disability!).

While editing for our audience is one approach to the advice-giving conundrum, it's not the only tool we have. After I gave birth to my son, I was in the hospital for a few days recovering from a C-section. If you've been through this early-newborn stage, particularly when the newborn in question has just emerged from your person, you may remember it as a time of tsunami-like hormones, crushing sleep deprivation, and hitherto unknown bodily fluids emerging (or not) at times of their own choosing.

Plus, there's a foreign little human to maintain. The combination of all the above made me more than a little out of it. People showed up in my room and I robotically spoke with them: parents, grandparents, lactation consultant, nurse, pediatrician, obstetrician, physical therapist . . . with all the visitors, it took me a little while to realize that I was getting more medical visitors than the other patients on the unit. The physical therapists in particular looked delighted to be in my room, admiring the baby and exclaiming that they *never* get invited to the maternity department and *Oh, this is sooo much fun!* as they directed me, with my freshly severed abdominal muscles, to demonstrate how I get up from the floor or perform any number of gross-motor activities.

Slowly it dawned that this was not a social call—they were assessing whether I had the capacity to parent my son. And rather than assume I had taken the initiative to prepare for motherhood, they treated me (oh so politely) as a novice who hadn't realized that I would need to get this kid out of my uterus and into a bathtub. Once I got wise to what they were up to, I explained that I had already initiated months of physical therapy prior to and during my pregnancy, and that my therapist and I had already worked out all the baby-related activities of daily living. This seemed to surprise them (*A new mom? Preparing for her baby? How novel!*), but it did mean that they left me alone after that. It also meant that when one of the nurses tried to be supportive, saying that maybe I'd be lucky enough for my baby to also have CP, I could roll my eyes and take it as a super-awkward attempt at cheering me on.

Interactions like these are frustrating and sometimes frightening, but they also made me recognize my own strength. No new parent knows how to do all the things involved with newborn care, but I had spent countless hours over many months preparing for everything I possibly could. Recognizing what would be a struggle and seeking qualified helpers had actually made me an unusually capable new mom. We had an adapted stroller waiting at home, a bassinet I knew I could navigate solo, and a weirdly rigid thrift-store chair that ironically fit my nursing needs perfectly.

The doubts of strangers were an invitation for me to describe to them, and more importantly to myself, my strengths and skills. It might be unfair to have to justify to the world why you're capable, but there's also some value in accepting any invitation to show off competence. If every new parent, or everyone in a relationship, was asked to share why they're qualified for the role, I think we'd all hold our heads a little higher.

Being clear about what I had confidence in also made me recognize what I did, in fact, need help with. Nursing was a hot mess—my kid was hungry, and due to a nonfunctioning thyroid and scheduled C-section, I had nothing in that department to offer. I rejected some of the unsolicited advice I was gifted with at the hospital, but not all of it. I did my best to be clear about what would truly be helpful, like extra sessions with the lactation consultant, formula-feeding guidance, and what turned out to be an obscenely long-term rental of an industrial-strength breast pump.

I think, disabled or not, being open to some kinds of advice from the right people at the right time can be freeing. We don't have to feign competence where we don't feel it; there's strength in vulnerability because it opens the door to support that we'll actually benefit from. When it comes to guidance from outside parties, perhaps one course of action is to reject sometimes, subvert where we can, but also keep a curious spirit. Part of busting through ableism is recognizing that "I know everything and I have nothing to learn" is a cage that traps us all in harmful ways of interacting.

"SO HOW DO YOU TWO KNOW EACH OTHER?"

Along with the joys of navigating advice, we disabled people tend to have our relationships questioned by all and sundry (and not just romantic relationships—a dude recently walked up to my son, pointed to me, and quipped, "Take good care of your sister, kid"). Shane and Hannah Burcaw, whom we've mentioned before, have spoken extensively about how often people assume that nondisabled Hannah is Shane's nurse or caregiver rather than his wife.[3] Candy, who has EDS, and her boyfriend, Max, who has CP, explained, "From strangers, the most common assumption is simply that we are not a couple . . . we have had every assumption, from me [Candy] being a paid carer or just a friend to people who assume I am his sister."[4]

For same-gender interabled couples, this confusion about status can be compounded: Christina, who has quadriplegia and is married to fellow professor Janet, reflected, "Our union isn't always immediately legible. . . . One of the things I hate most is when we're not taken as a *sexual* couple."[5] Jessica and I have cracked ourselves up imagining what would happen if disabled people rolled up to random strangers and started parroting the stuff that we hear all the time. Imagine going up to a couple making out on a park bench and asking, "Aw, is that your brother?" or inquiring of someone pushing a stroller if that is their actual child. People would be totally creeped out, and yet this is the stuff that our community navigates all the freaking time.

Along with questioning the status of a relationship, strangers mischaracterize what brings or holds people together. In interabled relationships, folks sometimes assume that the disabled partner must have developed the impairment after the relationship started (how else to explain the existence of a married disabled person?). Disability scholar Simi Linton's husband described this phenomenon: "The question that people always want to ask me, but are usually too cautious or polite to, is whether we met before or after her injury. They don't seem to accept that . . . her disability is a given in our relationship. This is the way that it's always been."[6]

People also suppose that the nondisabled half of the couple has ulterior motives in the relationship. One woman related the time that a stranger, observing her with her disabled husband, demanded to know how much she got paid for being with him. When she pushed back, the person countered, "You mean the government doesn't even pay you because you're with him and you take care of him?" In her shock, she found herself oversharing details about their family finances, justifying to this rude stranger why she loved her husband.[7] When interabled couples talk about their partnerships online, trolls comment that the relationship must be for money or faked for attention. These repeated assaults can take a real emotional toll on couples.

So what to do when people misjudge or make offensive assumptions about your relationship? For many people, it depends on the situation and what frame of mind you're in. Christina and Janet typically (but not always) blow off or ignore misconceptions, while others see ignorance as an opportunity to cultivate the virtues of patience or grace. Interabled couple and youth pastors John and Jade explained, "We're Christians, so we forgive people who make ignorant comments. . . . You just feel a little sorry for the people who ask those questions."[8] Others take a more active approach: Ariel Henley, who has a facial difference, tweeted about being out with her boyfriend: "Boyfriend and I went and got lunch today. I noticed a lady staring at me so I made eye contact & smiled. She responded with a dirty look—like she was disgusted by me. So I loudly said, 'I love when people stare at me so rudely!' I really do try to let these things go but couldn't!"[9]

Candy and Max approach it this way: "Our response to subtle ableist sentiment is to be loud and proud about our situation, to [have] public displays of affection, to be cute and sexy and silly, and really to just provide the world with the representation that we want to see."[10] They also see how confronting ableism as a pair brings them closer together as a couple: if you can't always win, you can at least commiserate with each other. Whether you ignore, reframe, challenge, make out in public, or, like disabled author Ben Mattlin, put a big wedding photo of yourself right at the front door of your house to head off any misconceptions, know that your relationship is no less valid or real because people habitually mistake your partner for your sister (gross).[11]

A confession/addendum: The other day, I was chatting with the mom of one of my son's friends. Our talk turned to travel, and she shared that she is a citizen of a very small country in Eastern Europe. I'd never met anyone from this country and found myself asking all kinds of questions: "Which languages do you speak? Is your husband also from this country? How did you meet?" More than half of what I asked could have easily been answered by a ten-second Google search, and yet, insatiably curious, I persisted. Reflecting on this encounter, I wonder whether, had the situation been reversed and instead of my asking her about her background, she was asking about my disability, I would have felt put on the spot. I'm not sure. The situation reminded me that humans are hardwired for connection and curiosity and that questions can be used to strengthen our ties with one another, not only to minimize or dismiss. Curiosity and cruelty are two different things, though when we've been bludgeoned with the second over and over, our tolerance for the first can be limited.

"YOU'RE such AN INSPIRATION!"

One persistent theme of disabled and interabled relationships is the idea that there's an element of heroism baked in. We can't just be out there bickering over whose turn it is to take out the trash; au contraire, we are living, breathing symbols of humanity's highest ideals, casting off the shackles of a consumer-minded, beauty-obsessed culture to live a great and powerful truth: love can conquer all. The idea that we're just hanging out watching *Modern Family* reruns is very off-brand in terms of the weighty mantle that's been bestowed upon us.

Assumptions of heroism show up in all kinds of ways, but interabled couples seem to be treated to this kind of commentary most often. Reflecting on people's reactions to her marriage to spinal-cord injury survivor Max Starkloff, his wife, Colleen, said with a laugh, "I was canonized many times." She explained, "I do get that people mean well, but to canonize me as if something beyond love—mutual love—was going on, just because I married a disabled guy, demeans Max and others with disabilities." In response, she said that she often found herself trying to flip the script, talking about herself in a self-effacing way and building up Max, though the two have a very egalitarian and mutually fulfilling relationship.[12] Similarly, Marna Michele, who was born with arthrogry-posis, described how her husband is often cast as an extraordinary man for marrying her: "For some reason, the majority of the world would portray Robert as a 'hero' for dating me and an even bigger 'hero' for marrying me! But what they don't take the time to see is how much I offer to this relationship. I am Rob's confidant, his best friend, his thera-pist, his nutritionist, his life coach."[13]

Sometimes observers take the hero commentary a step further and take the liberty of assigning a silver lining to the situation. Jessica shared one experience where this happened:

> A couple of years ago, I was seeing a neurologist with my husband, and we were talking about something quite serious. It's not unusual for a doc-tor to praise my husband for being with me, but this doctor took it one step further. He said, "She may be hard to be married to, but you're in luck. [Because of her EDS] she's going to age really well."

Another doctor, noting that Jessica's disability makes it difficult to digest food, said to her then boyfriend, "At least you know she'll always be thin!" Yuck. The side effects of an illness that create culturally val-ued traits, like thinness and youthful-looking skin, are not consolation prizes for being in a relationship with a disabled person.

Casting one member of the couple as the sacrificial victim is, in addi-tion to being false, a profound dismissal of the gifts that both people bring to a relationship. No healthy partnership is grounded in one per-son's profound need and the other's tolerance for charity. Even in situ-ations where one person is carrying more of the load in one area, or at one season of life, the other should, over time, provide balance.

While I don't subscribe to some people's value of complementarian-ism (where men have one defined role and women another), I do think that if you strip gender and a predetermined list of tasks from that world-view, there's some real value in a (flexible, shifting) view of partnerships in which each person has areas of expertise and strength. In her chapter on caregiving, Jessica talked about how her husband takes on most of the physical tasks, and she does the cerebral ones. My sister-in-law has a rock-star corporate job and provides for her family financially; her husband manages cooking, laundry, pets, cars, and home maintenance.

It might not be even, but I also don't know how one measures *even* when it comes to relationships: the work of sharing a life isn't so well-defined that it can be counted and sorted into discrete units. A better measure might be asking whether both people are fulfilled; whether, knowing what they know now, each person would choose the relationship again; and if the marriage is a consistent source of strength and comfort (when all the socks are picked up, that is).

WE JUST WANT TACOS, WE DON'T WANT ABLEISM AS A SIDE

Interabled relationships aren't always heroic, but sometimes even those of us who are fighting the stigma against them inadvertently impose an element of superhumanism on them. I know I sometimes feel pressure to be perfect (or perfectly imperfect); that because we are a disabled couple, our relationship has something to prove. That's my one qualm with the #100outof100 hashtag that emerged from the vile Dr. Phil segment where he argued that no romantic relationships with a caregiving component can survive: the counterargument that suggests that they *all* do can unintentionally play right into the superhuman narrative that we are trying so hard to dismiss. Obviously, not every relationship where one person is disabled lasts, because not every relationship endures forever. We disabled folks are not doomed to failure in love, nor are our partnerships fated for success. Relationships involve constantly discovering, forging, and renegotiating roles. The ability to do that in a world that often dismisses or mischaracterizes those relationships might be somewhat heroic, but no single person is.

But what about those relationships where both people are obviously disabled? Ryan Honick (of appendix doctor fame) observed that the reverse of desexualizing disabled relationships is also true: if he's out with a friend who also uses a wheelchair, everyone assumes that they *must* be a couple, even if they're not remotely interested in each other. Activist Imani Barbarin laughed at how two disabled people hanging out can mess with people's minds:

> I dated disabled men, and it's always funny when we go out to restaurants, or outside, people can't tell which of us is the pity date. There's like, "He, wait . . . her . . . what's happening here? Which one of them is the hero in this equation?" It's like, "We're just going out, we just want our tacos, leave us alone. We want some tacos and cheese, we want some queso, that's all we want, we don't want ableism as a side."[14]

My husband and I are not infrequently told that we are *so inspiring*; once we went out to a nice restaurant to celebrate some milestone, and when we asked for the check, the server said one of the other tables had covered our tab. We were both a bit offended at the charity (but, holding minimal principles, also very happy for the free dinner). We were also grateful there's someone out there, in this all-too-unkind world, making a serious, if somewhat offensive, attempt to be nice. Life's complicated, and ultimately (and unfortunately for a book that's supposed to offer some kind of guidance), I don't have a magical prescription for warding off all of the BS we receive from people. Part of being human is not having complete control over how one is perceived but finding a way to figure out which battles we fight and which we leave to others.

There are some risks to living our full disabled lives out of the shadows—humans being the curious, sometimes mean, always awkward creatures that we are, there will probably always be weird questions and offensive statements, and someone will be told how *marvelous* they are for going to the grocery store. Recognizing how thin-skinned I am, I'm in no rush to post my relationship details to social media and wait for the comments to roll in, though I'm deeply grateful to all of those disabled and interabled couples who are doing just that and changing the game for all of us. I love that for dozens of kids—my son's friends, the kids where I work—there is absolutely nothing interesting about my being disabled or being married to a disabled guy. We might be oddities or heroes to one generation, but we're an entirely boring, unremarkable disabled couple to the next, and for that, I'm deeply grateful.

A NOTE FROM US

WHEN WE CAME UP WITH THE IDEA FOR THIS BOOK, WE HAD A FEW thoughts about what we would cover. We imagined that it could be a source of solidarity for disabled and chronically ill daters and a practical guide to managing an often inaccessible world while looking for love. When we dated in our twenties and thirties, we wished there was something written by disabled people to reference as we were making the tough decisions about what photos to put on our profiles and how to explore our sexuality while staying safe.

What we didn't expect, and what has been a tremendous honor, is how much we would learn from the disabled people we interviewed for these chapters. Our vision of what it means to enjoy romantic connection and seek sexual fulfillment while disabled has grown immeasurably thanks to the dozens of people who shared their stories with us. The content of the book changed as our understanding of disabled dating expanded, and we know that all who read this book will benefit from the candor and vulnerability of those who shared their perspectives.

For example, we had never considered the beautiful intersection of kink and disability culture—the way kink communities embrace curiosity and consent and how perfectly that overlaps with the expansive and creative reality of disabled sex. Through our interviews, we also found that disabled people were in ethically nonmonogamous (ENM) relationships at a higher rate than we had previously imagined. Disabled people, living in a world not designed for our bodies and minds, are particularly open to considering relationship structures that deviate from the norm.

We found our own perspectives shifting as people told us beautiful stories of creating relationships that helped them thrive.

Writing this book forced us to take a step back and truly consider what dating is and how it's influenced by cultural context. Searching for someone to partner with, short term or long term, is vulnerable, scary, and brave. We are honored that you have read this book while you navigate love and sex as a disabled person or someone in a relationship with a disabled person.

And if we were to boil it all down? What do we want to leave you with after fourteen chapters covering everything from beauty culture to finances? It's this: *you are worthy*. You deserve to be loved and admired and enjoyed. There are messages everywhere that there is an ideal way to have a body and a mind, and those are wrong. They have sprouted from fear, and they are flimsy and false. Loving and being loved by you is not a sacrifice; it's a gift.

We also encourage you to consider what it is you really want. To try to remove your dreams from societal expectations or from a need to prove your worthiness and to consider what kind of relationship (or relationships!) would fit your desires and needs. There are interesting and powerful communities of disabled people rewriting love and intimacy. Find them.

We intended this book to be a guide and a source of connection, but what it turned into, for us, is a celebration. Disabled love is thoughtful, honest, and brilliant. Immersing ourselves in that world has been a privilege. We hope you found some practical advice in these chapters, and, more importantly, we hope you realized that you aren't alone.

Love,

Jessica and Caroline

ACKNOWLEDGMENTS

THIS BOOK IS THE RESULT OF THE LABORS OF MANY TO WHOM WE ARE deeply grateful. To our agent, Jill Marr, and her team at SDLA, who encouraged us to explore the intersections of disability and dating, we appreciate your faith in us and in the power of disabled voices. Many thanks to our editor Renee Seidler; we treasured our extended, laughter-filled conversations and your advocacy for so many authors who dare to try something new. Thank you to Connie Oehring, YY Liak, Amy Quinn, Nzinga Temu, Cisca Schreefel, Ashley Kiedrowski, Kindall Gant, and the whole team at Hachette Go for your unfailing support. Thank you also to Heather Corrina for reading an early draft of this manuscript.

To the disabled and chronically ill people and allies who shared your stories with us, thank you from the bottom of our hearts for your trust and wisdom. It was the honor of a lifetime to get to share the experiences of our community with the world. Thank you to Amanda, Amma, Anna, Charlotte, Christie, Daniel, D'Arcee, Elizabeth, Evan, Harriet, Heather, Jack, Jacqueline, James, Jessica, Kathleen, Katie, Kelly, Quinn, Ron, Rui Rui, Ryan, Sarah, Sarah Todd, and Vayl.

Thanks to all our dates over the years, the good and the memorable, for inspiring the original manuscript and to Davidson College for bringing us together.

And to Judy Heumann, who mothered generations and whom we were privileged to call a friend and colleague, thank you always for your support of and contributions to this book. Your memory is a blessing and a battle cry.

JESSICA

Writing a book as a parent simply isn't possible without childcare. Thank you to all of those who loved Khalil and kept her safe while I worked, especially Brittany, Angie, Jody, Leah, Laylin, and Monica. And to Khalil, my most perfect potato pumpkin pie. I love you all the way back. You are the sweetest part of my happily ever after. And to little Frances. I haven't met you yet, but I am so grateful that you will be the little nugget on my chest when this book comes out.

Two women whom I deeply admire told me to write for years before I tried, and I am grateful to Irene and Kathy for their encouragement and direction. And to Mama, whose loving encouragement I hear every time I do something hard.

To my sisters, Amy, Heather, and Megan. I am so lucky that you are mine. To the rest of my family, thank you for teaching me hard work, persistence, and honesty.

Dating wasn't always simple for me, but I have been lucky enough to have a nest of friends and loved ones holding me up throughout my life, and I am thrilled that I can celebrate them here. I love you, Amanda, Amelia, Ames, Ann Marie, Antwon, Carter, Casey, Donna, James, Jenna, Kate, Lauren, Lee, Michelle, Michi, Mona, Nataly, Nikki, Preston, Roxy, Sarah, Sharon, and Tianna.

Caroline, thank you for sending that first email about writing together in 2020. I am so grateful to have a writing partner I trust, respect, and like. Here's to many more!

And David. Your goodness, humor, and devotion have given me a life in which I can try new things and always have a place to land. Thank you for knowing me, loving me, and keeping me safe. I love you.

CAROLINE

Thank you to Kevin, who keeps me laughing and whose love (and back-office know-how) is my anchor. I am deeply grateful for all you do to support these writing endeavors in the midst of our already busy days. And to Henry, whose curiosity, kindness, and delight in the world fill me with joy. You are always and forever my favorite writing buddy. To my parents, Stuart and Suzanne Levy; my sister, Katie; all of the Cupps; and the piles of grandparents, aunts, uncles, cousins, and little ones whose steadfast love has given me deep roots and the confidence to go beyond my comfort zone, thank you. Thanks also to my ultra-talented cousin Elizabeth Hinson of Site Culture, who built me such a beautiful website.

I am grateful to the professors at Davidson College, especially Dr. Ann Fox, who first introduced me to disability studies and transformed my world forever, and to those at Yale Divinity School and the University of Pennsylvania's bioethics program who encouraged me to continue to explore these topics from a variety of perspectives.

Thank you to the spectacularly cool congregation and staff at First Presbyterian Church, West Chester, who were so supportive of their pastor writing a book about the realities of dating, and to Kathleen Skomorucha; Kaela Dakes; Peter, Elizabeth, and Laura Guman; Joe Fabiani; and Mary Pellack for your natural and inviting ways of embodying accessibility and inclusion. I am deeply privileged to serve alongside you.

I am grateful to the friends who have been so supportive of me throughout the writing of this book: Amanda Blevins, Emily McClure, Sara Pantazes, Lisa Horst, and Katey Zeh, and of course Jessica Slice, without whom this whole adventure never would have happened.

RESOURCES

SAFETY AND SEXUAL TRAUMA HOTLINES

The Anti-Violence Project 212-714-1141
Darkness to Light 1-866-FOR-LIGHT
Love Is Respect 1-866-331-9474
RAINN 800-656-HOPE
Safe Horizon 1-800-621-HOPE

INTRODUCTIONS TO DISABILITY CULTURE

If you're new to the world of disability history and justice and looking for a general overview, these books offer a good start.

Care Work: Dreaming Disability Justice by Leah Lakshmi Piepzna-Samarasinha
Claiming Disability Knowledge & Identity by Simi Linton
Demystifying Disability: What to Know, What to Say, and How to Be an Ally by Emily Ladau
A Disability History of the United States by Kim E. Nielsen
The Disability Studies Reader by Lennard J. Davis
Disability Visibility: First-Person Stories from the Twenty-First Century by Alice Wong
Not So Different: What You Really Want to Ask About Having a Disability by Shane Burcaw
Teen Vogue's Disability (In)Justice series—https://www.teenvogue.com/tag /disability-injustice

MEMOIRS

If you're feeling inspired to read more nonfiction by disabled and chronically ill authors, these are some folks to check out:

Beautiful People: My Thirteen Truths About Disability by Melissa Blake
Being Heumann: An Unrepentant Memoir of a Disability Rights Activist by Judith Heumann with Kristen Joiner
The Country of the Blind: A Memoir at the End of Sight by Andrew Leland
Deaf Utopia: A Memoir—and a Love Letter to a Way of Life by Nyle DiMarco
Easy Beauty by Chloé Cooper Jones
A Face for Picasso: Coming of Age with Crouzon Syndrome by Ariel Henley
I'm Special: And Other Lies We Tell Ourselves by Ryan O'Connell
Look Me in the Eye: My Life with Asperger's by John Elder Robison

Loving Our Own Bones: Disability Wisdom and the Spiritual Subversiveness of Knowing Ourselves Whole by Julia Watts Belser
The Pretty One: On Life, Pop Culture, Disability, and Other Reasons to Fall in Love with Me by Keah Brown
Sipping Dom Pérignon Through a Straw: Reimagining Success as a Disabled Achiever by Eddie Ndopu
Sitting Pretty: The View from My Ordinary, Resilient, Disabled Body by Rebekah Taussig
Smile: A Memoir by Sara Ruhl
An Unquiet Mind: A Memoir of Moods and Madness by Kay Jamison

FILMS, SHOWS, AND PODCASTS
Here are some scripted shows, documentaries, and podcasts that focus on disability.
Being Heumann (Podcast)
Crip Camp: A Disability Revolution (Netflix)
Crutches and Spice (Podcast)
Special (Netflix)
Unrest (Documentary)
Vision Portraits (Documentary)
Who Am I to Stop It (New Day Films)

DISABILITY ACTIVISTS AND INFLUENCERS
Alice Wong: @SFDirewolf
Blair Imani: @blairimani
Daniel M. Jones: @theaspieworld
Eddie Ndopu: @eddiendopu
Emily Ladau: @emilyladau
Haben Girma: @habengurba
Keah Brown: @keah_maria
Lauren "Lolo" Spencer: @itslololove
Rikki Poynter: @rikkipoynter
Ryan O'Connell: @ryanoconn
Samantha Renke: @samantharenke
Vilissa Thompson: @vilissathompson

The following resources are organized by topic and then by medium.

DISABLED BEAUTY
PRODUCTS
Auf Augenhoehe—A German company offering ready-to-wear fashion for little people. https://www.aufaugenhoehe.design/en
Guide Beauty—Makeup formulas and applicators designed for people with mobility impairments. https://www.guidebeauty.com/pages/about-us

HAPTA—A high-tech, motion-stabilizing device for lipstick and mascara application. https://www.loreal.com/en/articles/science-and-technology/hapta-lancome-innovation/

IZ Adaptive—Adaptive clothing with a focus on wheelchair users. https://izadaptive.com/

June Adaptive—Offers a wide variety of accessible clothing catering to specific areas of adaptability. https://www.juneadaptive.com/

Kohl Creatives—Makeup brushes for individuals with visual impairments. https://www.kohlkreatives.com/

Olive & June—An adaptive nail-polish brand that's hit the mainstream. https://oliveandjune.com/pages/meet-mani-system-lp

Slick Chicks—Super-cute undies with side closures. https://slickchicksonline.com/

INFLUENCERS

Ellie Goldstein—This British model with Down syndrome is a face of Gucci. @elliejg16_zebedeemodel

Jillian Mercado—A model with muscular dystrophy who has appeared with Beyoncé and in campaigns for Diesel, Nordstrom, and Target. @jillianmercado

Karin Hitselberger—Karin has cerebral palsy and a spinal-cord injury and posts about accessible and fat fashion. @karin_recovers

Melissa Blake—Melissa creates amazing content about life and beauty with a facial difference. @melissablake81

Nina Tame—Shares her colorful style along with general observations on her life as a wheelchair user. @nina_tame

Nyle DiMarco—Deaf fashion icon who won *America's Next Top Model* and *Dancing with the Stars*. @nyledimarco

Selma Blair—Actress, businesswoman, and fashionista with multiple sclerosis. @selmablair

Tess Daly—British model who posts about makeup and personal care. @tess.daly

Xian Horn—Disabled beauty influencer and founder of Give Beauty Wings. @xianforbeauty83

DISABILITY-FOCUSED DATING APPS

Dateability—dating app designed by disabled people

NOMI—friendship-first app for neurodivergent people

SEX
EDUCATORS

Eva Sweeney—Obviously, Eva Sweeney was going to get top billing on this list. She got her own section in the chapter! Eva's contributions to the world of disabled sex are incalculable. On her website (www.crippingupsexwitheva.com) you can find courses like Sex and Disability 101, How to Find Cool Sex-Posi Queer-Friendly Aides, Cripping Up Toys, Oral Sex and Disability, How to Talk to Your Doctor About Your Sexual Health, Dating for Disabled Youth, Chronic Pain and Sex, and Assisted Masturbation. There is a page devoted to sex questions and answers and a little shop where you can buy vibrators and other sex toys. Eva offers advice on navigating sex with a personal assistant.

Andrew Gurza—Andrew identifies as a "disability awareness consultant and the chief disability officer and cofounder of Bump'n, a sex-toy company for and by disabled people" and can be found at www.andrewgurza.com. You may have heard Andrew speak or read their work since they have been featured on BBC, CBC, Daily Xtra, Gay Times UK, *Huffington Post*, the *Advocate*, Everyday Feminism, Mashable, and Out.com as well as in several anthologies. They have also appeared as a guest on Dan Savage's *Savage Love* and Cameron Esposito's *Queery*. You can follow Andrew on Instagram and listen to their podcast for regular provocative and thoughtful content on sex and disability.

Robin Wilson-Beattie—Robin is another brilliant sex educator. You can find her on Twitter @sexAbled.

Heather Corinna—In 1998, Heather founded Scarleteen, a rich and inclusive website for sex education. They are disabled and have written a hilarious and inclusive guide to menopause. While Scarleteen has "inclusive, comprehensive, supportive sexuality and relationship info for teens and emerging adults," don't let the age range turn you off. It is informative and essential for readers of all ages, as is the companion book, *S.E.X.: The All-You-Need-to-Know Sexuality Guide to Get You Through High School and College*.

https://www.scarleteen.com/ (a bonus!)—You can find a guide on Scarleteen from Eva Sweeney for communicating with a nonvocal sex partner.

Trista Marie—You can find her beautiful art and photography celebrating disabled sexuality on her website and Instagram, www.tristamarie.com and @tristamariemcg.

JoEllen Notte—On her website, https://www.redheadbedhead.com/, JoEllen frankly discusses how mental illness can impact someone's sex life. Her book *The Monster Under the Bed* is an exploration of how to navigate sex and relationships while coping with depression.

Joslyn Nerdahl—Joslyn works as a sex educator and intimacy coach and has experience with sexual surrogacy in the United States and Canada. You can find her on her website, www.mojomediator.com.

Ignixia—Ignixia is a disabled kink educator. Find her on her website, www.kink-positive.com.

ORGANIZATIONS

Advocating for Sex Positive Education and Consent Culture (ASPECC) https://aspecc.ca/

National Center for Sexual Freedom (NCSF)—In our research, we found that many disabled people are drawn to kink and have found sexual liberation in the creativity and consent inherent in kink culture. Through NCSF, you can learn more about kink and find additional resources. https://ncsfreedom.org/

Real Talk—realtalk.org is designed to provide free and accessible sex education to people with cognitive or intellectual disabilities. On this easy-to-navigate website, you can find videos on everything from consent, online dating, and contraception to pubic hair.

Sexability—sexability.org is designed to help those with spinal-cord injuries have more satisfying sex lives. From the site, you can find links to support groups, product reviews, and coaching services.

Sins Invalid—This Bay Area organization has, through art, changed the conversation around disability and sexuality. According to its website, sinsinvalid.org, "Sins Invalid is a disability justice based performance project that incubates and celebrates artists with disabilities, centralizing artists of color and LGBTQ/gender-variant artists as communities who have been historically marginalized. Led by disabled people of color, Sins Invalid's performance work explores the themes of sexuality, embodiment and the disabled body, developing provocative work where paradigms of 'normal' and 'sexy' are challenged, offering instead a vision of beauty and sexuality inclusive of all bodies and communities."

Touching Base—This organization, based in Australia, helps match disabled people with sex workers (for sexual surrogacy) in an ethical and safe manner. It also provides comprehensive and useful resources about considering sexual needs. touchingbase.org/

BOOKS

Access, Autonomy, and Dignity: Comprehensive Sexuality Education for People with Disabilities—A helpful, inclusive, and free guide on sex education and disability published by the National Partnership for Women & Families and the Autistic Self Advocacy Network. www.nationalpartnership.org/our-work/resources/health-care/repro/repro-disability-sexed.pdf

Caregivers and Sex by Madison Parrotta—A practical guide to navigating assistance and sex. https://www.scarleteen.com/article/disability_parenting_relationships_sexuality/sex_and_parent_caregivers.

Come as You Are by Emily Nagoski—This book, while not disability focused, is a great guide to learning about your own sexual desires and needs. Emily has an upcoming follow-up book, *Come Together.*

Easy Beauty by Chloé Cooper Jones—This stunning memoir addresses Chloé's experiences as a disabled wife and mother.

A Quick and Easy Guide to Sex and Disability by A. Andrews—This short and powerful illustrated book is the perfect introduction and guide to disabled sex. We think every disabled (and nondisabled) person should have this on their shelves.

Sex and Disability ed. by Anna Mollow and Robert McRuer—For the more academic among us, this dense and thoughtful examination of disabled sex could help orient our own sexual experiences in a larger historical and social context.

Sitting Pretty: The View from My Ordinary Resilient Disabled Body by Rebekah Taussig—This memoir on life as a young disabled woman touches on dating and marriage.

PODCASTS

Disability After Dark—Hosted by Andrew Gurza, this podcast talks openly about disability and sexuality, with many discussions of nonmonogamy.

Making Polyamory Work—Libby Sinback's podcast takes deep dives into complex ENM-related issues.

Normalizing Non-Monogamy—Emma and Fun host this Wednesday podcast that features interviews with people practicing ENM, polyamory, swinging, etc.

Polyamory Weekly—Cunning Minx and Lusty Guy's sex-, kink-, and ENM-friendly podcast has been on for well over a decade and has hundreds of old episodes in the archive that look at communication, jealousy, race, family, etc.

Savage Love—Dan Savage's podcast on sex is, for many nonqueer people, their first introduction to the culture around nonmonogamy. Savage speaks frankly and realistically about monogamy.

Why Are People into That?—In this broad and inclusive podcast, Tina Horn explores kink, love, gender, and sexuality weekly.

PRODUCTS

BonBon Sex Toy Mount by Liberator
The Bump'n Joystick
Dame Pillo
Door Jam Sex Swing
Hot Octopus Pulse III
The Liberator Wedge
Lovehoney Colourplay Colour-Changing Silicone Nipple Suckers
Lovehoney Curved Silicone Suction Cup Dildo 5.5 Inch
Mage Flexible Massager Vibrator by Intimate Melody
Sex Chair by Intimate Rider
Sex Machine by Humpus
Sex Stool by Kinkly
Spare Parts Harness
Tongue Star Pleasure Tongue by Hott Products
Thigh Strap-On by SportSheets
Wearable by Ohnut

QUEER AND CRIP INFLUENCERS

Aaron Philip
Andrew Gurza
Asha

Ben-Oni
Carson Tueller
Chella Man
Corin Parsons
D'Arcee Charington Neal
Dominick Evans
Elle Rose
Farrah Garland
Jessica Kellgren-Fozard
Jillian Mercado
Julian Gavino
Karli Drew
Kenny Fries
Lady Francesca
Leo B. Allanach
Leah Lakshmi Piepzna-Samarasinha
Liam O'Dell
Lizzie Williams
Lydia X. Z. Brown
Nasreen Alkhateeb
Olu Niyi-Awosusi
Rosie Jones
Roy Jones
Ruby Allegra
Ryan O'Connell
Shona Louise
Spencer West
Stevie Boebi
Syrus Marcus Ware
Umber Ghauri

ORGANIZATIONS

ParaPride (parapride.org)—ParaPride makes life more accessible for LGBTQ+ disabled people. Through events, workshops and research, it advocates for the LGBTQ+ disabled community and their allies.

Scarleteen (scarleteen.com/article/disability)—Sex ed for the real world

SEXUAL TRAUMA
ORGANIZATIONS

Abused Deaf Women's Advocacy Services https://www.adwas.org/

The Breathe Network (a network of affordable therapists) https://www.thebreathe network.org/

Sisters of Color Ending Sexual Assault (SCESA) https://sisterslead.org/

ETHICAL NONMONOGAMY
ORGANIZATIONS
Black & Poly—A community run by and specifically for Black folks that provides a space to learn and connect. http://blackandpoly.org/

Kimchi Cuddles—Tikva Wolf's web comic, which often explores polyamorous relationship dynamics. Her art is an accessible and enjoyable introduction to ENM and queer culture. https://kimchicuddles.com/

Loving More—A nonprofit that started in the 1990s with a magazine and has expanded to a comprehensive educational and support organization for nontraditional relationship models. It offers professional listings and links to local organizations and support groups. https://www.lovingmorenonprofit.org/

Loving Without Boundaries—Kitty Chambliss's website, which contains the resources she wishes she had when first practicing polyamory. It includes a podcast, blog, courses, and terminology guides. https://lovingwithoutboundaries.com/

Polyamory Society—A nonprofit organization established to provide resources and support for ENM people and families. http://www.polyamorysociety.org/

BOOKS
Building Open Relationships by Dr. Liz Powell—A detailed guide on creating the relationship structure that's right for you.

The Ethical Slut by Janet Hardy and Dossie Easton—The most well-known and comprehensive guide on ENM. A great place to start.

Love's Not Color Blind by Kevin Patterson—Considers racism in polyamorous communities.

Mating in Captivity by Esther Perel—Explores the conflict between domesticity and sexual desire.

Opening Up by Tristan Taormino—An interview-based guide for creating an open relationship.

Polysecure by Jessica Fern—Examines attachment theory and nonmonogamy.

Sex at Dawn by Christopher Ryan and Cacilda Jetha—A historical perspective on monogamy.

MONEY
ORGANIZATIONS
Access Living—Financial Literacy for People with Disabilities—Offers online classes geared toward disabled people who want to learn more about budgeting and saving. https://www.accessliving.org/our-services/money-management-classes/

Center for Disability Rights—Run by and for disabled people, this advocacy organization supports people who wish to live independently in the community. https://cdrnys.org/about/

Help Advisor—Assists people in understanding their health benefits and eligibility for a variety of services. https://www.helpadvisor.com/

National Disability Institute Financial Empowerment—Dedicated to providing financial education, resources, and empowerment to disabled people. https://www.nationaldisabilityinstitute.org/financial-wellness/financial-capability/

Special Needs Alliance—A national alliance of attorneys who focus on disability benefits, assets, and health care. https://www.specialneedsalliance.org/

Your Money, Your Goals from the Consumer Financial Protection Bureau—A free guidebook on a variety of financial topics with a focus on disabled consumers. https://files.consumerfinance.gov/f/documents/cfpb_ymyg_focus-on-people-with-disabilities.pdf

PARTNERING UP

These books and movies focus on disabled and interabled long-term relationships and in families with young children.

BOOKS

Blessed Union: Breaking the Silence About Mental Illness and Marriage by Sarah Griffith Lund

In Sickness and in Health: Love, Disability, and a Quest to Understand the Perils and Pleasures of Interabled Romance by Ben Mattlin

Unfit Parent by Jessica Slice

SHOWS, DOCUMENTARIES, AND PODCASTS

CODA (Movie)

Junkyard Mayhem (Podcast); Squirmy and Grubs (YouTube) with Shane and Hannah Burcaw

Picture This (YouTube)

Rolling Through Life with TaLisha (YouTube)

Take a Look at This Heart (Prime)

Then Barbara Met Alan (Documentary)

NOTES

Introduction

1. Imani Barbarin, "Ableism in Dating with Marina Carlos," *Crutches and Spice* (podcast), transcript, 41:06, December 3, 2019, https://crutchesandspice.com/2019/12/03/ableism-in-dating-with-marina-carlos/.

2. Fortesa Latifi, "Spoon Theory: What It Is and How I Use It to Manage Chronic Illness," *Washington Post*, January 14, 2023, https://www.washingtonpost.com/wellness/2023/01/14/spoon-theory-chronic-illness-spoonie/.

3. Kimberlé Crenshaw, "Mapping the Margins: Intersectionality, Identity Politics, and Violence Against Women of Color," *Stanford Law Review* 43, no. 6 (1991): 1241–1299, https://doi.org/10.2307/1229039.

Chapter 1

1. Pamela Li, "Overprotective Parents—Causes, Signs and Effects," Parenting for Brain, August 28, 2023, https://doi.org/https://www.parentingforbrain.com/overprotective-parents/#:~:text=Besides%20higher%20occurrence%20of%20anxiety,in%20interactions%E2%80%8B16%E2%80%8B.

2. Laura Graham Holmes, "Comprehensive Sex Education for Youth with Disabilities: A Call to Action," Siecus, accessed January 5, 2024, https://siecus.org/resources/comprehensive-sex-education-for-youth-with-disabilities/.

3. Shanon S. Taylor and Tammy V. Abernathy, "Sexual Health Education for Youth with Disabilities: An Unmet Need," May 5, 2022, https://www.intechopen.com/chapters/81652.

4. Laura Schopp, Tiffany Sanford, and Kristopher Hagglund, "Removing Service Barriers for Women with Physical Disabilities: Promoting Accessibility in the Gynecologic Care Setting," *Journal of Midwifery & Women's Health* 47, no. 2 (2008): 112.

5. R. W. Blum, M. D. Resnick, and R. Nelson, "Family and Peer Issues Among Adolescents with Spina Bifida and Cerebral Palsy," *Pediatrics* 88, no. 2 (1991): 284.

6. Lauren Appelbaum, "Percentage of Characters with Disabilities on TV Reaches 11-Year Record High," RespectAbility, January 14, 2021, https://doi.org/https://www.respectability.org/2021/01/glaad-report-2020/.

Chapter 2

1. Patricia Berne, "Beauty Always Recognizes Itself: A Roundtable on Sins Invalid," *Women's Studies Quarterly* 46, no. 1/2 (2018): 241–252, https://www.jstor.org /stable/26421177.

2. Ryan O'Connell, *I'm Special: And Other Lies We Tell Ourselves* (New York: Simon & Schuster, 2015), 31.

3. Judy Heumann and Kristen Joiner, *Being Heumann: An Unrepentant Memoir of a Disability Rights Activist* (New York: Beacon Press, 2020).

4. Caroline B. Cupp, personal interview with Katie Kaplan, September 2, 2022.

5. Caroline B. Cupp, personal interview with Jack Oppen, September 16, 2022.

6. O'Connell, *I'm Special*, 18.

7. Cupp, Kaplan interview.

8. Jamie Feldman, "This Viral Hashtag Lets People with Disabilities Show Off Their Sexy Sides," *HuffPost*, March 12, 2019, https://doi.org/https://www.huffpost.com/entry /disabled-people-are-hot-hashtag_n_5c869242e4b08d5b78641b90.

9. Caroline B. Cupp and Jessica C. Slice, personal interview with Sarah Todd, September 5, 2022.

10. Emily Ladau, *Demystifying Disability: What to Know, What to Say, and How to Be an Ally* (New York: Ten Speed, 2021).

11. Jessica C. Slice, personal interview with D'Arcee Neal, October 4, 2022.

12. Robert McRuer and Anna Mollow, eds., *Sex and Disability* (Durham, NC: Duke University Press, 2012).

13. Jessica C. Slice, personal interview with Amanda Bock, September 22, 2022.

14. Berne, "Beauty Always Recognizes Itself."

15. Cupp and Slice, Todd interview.

Chapter 3

1. Caroline B. Cupp and Jessica C. Slice, personal interview with Melissa Blake, April 10, 2023; Caroline B. Cupp, personal interview with Gilead, April 10, 2023.

2. Andrew G., "Disability and Dating: I'm Sexy, Seated, and Single Forever," Scarleteen: Sex Ed for the Real World, March 7, 2019, https://www.scarleteen .com/article/disability_relationships_sexual_identity_sexuality/disability_and _dating_im_sexy_seated_and.

Chapter 4

1. Meredith Moore, Corey Heath, Troy McDaniel, and Sethuraman Panchanathan, "The Blind Date: Improving the Accessibility of Mobile Dating Applications for Individuals with Visual Impairments," in *2019 IEEE Global Conference on Signal and Information Processing (GlobalSIP)* (New York: IEEE, 2019), 1–5.

2. Jessica C. Slice, personal interview with Christie Faye Collins, April 6, 2023.

3. Steven Aquino, "Hiki Is Reimagining What It Means to Be a Dating App with Neurodiversity and Connectedness," *Forbes*, January 27, 2021, https://www.forbes

.com/sites/stevenaquino/2021/01/07/hiki-is-reimagining-what-it-means-to-be-a-dating -app-with-neurodiversity-and-connectedness/?sh=7c0443bc4a40.

Chapter 5

1. Caroline B. Cupp, personal interview with Rui Rui Bleifuss, October 11, 2022.

2. Imani Barbarin, "Ableism in Dating with Marina Carlos," *Crutches and Spice* (podcast), transcript, 41:06, December 3, 2019, https://crutchesandspice.com/2019/12/03 /ableism-in-dating-with-marina-carlos/.

3. Caroline B. Cupp, personal interview with Daniel Harris, October 15, 2022.

4. Caroline B. Cupp, personal interview with Kathleen Skomorucha, August 30, 2022.

5. Cupp, Bleifuss interview.

6. Barbarin, "Ableism in Dating with Marina Carlos."

7. Caroline B. Cupp, personal interview with Katie Kaplan, September 2, 2022.

8. Cupp, Bleifuss interview.

9. Cupp, Harris interview.

Chapter 6

1. Glennon Doyle, "How to Love Your Body Now with Carson Tueller," *We Can Do Hard Things*, July 28, 2022, https://momastery.com/blog/we-can-do-hard-things-ep -117.

2. Darryl Sellwood, Parimala Raghavendra, and Ruth Walker, "Facilitators and Barriers to Developing Romantic and Sexual Relationships: Lived Experiences of People with Complex Communication Needs," *Augmentative and Alternative Communication* 38, no. 1 (2022): 1–14, doi: 10.1080/07434618.2022.2046852.

3. Sonali Shah, "'Disabled People Are Sexual Citizens Too': Supporting Sexual Identity, Well-Being, and Safety for Disabled Young People," *Frontiers in Education*, vol. 2 (Lausanne, Switzerland: Frontiers Media SA, 2017), 46.

4. Angela Chen, *Ace: What Asexuality Reveals About Desire, Society, and the Meaning of Sex* (Boston: Beacon Press, 2020).

5. S. E. Smith, "Taking Your Body for a Ride: Masturbation and Disability," Scarleteen, July 28, 2017, https://www.scarleteen.com/taking_your_body_for_a_ride _masturbation_and_disability.

6. A. Andrews, *A Quick and Easy Guide to Sex and Disability* (Minneapolis, MN: Limerence Press, 2020).

7. Emily Nagoski, *The Come As You Are Workbook: The Surprising New Science That Will Transform Your Sex Life* (London: Simon & Schuster, 2015).

8. Jackie Lam, "We Talked to People Living with Disabilities About Sex, and Here's What They Had to Say," BuzzFeed, December 12, 2021, https://doi.org/https://www .buzzfeed.com/jackielam/people-living-with-disabilities-discuss-sex.

9. Andrews, *A Quick and Easy Guide to Sex and Disability*.

10. Angie Jones, "Kinks and Fetishes: An A to Z Guide," *Glamour*, February 28, 2023, https://www.glamour.com/story/a-to-z-kinks-and-fetishes.

11. Emmett Patterson, "How Practicing Kink Helps Keep People with Disabilities Connected to Their Desire," The Body, November 23, 2020, https://www.thebody.com /article/kink-managing-chronic-pain.

12. "Why BDSM Could Allow Anyone Disabled to Enjoy Sex," Disability Horizons, April 29, 2019, https://disabilityhorizons.com/2019/04/why-bdsm-could -allow-anyone-disabled-to-enjoy-sex/.

13. Mark O'Brien, "On Seeing a Sex Surrogate," *Sun* magazine, May 1990, https:// www.thesunmagazine.org/issues/174/on-seeing-a-sex-surrogate.

14. Sellwood, Raghavendra, and Walker, "Facilitators and Barriers to Developing Romantic and Sexual Relationships."

15. Emma McGowan, "This Sex Ed Platform Offers Info About Sex & Disability That's Hard to Get Anywhere Else," Bustle, September 16, 2019, https://www .bustle.com/p/cripping-up-sex-with-eva-offers-info-about-sex-disability-thats-hard -to-get-anywhere-else-18201540.

16. Madison Parrotta, "Sex and Parent Caregivers," Scarleteen, June 20, 2019, https://www.scarleteen.com/article/disability_parenting_relationships_sexuality /sex_and_parent_caregivers.

17. Suzannah Weiss, "How to Have Great Sex When You're on the Autism Spectrum," *Vice*, July 22, 2022, https://www.vice.com/en/article/g5vqky/how-to-have-great -sex-when-youre-on-the-autism-spectrum.

Chapter 8

1. Vilissa Thompson, Nora Ellman, and Rebecca Cokley, "Sexual Violence and the Disability Community," Center for American Progress, February 12, 2021, https:// doi.org/https://www.americanprogress.org/article/sexual-violence-disability -community/.

2. "Sexual Abuse," Disability Justice, 2023, https://disabilityjustice.org/sexual -abuse/#:~:text=Approximately%2080%25%20of%20women%20and,assaulted %20more%20than%2010%20times.

3. Ariel Henley, "Why Sex Education for Disabled People Is So Important," *Teen Vogue*, January 1, 2017, https://doi.org/https://www.teenvogue.com/story/disabled-sex-ed.

4. Laura Graham Holmes, *Comprehensive Sex Education for Youth with Disabilities: A Call to Action*, Siecus, https://siecus.org/wp-content/uploads/2021/03 /SIECUS-2021-Youth-with-Disabilities-CTA-1.pdf.

5. Suzanne Smeltzer, Monika Mitra, and Linda Long-Bellil, "Obstetric Clinicians' Experiences and Educational Preparation for Caring for Pregnant Women with Physical Disabilities: A Qualitative Study," *Disability Health* 11, no. 1 (2018): 8–13, https:// doi.org/10.1016/j.dhjo.2017.07.004.

6. Amy Houtrow and Ellen R. Elias, "Promoting Healthy Sexuality for Children and Adolescents with Disabilities," *Pediatrics* 148, no. 1 (2021), https://doi.org/10.1542 /peds.2021-052043.

7. Rebekah L. Rollston, "Comprehensive Sex Education as Violence Prevention," Harvard Medical School Primary Care Review, May 29, 2020, https://doi

.org/https://info.primarycare.hms.harvard.edu/review/sexual-education-violence-prevention.

8. Caroline B. Cupp, personal interview with Kathleen Skomorucha, August 30, 2022.

9. "Abuse and Exploitation of People with Developmental Disabilities," Disability Justice, 2023, https://doi.org/https://disabilityjustice.org/justice-denied/abuse-and-exploitation/.

10. Ibid.

11. "What Is Sexual Abuse?," Love Is Respect.org, accessed September 1, 2023, https://www.loveisrespect.org/pdf/What_Is_Sexual_Abuse.pdf.

12. US Department of Education, Office of Civil Rights, Philadelphia Office, "Verbal and Psychological Abuse." Disability Justice, December 1, 2017, https://disabilityjustice.org/verbal-and-psychological-abuse/.

13. S. M. Caraballo, "Creeped Out: My Daughter Is 22 but Looks Like She's 8 Years Old—I Worry Whenever Guys Show Any Romantic Interest in Her," *U.S. Sun*, February 7, 2022, https://www.the-sun.com/lifestyle/4632540/shauna-rae-mom-worries-guys-dating-her/.

14. Caroline B. Cupp and Jessica C. Slice, personal interview with John Adams, April 25, 2022.

15. Alison Kafer, "Desire and Disgust: My Ambivalent Adventures in Devoteeism," in *Sex and Disability*, ed. Anna Mollow and Robert McRuer (Durham, NC: Duke University Press, 2012), 331–354.

16. "Your Body Is Not a Sex Object: Devotees and Disability," Scarleteen, July 28, 2017, https://www.scarleteen.com/your_body_is_not_a_sex_object_devotees_and_disability.

Chapter 9

1. Janet Hardy and Dossie Easton, *The Ethical Slut: A Practical Guide to Polyamory, Open Relationships and Other Adventures*, 3rd ed. (Berkeley, CA: Ten Speed Press, 2017).

2. Jillian Weise, "I Approach Polyamory with the Same Drive I Do My Work," The Cut, March 7, 2022, https://www.thecut.com/2022/03/polyamory-ambition-disability.html.

3. Amanda Van Slyke, "How Polyamory Helped Me Advocate for My Needs as a Disabled Person," Thought Catalog, November 27, 2017, https://thoughtcatalog.com/amanda-van-slyke/2017/11/how-polyamory-helped-me-advocate-for-my-needs-as-a-disabled-person/.

4. Ibid.

5. Morgan Mac Caisín, "What I Wish People Understood About Polyamory and Disability," The Mighty, July 19, 2022, https://themighty.com/topic/disability/having-a-polyamorous-relationship-as-a-person-with-a-disability/.

6. Teighlor McGee, "As a Black, Fat, Disabled Person in Love, My Monogamy Feels Radical," Autostraddle, January 25, 2022, https://www.autostraddle.com/as-a-black-fat-disabled-person-in-love-my-monogamy-feels-radical/.

7. "Rest in Power: Joint Statement on the Life of Teighlor McGee—YWCA St. Paul," April 15, 2022, https://www.ywcastpaul.org/rest-in-power-joint-statement -on-the-life-of-teighlor-mcgee/.

Chapter 10

1. Alexander Cheves, "9 LGBTQ+ People Explain How They Love, Hate, and Understand the Word 'Queer,'" Them, June 4, 2019, https://www.them.us/story /what-does-queer-mean.

2. "LGBTQ+ Glossary," It Gets Better, accessed August 18, 2023, https:// itgetsbetter.org/glossary/?gclid=CjoKCQjwlPWgBhDHARIsAH2xdNfPIKUf b8j3h4eubR8IjtG85_NN_U1mC6xlfi62GJFoo-O9GcAa-1MaAgp7EALw_wcB.

3. "Built-in Ableism Makes Queer Spaces Inaccessible to Disabled People," Bitch Media, 2018.

4. Ace Ratcliff, "This Year, Pride Returned to Its Radical Roots," Bitch Media, 2020.

5. Raven Ishak, "A Lack of Accessibility in Queer Spaces Crushes Community Pride," HelloGiggles, June 9, 2021, https://hellogiggles.com/disabled -people-pride-events-lgbtq/.

6. Miles Griffis, "As Queer Spaces Return to 'Normal,' Disabled LGBTQ+ People Are Being Left Behind," Them, February 17, 2023, https://www.them.us/story /queer-spaces-covid-disability-disabled-creating-change-conference.

7. Jones, "Disability Activists Push for More Inclusive Pride Celebrations."

8. Alaina Leary, "Activist Spotlight: Annie Segarra – YouTuber, Artist, Activist," Rooted in Rights, August 30, 2017, https://rootedinrights.org/activist -spotlight-annie-segarra-youtuber-artist-activist/

9. Zoe Christen Jones, "Disability Activists Push for More Inclusive Pride Celebration," CBS News, June 29, 2021, https://www.cbsnews.com/news /disability-activists-push-for-more-inclusive-pride-celebrations/

10. Penny Pepper, "Treating Disabled People as Asexual Is Exasperating and Offensive," Guardian, November 23, 2017, https://www.theguardian.com/commentisfree /2016/jun/08/disabled-people-asexual-sex-lives-you-before-me-sexuality.

11. Sarah Neilson, "Angela Chen's 'Ace' Reveals What It Means to Be Asexual in a Society Obsessed with Sexuality," Washington Post, September 28, 2020, https:// www.washingtonpost.com/entertainment/books/angela-chens-ace-reveals-what-it -means-to-be-asexual-in-a-society-obsessed-with-sexuality/2020/09/28/d211 780a-fdaa-11ea-9ceb-061d646d9c67_story.html.

12. "Welcome," Asexual Visibility and Education Network, accessed April 27, 2023, https://www.asexuality.org/.

13. Angela Chen, Ace: What Asexuality Reveals About Desire, Society, and the Meaning of Sex (Boston: Beacon Press, 2020).

14. Maria Elena Fernandez, "'You Don't Have to Have Cerebral Palsy to Relate to My Story': Ryan O'Connell's Show About Gay, Disabled Life Is Netflix's First 15-Minute Sitcom," Vulture, April 12, 2019, https://www.vulture.com/2019/04/ryan -oconnell-special-netflix.html.

15. Ryan O'Connell, "Coming Out of the Disabled Closet," Thought Catalog, January 6, 2015, https://thoughtcatalog.com/ryan-oconnell/2015/01/coming-out-of-the-disabled-closet/.

16. Ryan O'Connell, "I Wouldn't Fuck Me: My Life as a Gay and Disabled Man," *Vice*, September 16, 2015, https://www.vice.com/en/article/3k889n/i-wouldnt-fuck-me-my-life-as-a-gay-and-disabled-man.

17. Ibid.

18. Ibid.

19. Ibid.

20. Allison Zoller, "'They Are Socialized Differently': People with Autism More Likely to Identify as LGBTQ+," UNC Autism Research Center, August 4, 2022, https://autism.unc.edu/2022/08/they-are-socialized-differently-people-with-autism-more-likely-to-identify-as-lgbtq/.

21. Dayna Troisi, "How Having a Disability Influenced My Queer Dating Life," Buzzfeed, May 7, 2017, https://www.buzzfeed.com/daynatroisi/queer-dating-with-a-disability.

Chapter 11

1. Caroline B. Cupp and Jessica C. Slice, personal interview with John Adams, April 25, 2022.

2. Rebekah Taussig, "My Almost Endless Quest for an Accessible-ish and (Somewhat) Charming Home," Dwell, February 1, 2023, https://doi.org/https://www.dwell.com/article/my-almost-endless-quest-for-an-accessible-ish-and-somewhat-charming-home-0672c1cd.

3. Caroline B. Cupp, personal interview with Katie Kaplan, September 2, 2022.

4. Chloé Cooper Jones, *Easy Beauty* (New York: Avid Reader Press, 2022), 89.

5. Caroline B. Cupp, personal interview with Judy Heumann, August 30, 2022.

6. Jessica C. Slice, personal interview with Sarah Napoli, August 22, 2022.

7. Jessica C. Slice, personal interview with "Heather," August 26, 2022.

8. Jordan Reed, "Interabled Couples Share How They Make Their Relationships Work," Brain & Life, October 1, 2021, https://doi.org/https://www.brainandlife.org/articles/interabled-couples-share-how-their-relationships-work.

9. Slice, "Heather" interview.

10. Caroline B. Cupp, personal interview with Ron Sandison, September 14, 2022.

11. Shane and Hannah Burcaw, "We're Hiring a Caregiver?!," YouTube, April 19, 2023, 15:53–31:06, https://www.youtube.com/watch?v=mPQzuRMGyxw.

12. Cupp, Heumann interview.

13. Ben Mattlin, *In Sickness and in Health: Love, Disability, and a Quest to Understand the Perils and Pleasures of Interabled Romance* (Boston: Beacon Press, 2019).

14. Burcaw, "We're Hiring a Caregiver?!"

15. Cupp, Heumann interview.

16. Rebekah Taussig, "My Disabled Body Prepared Me for Motherhood Like Nothing Else Could," Romper, June 27, 2023, https://doi.org/https://www.romper.com/parenting/disabled-parents-weve-got-this.

Notes

Chapter 12

1. Ben Mattlin, "Dr. Phil's Offensive, Reductive View of Interabled Love," Beacon Broadside: A Project of Beacon Press, April 4, 2019, https://www.beaconbroadside .com/broadside/2019/04/dr-phils-offensive-reductive-view-of-interabled-love.html.

2. "Tips for Success in an Interabled Relationship," BraunAbility, accessed August 21, 2023, https://www.braunability.com/us/en/community/the-driving-force/tips-for -success-interabled-relationship.html.

3. Ibid.

4. Ibid.

5. Pema Chödrön, *When Things Fall Apart: Heart Advice for Difficult Times* (London: Thorsons Classics, 2017).

6. Sarah Smith Rainey, *Love, Sex, and Disability: The Pleasures of Care* (Boulder, CO: Lynne Rienner Publishers, 2011).

Chapter 13

1. Caroline B. Cupp, personal interview with "Shoshanna," April 21, 2023.

2. Ibid.

3. Caroline B. Cupp, personal interview with "Gilead," April 10, 2023.

4. Caroline B. Cupp, personal interview with Jack Oppen, September 16, 2022.

5. Laura Silver, "These Couples Say They Can't Move In Together Because One of Them Will Lose Their Disability Benefits," BuzzFeed, August 6, 2017, https://www .buzzfeed.com/laurasilver/these-couples-say-the-disability-benefits-system-is.

6. Dominick Evans, "Disabled People Penalized for Getting Married," *Audacity* magazine, January 2, 2019, https://www.audacitymagazine.com/disabled-people -penalized-for-getting-married/.

7. Gabriella Garbero, "The 'Fundamental' Right to Marriage," The Girl Who Sits, January 10, 2021, https://thegirlwhosits.com/2021/01/10/the-fundamental-right-to -marriage/.

8. Tammy LaGorce, "Seeking Marriage Equality for People with Disabilities," *New York Times*, August 25, 2022, https://www.nytimes.com/2022/08/25/style /marriage-equality-disabled-people.html.

9. Garbero, "The 'Fundamental' Right to Marriage."

10. Marriage Equality for Disabled Adults Act, H.R., 117th Cong. (2022), https://www .congress.gov/bill/117th-congress/house-bill/6405/text?q=%7B.

Chapter 14

1. Caroline B. Cupp, personal interview with Ryan Honick, April 8, 2022.

2. Caroline B. Cupp, personal interview with "Gilead," April 10, 2023.

3. Abigail Wilson, "Trolls Say My Disabled Husband Can't Satisfy Me but They're Wrong," *New York Sun*, January 27, 2022, https://nypost.com/2022/01/27 /trolls-say-my-disabled-husband-cant-satisfy-me-but-theyre-wrong/.

Notes

4. Laura Dorwart, "The Profoundly Ignorant Questions I Get Asked About My Disabled Husband," MIC, September 25, 2019, https://doi.org/https://www.mic.com/life/these-misconceptions-about-disabled-peoples-relationships-cut-deep-18802804.

5. Ben Mattlin, *In Sickness and in Health: Love, Disability, and a Quest to Understand the Perils and Pleasures of Interabled Romance* (Boston: Beacon Press, 2019).

6. Ibid.

7. Dorwart, "The Profoundly Ignorant Questions."

8. Ellen Coughlan, "Man Whose Wife Is Disabled Reveals the Most Outrageous Questions He's Asked by Strangers—Including Whether the Couple Can Have Sex or If He 'Has a Thing' for People in Wheelchairs," *Daily Mail*, July 4, 2022, https://www.dailymail.co.uk/femail/article-10979771/Man-wife-disabled-reveals-outrageous-questions-hes-asked.html.

9. Ariel Henley (@ariel_henley9), Twitter, August 13, 2019.

10. Dorwart, "The Profoundly Ignorant Questions."

11. Mattlin, *In Sickness and in Health*.

12. Ibid.

13. Devon Ledbetter, "'You Know I'm in a Wheelchair, Right?' 'I Limited Myself on the Love I Truly Deserved': Interabled Couple Share Love Story, 'Our Relationship Is 50/50, No Matter What Society Thinks,'" Love What Matters, February 8, 2022, https://www.lovewhatmatters.com/you-know-im-in-a-wheelchair-right-i-canceled-our-date-i-limited-myself-on-the-love-i-truly-deserved-interabled-couple-share-love-story/.

14. Imani Barbarin, "Ableism in Dating with Marina Carlos," *Crutches and Spice* (podcast), transcript, 41:06, December 3, 2019, https://crutchesandspice.com/2019/12/03/ableism-in-dating-with-marina-carlos/.

INDEX

Index

androgynous, 146

anger issues, 98–99

apps. *See* dating apps

Arizona State University, 39

arthrogryposis, 220

asexuality, 152–153

  assumptions about, 76, 144, 152–153, 156

  definition of, 147

Asexual Visibility and Education

    Network (AVEN), 152

assisted masturbation, 87

assumptions

  about asexuality, 76, 144, 152–153, 156

  about autistic people, 156

  about caregiving, 189–190

  about heroism, 190, 219–221

  about hypersexuality, 76, 144

  about incompetence, 214–216

  about innocence, 212–214

  about sexual frequency, 82

  about superhuman narrative, 221–223

attention

  compliments and, 25

  in devoteeism, 121

  harassment as, 5

  patronizing, 5

  true, 115

augmentative and alternative

    communication (AAC) device,

    during sex, 75

authentic communication, 169–170

autistic people

  assumptions about, 156

  and chores, 172

  and ethical nonmonogamy, 130–131,

    136, 137

  and noise, 67

and queerness, 155–156

and sensation during sex, 80, 89

and sex, 80, 88–90

using email with, 49

See also neurodivergent people

autonomy, 186, 190

Autostraddle (magazine), 140–141

Aylward, Hannah, 11

background-check reporting systems, 114

Barbarin, Imani, 222

bar seating, 64

bathrooms, 21–22, 66

BDSM, 85, 89

beauty/beauty standards

  and disability hierarchy, 23

  and disability rights movement, 16–17

  and disabled people, 14, 24, 27

  and gay men, 153–155

  and healthy relationships, 16

  and insecurity, 15

  and relationship with our bodies, 15–16

  Western cultural ideal and, 24

  widening views of, 14

Berne, Patricia, 16

birth-control methods, 78

bisexual, definition of, 147

Blackstock, Oni, 151

Blake, Melissa, 31, 32, 33–34

blind people, dating apps inaccessible

  to, 39

Blue, Lionel, 162

Body Bouncer (sex tool), 84

book clubs, 47

boundaries, 74

brain injury, 193–194

BraunAbility, 182–183

Index

Index

Index

Index

Index

masc, 146

masturbation, 77, 87

Mattlin, Ben, 174, 218

McGee, Teighlor, 140–141

media/tv

  on beauty standards for gay men, 154

  on caregiving, 180–182

  disabled characters on, 4–5, 10–11

  disabled relationships on, 29, 30

  lack of disabled characters on, 2–4

  sex in, 72

  See also social media

Medicaid, 138, 195, 199, 201–204

meeting up, 53–68

  disclosing disability before, 56–58

  food and eating, 66–67

  locations for, 60–65

  noise levels, 67

  safety tips for, 118–119

  toileting, 66

  on video chat, 58–59

  See also first dates

metamour, 133

Michele, Marna, 220

The Mighty (magazine), 139–140

migraines, 169

mobility issues, and false presumption of drunkenness, 67–68

mobility needs

  and choosing meetup locations, 60–65

  hiding from others, 22–23

money. *See* finances

monogamish, 134

monogamy

  definition of, 132

  structure of, 133

movies, 63

moving in

  accessible housing, 164–165

  big issues in, 161–162

  dating stories, 162–163

  practicality of, 163–164

  when you know, you know phenomenon, 165–167

  See also partnering up

munch, 134

mutual-aid mindset, 131–132, 191–192

Nagoski, Emily, 82

National Center for Sexual Freedom (NCSF), 85

National Center for the Victims of Crime, 128

National Domestic Violence Hotline, 107, 126

National Sexual Assault Hotline, 107, 126, 127

neurodivergent people

  and consent, 120

  dating app for, 39–42, 156

  and ethical nonmonogamy, 130–131, 136, 137

  identifying as LGBTQIA+, 40, 155–156

  and noise, 67

  and sensation during sex, 80, 89

  and sex, 88–90

  using email with, 49

new relationship energy (NRE), 134

noise, on dates, 67

NOMI (dating app), 39–41, 42, 156

nonsexual committed partnerships, 137–138

nursing, advice on, 216

Index

Index

Index

Index

Index